Gender Equality in the Mirror

World Trade Institute Advanced Studies

VOLUME 10

The titles published in this series are listed at *brill.com/wtia*

Gender Equality in the Mirror

Reflecting on Power, Participation and Global Justice

Edited by

Elisa Fornalé

BRILL
NIJHOFF

LEIDEN | BOSTON

Open access publication of this book has been made possible by the Swiss National Science Foundation.

The Library of Congress Cataloging-in-Publication Data is available online at https://catalog.loc.gov
LC record available at https://lccn.loc.gov/2022938312

Typeface for the Latin, Greek, and Cyrillic scripts: "Brill". See and download: brill.com/brill-typeface.

ISSN 2405-9331
ISBN 978-90-04-46767-5 (hardback)
ISBN 978-90-04-46768-2 (e-book)

This book is printed on acid-free paper and produced in a sustainable manner.

Contents

Preface

Both the concept and reality of inequality have many facets. These include unequal economic opportunities, social exclusion, and limits on rights to political participation. They also cut across different demographic categories, including race, gender, religion, and even linguistic groups. This volume takes the institutional structures framing gender inequality as its starting point, exploring issues ranging from socio-economic rights under domestic law to the participation of women in international institutions. The topics covered are highly relevant, and the chapters themselves offer valuable insight.

This volume has grown out of recent efforts at the University of Bern, led by Professor Elisa Fornalé at the World Trade Institute (WTI), to better integrate an awareness of gender-related issues into what we do. The WTI is an institute focused on the rules and political systems governing the global economy. These are important determinants of the institutional mechanisms that drive changes (or lack thereof) in gender inequality. As the WTI is a university institute, Professor Fornalé's efforts have had a direct impact through coursework, periodic seminars on the topic, and better focus in our research programmes. As COVID-19 restrictions limited scope for direct personal interaction, these efforts were taken online. While important steps have been taken, more remains to be done

Our collective experience with COVID-19 has served to highlight structural drivers of gender inequality, as seen in the distribution of the burden of adjustment to societal and economic shocks. It has also shown that we cannot really separate the economic from the social and political dimensions of response to such events. While some aspects of the interaction between structural inequalities and the systemic shocks caused by COVID-19 are examined in this volume, others will require more time to study and deconstruct. In this sense, this volume is a valuable reference, but much more work needs to be done. As COVID-19 will not be the last major structural shock (consider for example the possibilities for future climate driven shocks), understanding and addressing such issues will remain important as we move past the current crisis and on to new ones.

Finally, I must say that I am both honoured and humbled to have been asked to write a preface to this volume. It represents hard work on an important set of issues and will provide the reader with valuable lessons and insight. Reading the chapters collected here should be time well spent.

Joseph Francois
Managing Director, World Trade Institute
Professor of Economics, University of Bern

Acknowledgments

I express my gratitude to the Office for Gender Equality of the University of Bern for encouraging us to develop our Gender Lecture Series and for funding activities that led to this manuscript. Special thanks go to Karin Beyeler who has always been very helpful. Thanks are also due to the WTI team who provided me with the perfect environment for implementing our gender activities over the past three years. In particular, I am grateful to Sophia Thompson, Rebecca Gilgen, Francesco De Fino, and Pablo Rahul Das for always being supportive and a willing source of help. I also wish to thank the participants at our Gender Lectures who, through their engagement and participation in fruitful debates, have played an influential part in shaping this book project.

I gratefully acknowledge the grant received from the Swiss National Science Foundation for the project "Gender Equality in the Mirror: Clothing the Invisibility of Women's Participation at International Level" (No. 100011_200462/1 - www.womenandparticipation.org), the grant received from the Swiss National Foundation for Open Access publication (No. 10BP12_211239/1), and the grant received from the Region of Piedmont, Equality Office, which supported the publication process. I would like to express my gratitude to all the staff of Brill Press, Kelley Baylis and Mary Sheldon for their valuable support and rewarding working relationship. I must also thank the authors who have always showed an incredible degree of commitment to this joint effort. Their contributions of original research and their patience during the editorial process made this excellent publication possible. Finally, many thanks to Tamara Koehler for research assistance and Susan Kaplan for assisting with the editing and proofreading the manuscript.

Illustrations

Figures

Tables

Notes on Contributors

Valentina Beghini

is a lawyer by training, with a PhD in European and Comparative Legal Studies and more than 10 years of experience working at the national and international level – including with governmental agencies, the United Nations, non-governmental organisations and in the private sector in Europe, South-East Asia and sub-Saharan Africa. She has worked extensively on fundamental principles and rights at work, international labour standards, gender equality and children's rights. She is currently working as a Technical Specialist on Gender Equality and Non-Discrimination, at the International Labour Organization (ILO) in Geneva, coordinating the work on the promotion of the ratification and implementation of the ILO Violence and Harassment Convention, 2019 (No. 190) and its accompanying Recommendation.

Zsuzsa Blaskó

is a senior research fellow at the European Commission's Joint Research Centre. She is a sociologist by background and her main research interest lies in social inequalities, with a particular focus on education and gender relations. Her work includes analyses of gender role attitudes, maternal employment and girls' expectations about working in science, technology, engineering and mathematics. In April 2020, she published the Joint Research Centre (JRC) Technical Report, *How will the COVID-19 crisis affect existing gender divides in Europe?*.

Flavia Bustreo

is a leading physician, public health professional and advocate for the health and human rights of women, children, adolescents and the elderly. She is known for taking action on the social and environmental determinants of health, including the health impacts of climate change. She is currently the Chair of the Governance and Nomination Committee at the Partnership for Maternal, Newborn and Child Health and advises several governmental and non-governmental entities including the International Federation of Gynecology and Obstetrics. Dr Bustreo was the former Assistant Director-General for Family, Women's and Children's Health for the World Health Organization (WHO) from 2010 to 2017. At WHO she led the organization's work on reproductive, maternal, child and adolescent health, climate change, ageing, vaccinations, health and human rights, health and gender equity, and the social determinants of health. Dr Bustreo's contributions to global health have been recognised with numerous awards, including an honorary doctorate from the University of Essex in 2018.

Umberto Cattaneo
is an economist in the Gender, Equality, Diversity and Inclusion Branch of the International Labour Organization (ILO) in Geneva. Umberto has advanced ILO research and advised ILO constituents on gender equality and non-discrimination at work, including on the care economy, violence and harassment in the world of work and equal pay for work of equal value. Umberto is closely involved in providing support to the G20 Employment Working Group. He is currently the lead author of the new ILO Care Report 2.0, which will provide an update regarding legal provisions on care leave policies and care services, as well as cost/benefit policy simulations. Prior joining the ILO, Umberto worked for two years in the Office of the Chief Economist for Africa at the World Bank and obtained his PhD in economics from the University of Genova in Italy.

Federica Cristani
is a senior researcher at the Institute of International Relations in Prague, Czech Republic, and a visiting senior researcher at the Arctic Centre of the University of Lapland, Finland. She holds a PhD in international law from the University of Verona, Italy. She previously worked as a post-doctoral researcher at the World Trade Institute of the University of Bern, Switzerland, and at the University of Verona, and has been a visiting scholar at several universities and research centres in Europe. Her main research interests include international economic law and international law of cyberspace. She has published in peer-reviewed journals and has contributed to several book chapters. She is a Co-Chair of the Coordinating Committee of the Interest Group on International Economic Law of the European Society of International Law.

Elisa Fornalé
is a Swiss National Science Foundation (SNSF) Professor at the World Trade Institute (WTI), University of Bern. She holds a law degree from the University of Trento, Italy, and a PhD in law from the University of Palermo, Italy, and she specialises in international law, human rights and migration. Since April 2021, she has been the Principal Investigator of the project "Gender Equality in the Mirror (GEM)" which explores women's participatory rights. She is the Gender Coordinator of the Gender Team at the WTI and she initiated the Gender Lecture Series – Know the GAP. In parallel, she is implementing the "Framing Environmental Degradation, Human Mobility and Human Development as

a Matter of Common Concern" (CLI_M_CO2), which is exploring the adverse impacts of climate change through a pilot case study in the Small Pacific Island States. Since 2021, she has been the appointed co-Rapporteur of the International Law Association (ILA) Committee on International Law and Sea Level Rise.

Joseph Francois
is managing director and professor of economics at the World Trade Institute, University of Bern, Switzerland. He served as deputy director of the National Centre of Competence in Research: Trade Regulation from 2015 to 2017. Previously he was professor of economics (with a chair in economic theory) at the Johannes Kepler University Linz. He is a fellow of the Centre for Economic Policy Research (London), director of the European Trade Study Group and the Institute for International and Development Economics, senior research fellow with the Vienna Institute for International Economic Studies, and a board member of the Global Trade Analysis Project. He serves on the editorial board of the *Review of Development Economics*, and the *World Trade Review*. Past professional incarnations have included professor of economics at Erasmus University Rotterdam, research economist for the World Trade Organization, and chief of research and acting director of economics for the US International Trade Commission.

Asuncion Fresnoza-Flot
is a tenured research associate of the Fund for Scientific Research in Belgium and senior lecturer (*maîtresse d'enseignement*) at the Laboratory of Anthropology of Contemporary Worlds of the Université Libre de Bruxelles. Her recent publications include the edited Special Issues "Mobilités dans le Sud globalisé: altérité, racialisation et fabrique des identités" [Racialisation and othering in the context of mobilities: a focus on the globalised South] (with Julian Debonneville and Gwénola Ricordeau, *Civilisations* 2019) and "Asia-Europe intimate links: family migration, binational couples and mixed-parentage children" (with Simeng Wang, *Asian and Pacific Migration Journal* 2021). Her ongoing research project examines the contextual mobility of Belgian-Asian couples in their cross-border social spaces.

Chiara Germano
is an Italian lawyer specialised in commercial and labour law, who has been practising in Turin since 2006. Always interested in gender equality issues, in 2016 she was nominated by the Italian Ministry of Labour as Vice-Counsellor for Equal Opportunities in the Piedmont Region. This institution is responsible for supervising the correct application of the rules on gender discrimination in

the workplace. She served in the role until 2021 carrying out a variety of tasks, including dealing with legal claims for gender equality violations before the municipal courts, advocacy actions, training programmes and conferences on the topic of gender equality. She has edited publications on the subject and attended specialist seminars at national and European level. Since 2007, she has also been a member of the *Centro Studi Domenico Napoletano*, an association focused on the study of labour law.

Anna Giulia Ponchia
is an international development professional and advocate for gender equality and for the rights of women and girls in humanitarian and conflict settings. She is currently part of the Innovation Team at Results for Development, working to identify and scale up innovative solutions to address systemic challenges in health, education and nutrition in low- and middle-income countries. Previously, Anna Giulia worked for the governance team at the Partnership for Maternal, Newborn and Child Health, hosted by the World Health Organization. She was also a trade officer at the British Chamber of Commerce in Mexico, specialising in Latin American trade and development. Her research interests lie in the application of innovations in humanitarian settings through the integration of a localisation and gender lens. Anna Giulia holds an MSc in International Development and Humanitarian Emergencies from the London School of Economics and Political Science, and a BA from the University of Warwick.

Mara Catherine Harvey
is driven by two fundamental beliefs: that daily money decisions are an untapped source of positive social and environmental impact, and that we cannot wait another 100+ years to achieve economic gender equality. As senior manager in finance with more than 21 years of experience in Wealth Management at UBS, she has had the privilege to transform the world of finance to better address women's needs, and to support clients from all around the world to make more impact with their wealth. Above all, she is a passionate advocate for financial literacy, equality and female economic empowerment. She holds a doctorate with highest honours in Political Economy from Fribourg University, Switzerland, and she speaks English, Italian, French and German fluently. Since 2014, she has lived in Zurich and she enjoys spending her free time writing. She is the author of *Women and Risk – Rewriting the Rules* (2018) and *A Smart Way to Start* (2018–2020), a rhyming book series for children on money, equality and sustainability. Her vision is to redefine financial parenting and shape our children's financial future, to empower all girls to talk about

money, to know their worth and to feel comfortable negotiating their pay, so they can enter the workforce on equal terms to the boys. Her latest rhyming children's book, *Start Doing Good*, explains the 17 Sustainable Development Goals and has been endorsed by the United Nations.

Rachael Hinton
is a social scientist and researcher with more than 20 years of experience in international health and development, including women's, children's and adolescents' health, human rights, and peace building and conflict reduction in humanitarian and fragile settings. Rachael has wide-ranging professional experience, including over ten years leading research teams in Papua New Guinea and working with the Partnership for Maternal and Child Health and the World Health Organization on a range of technical, policy and advocacy-related products. Dr Hinton leads an independent consultancy company, focusing on writing and publishing projects in the fields of global health and development.

Catherine Kessedjian
is Professor Emerita of the University Panthéon-Assas Paris II. She acts as arbitrator in selected international commercial and investment disputes. She also acts as a mediator in French and English. She is listed as International Centre for Settlement of Investment Disputes Conciliator (list of France). She is a member of numerous professional organisations, notably the American Law Institute (ALI) and the Institut de droit international. For ALI, she currently acts as a member of the International Advisers Committee for the Restatement on Foreign Relations Law. She is the President of the French Branch of the International Law Association (ILA) and Vice Chair of the global ILA. Until 2016, she was the Deputy Director of the European College of Paris and Director of Studies of the LLM in European Law. In 2016, she was visiting professor at Padova University (Italy) and in 2017 Wainwright Senior Fellow and Visiting Professor at McGill Faculty of Law.

Sandra Mantu
is assistant professor at the Centre for Migration Law (CMR), Faculty of Law, Radboud University, the Netherlands and co-managing editor of the *European Journal of Migration and Law*. Her research and teaching focuses on European Union (EU) citizenship, free movement of persons, implementation of EU law, social rights, equality, and nationality law. In 2014, Sandra defended her PhD thesis, which dealt with the legal rules and practices of citizenship deprivation in a selection of EU Member States and their link with EU citizenship. She

has been involved in several EU-funded projects looking at the legal aspects of EU citizenship and EU migration and a key staff member in two Jean Monnet Centre of Excellence work programmes implemented by the Centre for Migration Law. Sandra's latest book, with P. Minderhoud and E. Guild is *EU Citizenship and Free Movement Rights: Taking Supranational Citizenship Seriously*, published by Brill (2020).

Lidia Katia C. Manzo
has recently been awarded the Marie Sklodowska Curie European Individual Fellowship 2020–2022 to develop the project CITY-OF-CARE at the Department of Social and Political Sciences of the University of Milan. She is interested in the application of ethnography and participatory methods in critical urban cultural studies to reinforce our knowledge of how discrimination, segregation and hegemony work spatially. She teaches urban and environmental sociology and general sociology at the University of Milan. Among her latest publications, 'Mothers, Childcare Duties, and Remote Working Under COVID-19 Lockdown in Italy: Cultivating Communities of Care' (with Manzo, A. and Minello, A) in Dialogues in Human Geography (2020).

Sara Martucci
is an assistant professor of social and behavioral sciences at Mercy College in New York. Her research is typically focused on everyday experiences of gentrification in New York City. She is currently researching the gendered division of labour in the home during the COVID-19 lockdown and how these experiences differed for mothers by profession. Sara regularly presents her work at the Urban Affairs Association annual conference. She recently published the article 'He's Working from Home and I'm at Home Trying to Work: Experiences of Childcare and the Work–Family Balance Among Mothers During COVID-19' in the *Journal of Family Issues*. Dr Sara Martucci holds a PhD in Sociology from the CUNY Graduate Center.

Alessandra Minello
is assistant professor of demography at the Department of Statistical Sciences of the University of Padua. Her academic research focuses on gender differences in several domains. She received her PhD in Sociology and Social Research from the University of Trento, Italy, where she compared the factors affecting the educational expectations and aspirations of children of immigrant and native students in Italy and Europe. During her PhD, she also worked as an associate researcher at the Dondena Centre for Research on Social Dynamics and Public Policy (Bocconi University of Milan, Italy), where she

analysed data on human capital with respect to the children of immigrants and second-generation Italians, and proposed a comparison to native Italian children. As a postdoctoral researcher at the European University Institute in Florence, Italy, she engaged in a project on the determinants of gender-specific competencies and decision-making with respect to educational trajectories and their consequences on job entry and careers in Germany. She currently works mainly on academic trajectories of women and men. She also works on fertility intentions, education, sexuality and homicides.

Emanuela Pozzan
is a senior gender and non-discrimination specialist at the International Labour Organization with more than 18 years of experience working in the Middle East, Africa and Asia on gender equality, diversity and inclusion in the world of work. Her educational background includes a degree in Middle Eastern Studies and a Master of Science in Development Studies from SOAS with a focus on gender equality and forced migration. Her career has included serving in the Italian Ministry of Foreign Affairs, non-governmental organisations, United Nations Population Fund and the International Labour Organization (ILO). She is now working in the Gender, Equality, Diversity and Inclusion Branch at the ILO headquarters where she coordinates a portfolio of initiatives in the area of access to work for women, care economy, pay equity, and violence and harassment in the world of work. Among her latest publications, *A Quantum Leap for Gender Equality: For a Better Future of Work for All* (ILO, 2019).

Cecilia Rocco
is a consultant with expertise on international relations, diplomacy, and gender equality. Rocco has worked as a consultant for the Partnership for Maternal, Newborn and Child Health, hosted by the World Health Organization and the International Federation of Gynecology and Obstetrics. Her research focuses on the effect of multilevel actions and integrated policies to ensure for women, children, adolescents and newborns the highest attainable standard of physical and mental health. Her main areas of work cover diplomacy, women's rights and Sustainable Development Goal (SDG)5 Gender Equality, with a specific focus on target 5.2 and the role of global governance and international platforms in creating synergies to address gender-based violence and maltreatment of young people, especially from a socio-economic perspective. Rocco holds an MSc in International Relations and Diplomacy, and a BA in International Relations from the University of Trieste.

Patricia Schulz
is a Swiss lawyer. She practised law with the Geneva bar, later worked with the International Labour Organization in Madagascar and then taught at the Faculty of Law of Geneva. She headed the Federal Office for Gender Equality from 1994 to 2010 and represented Switzerland at the United Nations (UN) and Council of Europe, including in major meetings on gender equality. She did two mandates as expert in the UN Committee on the Elimination of Discrimination against Women (CEDAW, 2011–2018), including being its Rapporteur and chairing the Working Group on Individual Communications. She joined the Board of the United Nations Research Institute for Social Development (2011–2016), where she is now a Senior Research Associate. Her latest publication is *The UN Convention on the Elimination of All Forms of Discrimination Against Women and its Optional Protocol: A Commentary. Second Edition* edited by P. Schulz, R. Halperin-Kaddari, B. Rudolf and M. Freeman (2nd edn, OUP forthcoming 2022).

Introduction

Reflecting on Power, Participation and Global Justice

Elisa Fornalé

1 Introduction

The coronavirus pandemic crisis, in all its multifold manifestations, has clearly demonstrated how current structures of power risk perpetuating inequality between men and women.[1] As stressed by de Búrca 'we live in a time of global turbulence'.[2] But, despite the uncertainty, this era offers us a unique opportunity to embrace contemporary challenges and engage in progressive change by rethinking the ways in which the realisation of women's rights could be better consolidated in the struggle for global justice.

Our book seizes the momentum of this time of transformation to offer a novel view of the ways in which women's invisibility and exclusion in the post-pandemic future can be redressed. The book seeks to explore the potential of the gender–power nexus, drawing on its different dimensions to provide a closer look at how we can accelerate the path towards gender equality and influence the gendered structures that dictate the distribution of socio-economic resources.[3] In line with D'Ignazio and Klein, the term 'power' is used here to describe the interconnected domains (structural, disciplinary, hegemonic, and interpersonal) that confer advantages and privileges on some groups (in this case, men) and systematic disadvantages on others (i.e. women).[4]

---

1 Hilary Charlesworth and Christine Chinkin, *The Boundaries of International Law: A Feminist Analysis* (Manchester University Press 2000); United Nations (UN), 'Policy Brief: The Impact of COVID-19 on Women' (2020); United Nations Experts, 'COVID-19: States Should Not Abuse Emergency Measures to Suppress Human Rights' (2020); Bram Büscher et al., 'Planning for a World beyond COVID-19: Five Pillars for Post-Neoliberal Development' (2021) 140 World Development 1.

2 Gráinne de Búrca, *Reframing Human Rights in a Turbulent Era* (OUP 2021) 1.

3 As highlighted by Chinkin 'a comprehensive approach to gender analysis is sought with a view to transformation of prevailing social structures – the workplace, the family, the global economy', Christine Chinkin, 'Gender and Economic, Social, and Cultural Rights' in Eibe Riedel et al. (eds), *Economic, Social and Cultural Rights in International Law* (OUP 2014) 159.

4 In their work, D'Ignazio and Klein describe 'the structural domain' as the laws and policies that contribute to 'organize oppression'; the 'disciplinary domain' which includes those

This book starts with a historical account of concepts, principles, sources, and the institutional framework that define the contours of a 'gender-positive environment' and provide new opportunities for removing resilient barriers to economic empowerment and equal participation of women.

The second part of the volume introduces some contemporary developments in women's socio-economic participation. Specific thematic areas (financial equality and gendered division of labour), which require direct action to move forward the parity debate are covered.[5] These dimensions have been identified to demonstrate how power is not distributed equally – in terms of access to resources and opportunities – and to trace the interlocking structural factors that embody 'gender norms and produce systematically unjust relationships'.[6] The final part concentrates on the gendered dimensions of institutional cultures and practices.[7] The proportion of women currently occupying positions in international institutions, such as United Nations (UN) treaty bodies, among others, is still very low.[8] The analysis will provide some insights in terms of the legitimacy and representativeness of institutional environments to identify best practices for moving from *de jure* to *de facto* equality through and within gender policy.[9]

---

who implement normative measures that 'encode inequality'; the 'hegemonic domain' which refers to the cultural ideas that are circulated including by the media; and, finally, the 'interpersonal domain' which includes the personal experience of individuals who are part of the less powerful group. These four domains configure what the authors identify as the 'matrix of domination', building on the work of Collins: Patricia Hill Collins, *Black Feminist Thought: Knowledge, Consciousness, and the Politics of Empowerment* (Routledge 2008). D'Ignazio and Lauren Klein, *Data Feminism* (The MIT Press 2020) 24–26.

5 Rebecca Adami, 'International Welfare Feminism CSW Navigating Cold War Tensions 1949' in Rebecca Adami and Dan Plesch (eds), *Women and the UN. A New History of Women's International Human Rights* (Routledge 2021) 55.

6 Alison M Jaggar 'Global Gender Justice' in Thom Brooks (ed), *The Oxford Handbook of Global Justice* (OUP 2020); Nico Krisch 'International Law in Times of Hegemony: Unequal Power and the Shaping of the International Legal Order' (2005) 16 European Journal of International Law 369.

7 'Institutional practices may not directly discriminate against women, but they can effectively inhibit women's participation by reflecting male life patterns as benchmarks of eligibility and success'. Hilary Charlesworth 'Transforming the United Men's Club: Feminist Futures for the United Nations' (1994) 4 (2) Transnational Law and Contemporary Problems 421, 440.

8 Dianne Otto, 'The Exile of Inclusion: Reflections on Gender Issues in International Law Over the Last Decade' (2009) Legal Studies Research Paper n. 431.

9 Anne-Marie Slaughter and Hilary Charlesworth, 'The Gender of International Institutions' Proceedings of the Annual Meeting (American Society of International Law), April 5–8, (1998) Structure of World Order 79.

2 The Status of Women's Empowerment: Moving from Powerless Equality to Powerful Equality

In recent years, domestic and international policies in different frameworks have been grappling with gender equality and women's empowerment. Extremely influential in this regard, is the Buenos Aires Declaration on Trade and Women's Economic Empowerment, which was adopted in 2017.[10] This Declaration, for the first time, expressly linked equal participation of women and men to the notions of inclusive economic growth and sustainable development.[11]

It is significant that the sixty-fifth session of the Commission on the Status of Women (CSW) focused on: 'women's full and effective participation and decision making in public life'. The aim was to identify persistent barriers as well as opportunities for achieving, as suggested by Norris, cultural, civic, normative, and decision-making empowerment.[12] The CSW 'recognizes that progress in achieving gender equality and the empowerment of all women and girls, and the full enjoyment of their human rights has been held back owing to the persistence of historical and structural unequal power relations between women

10 The 'Buenos Aires Declaration on Trade and Women's Economic Empowerment' (hereinafter the 'Declaration') was presented at the Eleventh World Trade Organization (WTO) Ministerial Conference, on 12 December 2017, and 118 WTO Members agreed to support it. The WTO appointed a 'Trade and Gender Focal Point' in 2017. In 2020, an 'Informal Working Group on Trade and Gender' was established by WTO Members, and Botswana, El Salvador and Iceland are chairing this initiative.

11 At the WTO's 12th Ministerial Conference an outcome document, drafted by the 'Friends of Gender' group, which includes 19 WTO Members, four international organizations, and the WTO Secretariat, presented draft recommendations for WTO Members. In 2021, a WTO technical assistance programme on trade and gender dedicated to government officials was created together with the launch of the 'Gender Research Hub' to improve the understanding of the trade and gender nexus.

12 Women's empowerment is highly prominent as a priority theme for strengthening women's participation in public life worldwide. See: Pippa Norris, 'The State of Women's Participation and Empowerment: New Challenges to Gender Equality' Background Paper in UN Women Expert Group Meeting; CSW, E/CN.6/2021/3, 'Women's Full and Effective Participation and Decision-Making in Public Life, as Well as the Elimination of Violence, for Achieving Gender Equality and the Empowerment of all Women and Girls' (21 December 2020) Report of the Secretary-General; Jill Steans and Daniela Tepe-Belfrage (eds), *Handbook on Gender in World Politics* (Edward Elgar 2013); Michelle Bachelet, 'Statement on Strengthening the Treaty Bodies, Guardians of the World's Human Rights Covenants and Treaties' (2020) United Nations High Commissioner for Human Rights; Knop Karen (ed), *Gender and Human Rights* (OUP 2004).

and men'.[13] The priority theme of the sixty-sixth session of the CSW (March 2022) also focuses on 'achieving gender equality and women's empowerment', this time in the context of climate change.[14] This requires efforts to improve the socio-economic conditions and also to redress the inadequate representation of women in governance. Let us consider briefly the conceptual framework elaborated by van Eerdewijk et al. to introduce how women's empowerment may be achieved.[15] Interestingly, they illustrate it as a 'process' and an 'outcome' that could be achieved by the 'expansion of choice and strengthening of voice through the transformation of power relations, so women have more control over their lives and futures'.[16] Achievement of this outcome would require the following actions: i) identifying measures to increase women's and girls' capacity to 'take action' (agency elements), ii) revising formal and informal arrangements to include a gender analysis (institutional structures), and, finally, iii) increasing both 'tangible and intangible capital and sources of

13 Commission on the Status of Women (CSW), E/CN.6/2021/L.3, 'Women's Full and Effective Participation and Decision-Making in Public Life, as Well as the Elimination of Violence, for Achieving Gender Equality and the Empowerment of all Women and Girls. Agreed Conclusions' (30 March 2021) para 33.

14 Expert Group Meeting, EGM/CSW/2022/CN, 'Achieving Gender Equality and the Empowerment of all Women and Girls in the Context of Climate Change, Environmental and Disaster Risk Reduction Policies and Programmes' (11–14 October 2021) Concept Note; Bernadette P Resurreccion, 'Gender, Climate Change and Disasters: Vulnerabilities, Responses, and Imagining a More Caring and Better World' (September 2021) EGM/ENV/BP.2, Background Paper, in Expert Group Meeting, 'Achieving Gender Equality and the Empowerment of all Women and Girls in the Context of Climate Change, Environmental and Disaster Risk Reduction Policies and Programmes' (11–14 October 2021).

15 Their framework is illustrated by Mary Picard, 'Empowering Women in Climate, Environment and Disaster Risk Governance: from National Policy to Local Action' EGM/ENV/BP.1, and it builds on the work of Kaaber. Anouka van Eerdewijk et al. 'White Paper: A Conceptual Model of Women and Girls' Empowerment' KIT Gender, Bill & Melinda Gates Foundation (March 2017).

16 Van Erdewijk et al. describe empowerment as 'contingent on the interaction between three elements: agency, institutional structure and resources'. Interesting in their model is the conceptualisation of power that they place at the heart of women and girls' ability to act as part of the empowerment process. Expressions of power include 'power-to' (the individual ability to have a positive influence), 'power-within' (refers to the sense of self-confidence and self-awareness to be able to have influence) and 'power-with' (collaborative power that could derive from collaborative action). In line with their conceptualisation 'empowerment of women and girls occurs when women and girls exercise agency and have more control over resources and when institutional structures are more enabling to their choice and voice, and ultimately their lives and future. Transformation of power relations is not by definition a harmonious process'. Van Eerdewijk et al. (n 15) 13–14, 23–24.

power' that must be sought to foster adequate responses (resources).[17] This framework suggests that achieving gender equality[18] is a complex process that requires taking steps to deal with the lack of political will and resources. It is also necessary to invest in remedying our lack of knowledge about how to reform existing governance structures and create the institutional preconditions required for the realisation of equality.[19]

Academic interest in women's empowerment has undergone a significant expansion, in particular, in the fields of human rights, development studies and gender politics. This has resulted in the elaboration of specific concepts that could play a concrete role in shaping meaningful responses.[20] The three-volume compilation edited by Otto, *Gender Issues and Human Rights*, presents evidence of how human rights law has been applied to improve women's position since 1990.[21] The overview of theoretical approaches, legal and institutional developments provides invaluable support to our work from at least two angles: first by paving the way to an emancipatory conception of equality and secondly by guiding a gender-oriented interpretation of international law aimed at stimulating new institutional and normative developments. However, the global COVID-19 pandemic has reminded us that, in reality, translating human rights and abstract legal principles is more complex than we would expect. Human rights could be limited and weakened, and women's voices could be silenced if we do not engage with the complexities associated with the realities of gendered hierarchies of powers

---

17 See the analysis conducted by Adami of 'international welfare feminism', which she describes as the 'advancement of women's rights with the understanding of women's equality and political freedom is linked with and dependent upon their economic liberation from unpaid or forced labour under capitalist, colonial, and patriarchal power structures', Adami (n 5) 65.

18 'The Commission also recognizes that women's full and effective participation in public life depends on enabling factors such as economic independence and full and equal access to quality education, training, decent work and equal value, universal health coverage [...]' CSW (n 13) para 40.

19 ibid.

20 Wendy Harcourt (ed), *The Palgrave Handbook of Gender and Development. Critical Engagements in Feminist Theory and Practice* (Palgrave Macmillan 2016); Susan Franceschet et al. (eds), *The Palgrave Handbook of Women's Political Rights* (Palgrave Macmillan 2019); Ilona CMD Cairns 'The Costs of (Partial) Inclusion: The Evolution, Limits and Biases of Principal Feminist Challenges to International Law', in Maarit Jänterä-Jareborg and Hélène Tigroudja (eds.) *Women's Human Rights and the Elimination of Discrimination* (Hague Academy of International Law, Brill 2015) 153; Rebecca Adami, *Women and the Universal Declaration of Human Rights* (Routledge 2019).

21 Diane Otto (ed), *Gender Issues and Human Rights* (Edward Elgar 2013).

that render the search for justice ineffective and inadequate.[22] Scholars have warned of the challenges that persist in translating *de jure* equality into *de facto* empowerment.[23] Some scholars, such as Adami, Plesch and Acharya, suggest that progress towards substantive equality requires the inclusion of new narratives able to open up space for advancing from disempowerment to empowerment.[24]

Our edited volume has the aim of 'seeing the unseen'[25] and adding lived experiences to investigate the limits and boundaries of human rights law. To this end, it focuses on ways of shifting from powerless to powerful equality through implementation of the law and emancipatory purposes in redistributing powers and resources.[26] After demonstrating how the gender–power nexus helps in unpacking the *de facto* mechanisms (informal and formal) that matter for women's inclusion, we outline practical steps towards a larger and historically informed, post-pandemic 'powerful equality' framework that engages the world beyond academia. Our book focuses on complementary dimensions (socio-economic, cultural, public, and decision-making) to offer a useful framework that connects human rights, participation and institutionalisation as building blocks for the pursuit of women's advancement around the world. We will explore these dimensions with the ultimate aim of raising broad awareness of the need to invest in gender equality for the construction of our society (representativeness), human development (economic and social rights), and sustainability (inclusiveness).

The achievement of gender equality and women's empowerment is crucial to strengthen our ability to face emerging global challenges, especially those that could exacerbate pre-existing disadvantages. Thus, building resilience

22 Mary Picard, 'Empowering Women in Climate, Environment and Disaster Risk Governance: from National Policy to Local Action' EGM/ENV/BP.1, Background Paper; De Búrca (n 2).

23 Pippa Norris, 'The State of Women's Participation and Empowerment: New Challenges to Gender Equality' Background Paper in UN Women Expert Group Meeting.

24 Rebecca Adami et al., 'Commentary – The Restorative Archeology of Knowledge about the Role of Women in the History of the UN – Theoretical Implications for International Relations' in Rebecca Adami and Dan Plesch (eds), *Women and the UN: A New History of Women's International Human Rights* (Routledge 2021) 161.

25 Fareda Banda, 'The Limits of Law' in Bardo Fassbender and Knut Traisbach (eds), *The Limits of Human Rights* (OUP 2019) 268.

26 Hanna Beate Schöpp-Schilling and Cees Flinterman (eds), *The Circle of Empowerment: Twenty-Five Years of the UN Committee on the Elimination of Discrimination against Women* (The Feminist Press at the City University of New York 2007).

to face the adverse impacts of climate change, the rapid spread of digitalisation and inequality, as well as the emergence of anti-gender movements is essential.[27]

3 Non-ideal Theory and Global Gender Justice

We adopt a non-ideal gender theory as the methodological approach to analyse some of the unresolved and less well-explored issues related to gender inequality.[28] This approach has been used in various contexts, including more recently in the context of gender studies, to connect with global justice.[29] As highlighted by Jaggar, the appeal of non-ideal theory is that it starts from the reality of women's situation in all its variety, informed by 'direct experience and by a commitment to action'.[30] Instead of the 'picture of an ideal world',[31] this approach calls for capturing gender concerns and inequality as it emerges from a combination of micro and macro dynamics. In this way, it is possible to shed new light on ways of redressing gender injustice and identifying political responsibilities that can only arise from discussions that are 'more gender-just'.[32] It allows the readers to put themselves in women's shoes and to understand the impact of gender inequality on different scales in the workplace, politics, and everyday life. Rather than sticking to the traditional method of analysis from the outside, our ambitious exercise allows us to share the real-life stories of women who have been able to step out from the shadows using

27 As highlighted by the UN Secretary-General '64. Transforming the balance of power is essential for promoting and protecting women's human rights and solving the urgent challenges of the current age, from deepening inequalities and polarization, to the climate crisis and the COVID-19 pandemic' (CSW n (13)). Several developments will help to face these specific challenges posed to women's rights in this turbulent and rapidly changing era, where the risk of rising inequality and invisibility is high. For instance, the CEDAW Committee opted not to keep silent on these issues by adopting Recommendation No. 37, which specifically urges states to promote participation and empowerment in disaster risk reduction. CEDAW, General Recommendation No. 37 (2018) on Gender-related Dimensions of Disaster Risk Reduction in the Context of Climate Change, 7 February 2018, UN Doc CEDAW/C/GR/37.

28 Alison M Jaggar 'Global Gender Justice' in Thom Brooks (ed), *The Oxford Handbook of Global Justice* (OUP 2020).

29 Clare Heyward and Dominic Roser (eds), *Climate Justice in a Non-Ideal World* (OUP 2016).

30 Jaggar (n 28); Elisabeth Anderson, *The Imperative of Integration* (Princeton University Press 2013); D'Ignazio and Klein (n 4).

31 Anderson (n 30).

32 Jaggar (n 28).

their experience to bring a change in perspective – what Gurumurthy called 'the empiricism of lived experience'.[33] Accordingly, gender is seen through the prism of day-to-day interactions to identify existing problems and to overcome what D'Ignazio and Klein describe as the 'privilege hazard': 'the phenomenon that makes those who occupy the most privileged positions among us […] so poorly equipped to recognize instances of oppression in the world'.[34] Through the voices of women whose lives and work are contributing to the fulfilment of the collective task of inclusion, this edited volume provides an original analysis of the socio-economic and political ingredients of global gender justice.

Our overall aim is to encourage a rethink of the unequal position of women around the world, broadening the scope of traditional gender studies by applying 'action guiding non-ideal theory', which could result in recommendations on ways to move towards a 'more just world'.[35] This could be achieved through calling attention to the most pressing 'imbalanced sets of life options' and perspectives for women;[36] through our questioning of traditional and ossified institutional structures, and through demonstrating how scholars and practitioners in an 'expanding set of allied fields' can contribute in meaningful and practical ways to improving the situation of women most affected by the power bias.

4 Structure of the Book

The structure of our book mirrors the inequality of this present and unique moment to provide an original reflection around three major lines of enquiry. Each of these is presented in a separate part of the book as described in detail in the following sections.

4.1 *Women and Resilient Inequalities*

The book starts with a historical account of gender (in)equalities in the area of women's rights by focusing on the conceptual limits for women's empowerment

33 D'Ignazio and Klein (n 4) 29. D'Ignazio and Klein refer to the keynote lecture given by Anita Gurumurthy (IT for Change, India) at the Data Justice Conference, 2018, Cardiff University (the recordings are available at https://cardiff.cloud.panopto.eu/Panopto/Pages/Viewer.aspx?id=bdcb2ca7-1e69-48b8-8c95-a8e700c494cf).

34 ibid 29.

35 Clare Heyward and Dominic Roser 'Introduction', in Clare Heyward and Dominic Roser (eds), *Climate Justice in a Non-Ideal World* (OUP 2016) 8–9.

36 Jaggar (n 28).

emerging in the human rights field. The first section examines the intersection with power and draws attention to the structural bases of women's exclusion.[37]

Patricia Schulz's chapter 'Progress in and Challenges to the Rights of Women to Non-Discrimination and Gender Equality' introduces the edited volume by reviewing the international legal framework on women's human rights and linking it to the political objectives contained in the UN Sustainable Development Goals adopted in 2015. Schulz describes the progress made at national level with the adoption of laws conforming to international human rights standards, mainly the Convention on the Elimination of Discrimination Against Women (CEDAW) and its double requirement for formal and substantive equality. She illustrates challenges to the implementation of the principles of non-discrimination and gender equality including insufficient resources, regressive policies, lack of political will, and attacks against women human rights defenders, which states need to overcome when moving towards powerful equality.

In the second chapter 'A Quantum Leap for Gender Equality: For a Better Future of Work for All' Beghini, Cattaneo, and Pozzan offer a timely contribution on the role of the International Labour Organization (ILO) in challenging inequality through the protection of women's socio-economic rights.[38] In 1919, the ILO adopted the first conventions on women and work. A century later, women are a force in the labour market, breaking down boundaries that at one time would have been considered unbreakable.[39] Despite the significant advances made for women at work over the past century, 'there is no room for complacency'.[40] Beghini, Pozzan, and Cattaneo base their analysis on the insights from the ILO's report that is the culmination of the extensive and often ground-breaking work undertaken in the context of the ILO's Women at Work Centenary Initiative.[41] The findings and recommendations of the Initiative resonate with the 2030 Agenda for Sustainable Development, which was adopted by the UN General Assembly in 2015.[42] The realisation of the 2030 Agenda depends on the achievement of gender equality in the world of work.

37 Otto (n 8); Martha C Nussbaum, 'Women's Progress and Women's Human Rights' in Fassbender and Traisbach (eds) (n 25).

38 ILO, 'A Quantum Leap for Gender Equality: For a Better Future of Work for All' (2019).

39 Eileen Boris et al., *Women's ILO: Transnational Networks, Global Labour Standards, and Gender Equity, 1919 to Present* (Brill 2018).

40 ILO (n 38) ; See also Adami (n 5).

41 ILO (n 38).

42 United Nations, 'Beijing Declaration and Platform for Action, The Fourth World Conference on Women' (1995); Pascale Allotey et al., 'Doing Gender Better: Can the UN Step Up?' (2019) 393 (10189) The Lancet 2371.

By highlighting key gender gaps and obstacles to decent work for women, the chapter aims to reinforce the need for a multifaceted approach. It also points out the measures that can, and should, be taken to seize the opportunities presented by the changing world of work. To this end, Beghini, Cattaneo, and Pozzan explore the structural barriers, including unpaid care work, that shape the nature and extent of women's engagement in paid employment, and how the challenges posed by the COVID-19 pandemic are being taken into account.

A broad understanding of how human rights law can be used to support change is based on an examination of the intersection of key concepts such as non-discrimination and gender mainstreaming to reveal the tensions between emancipatory change and institutional commitments on further organisational efforts.[43] Bustreo et al.'s chapter 'Gender Mainstreaming at the World Health Organization: Experiences, Challenges and Pitfalls in Global Health' presents a more precise 'conceptual vocabulary' by reviewing the history of gender mainstreaming in one of the United Nations (UN) specialised agencies, the World Health Organization (WHO).[44] The authors rigorously investigate how the concept of gender mainstreaming has been recognised as a critical and strategic approach for achieving gender equality commitments within the UN.[45] WHO began initiatives to operationalise gender and human rights after the 1995 Beijing Platform for Action, largely focusing on women and reproductive health.[46] In 2000, WHO created the Department of Gender and Women's Health and subsequently, in 2007, the World Health Assembly endorsed the 'Strategy for integrating gender analysis and actions into the work of WHO'. Bustreo et al. discuss the pioneering experience of WHO in its attempt to mainstream gender as a relational concept across the organisation

43 As described by Caglar et al. 'from an institutional perspective, GM is intended to create the conditions for institutional learning, for instance by building up gender expertise within organizations. The idea is to enable bureaucrats to reorganize institutional procedures and to redefine policy values in ways to achieve gender equality', Gulay Caglar et al., 'Gender in International Governance' in Steans and Tepe-Belfrage (n 12) 409.

44 Veronica Magar et al., 'Gender Mainstreaming within WHO: Not without Equity and Human Rights' (2019) 393 (10182) The Lancet 1678; C Nivedita and Madhumati Deshpande, 'Role of Feminist Movements in Gender Mainstreaming Policies: The Case of UN' (2019) 6(1) International Journal of Research and Analytical Reviews (IJRAR) 289.

45 As recalled by Otto 'after many years of marginalization in institutions devoted specifically to issues of concern to women, there are now many signs that "women's issues" are in the process of becoming institutionally "mainstreamed" in the UN, at least in the sense of integrating them into existing systems', Otto (n 8) 5; Sari Kuovo 'The United Nations and Gender Mainstreaming: Limits and Possibilities' in Doris Buss and Ambreena Manji (eds), *International Law: Modern Feminist Approaches* (Hart 2005) 237, 252.

46 Sundari Ravindran and A Kelkar-Khambete, 'Gender Mainstreaming in Health: Looking Back, Looking Forward' (2008) 3 Global Public Health 121.

and its programmes.[47] With their innovative analysis the authors contribute to highlight key factors for implementing innovative mainstreaming strategies to tackle the structural causes of gender inequalities and to achieve real transformative social change.

4.2 *Women and Socio-economic Equality*

The second part of the volume introduces some contemporary developments in women's socio-economic participation. It covers specific thematic areas (financial equality and gendered division of labour) that require direct action to move forward the parity debate.[48] To this end the chapters in Part 2 explore how current frameworks fail to capture the importance to the economic sphere of women's power and active agency.[49] The authors examine the relevance of addressing status bias (citizenship – chapters 4 and 5) and economic disadvantages (e.g. gendered division of labour – chapters 6 and 7 and financial literacy – chapter 8) to address women's unequal roles in decision-making.

The chapter by Mantu '(En)gendering EU Citizenship' addresses the role of European Union (EU) citizenship for mobile women. Mantu argues that within the EU, citizenship is considered to be the fundamental status of the nationals of the Member States, allowing them to enjoy a privileged legal position

47 Flavia Bustreo, Anna Giulia Ponchia, Cecilia Rocco, Rachael Hinton, 'Strengthening the Transformative Potential of Gender Mainstreaming in Global Health' (14 April 2021) 34 (100858) EClinicalMedicine.

48 Larking, in her analysis, focuses for instance on the role of trade and investment regimes in institutionalising 'gendered economic and social inequalities', Emma Larking 'Challenging Gendered Economic and Social Inequalities: An Analysis of the Role of Trade and Financial Liberalisation in Deepening Inequalities, and of the Capacity of Economic and Social Rights to Redress Them' in Rimmer H and Ogg K (eds), *Research Handbook on Feminist Engagement with International Law* (Edward Elgar 2019) 306; Anne-Catherine Fortas, 'Droit International Economique et Genre' in Jänterä-Jareborg and Tigroudja (eds.) (n 20); D'Ignazio and Klein (n 4); Kathryn Sikkink, *Evidence for Hope: Making Human Rights Work in the 21st Century* (Princeton University Press 2017).

49 Erturk adopts a political economy approach to reveal how 'power operated not only through coercion but also through the structured relations of production and reproduction that govern the distribution and use of resources, benefits, privileges and authority within the home and society at large. Political economy interacts with, alters and reconfigures the institutional and ideological formations of society where gender identities and statuses are shaped and the boundaries of rights and freedoms demarcated', Human Rights Council (HRC), A/HRC/11/6, 'Promotion and Protection of All Human Rights, Civil, Political, Economic, Social and Cultural Rights, Including the Right to Development' (18 May 2019) Report of the Special Rapporteur on Violence Against Women, Its Causes and Consequences, Yakin Erturk, 'Political Economy of Women's Human Rights' para 27.

in comparison with non-EU migrants.[50] Although EU citizens have a fundamental right to move and reside freely within the territory of other EU states, their mobility depends on their capacity for financial self-sufficiency, either as EU workers or by possessing sufficient resources. Mantu shows that the legal categories and rules on the exercise of free movement rights are not designed to take women's specificities into account. Issues such as the value of care work, opting out of employment for family reasons, concentration in low-paid, short-term and insecure jobs, and interruptions to working life have legal consequences that constrain mobility for EU women as well as impacting on their residence status and access to the welfare state. Yet, gender considerations remain largely absent in EU citizenship law and case law, raising questions as to the gendered nature of this status and the best way to prevent gender discrimination in the enjoyment of EU citizenship rights. The chapter by Fresnoza-Flot 'Gender Gaps in Migration Studies: Recent Developments and Prospects' describes how feminist scholars have contributed to the burgeoning of 'gender and migration' scholarship by reworking the introduction of gender perspectives in migration studies. In her chapter, Fresnoza conducts a comprehensive qualitative review of the 'gender and migration' scholarship and a quantitative analysis of the broader migration literature using a bibliometric approach. Through this combination of analytical methods, Frensnoza-Flot identifies three major gender gaps: feminised gender, which overlooks other socially constructed categories; heteronormativity, which impedes the inclusion of sexuality and queer perspectives in migration research; and the incomplete engendering of this field. Fresnoza-Flot demonstrates the need for strengthening collaborative actions to raise migration studies to the next level by making them more interdisciplinary, diversified, and gender sensitive.

Two chapters in this section analyse a specific set of challenges posed by the COVID-19 pandemic for progress of women's rights: the threat that existing inequalities will be exacerbated and that new difficulties will be created. Blasko's chapter 'Unpaid Work during the COVID-19 Pandemic: Amount, Allocation and the Aftermath: A European Perspective' offers a timely review of the consequences of COVID-19 stressing the socio-economic implications.[51] Gender

50 Sylvia Walby, 'The European Union and Gender Equality: Emergent Varieties of Gender Regimes' (2004) 11 (1) Social Politics: International Studies in Gender, State & Society 4; Jo Shaw, 'The European Union and Gender Mainstreaming: Constitutionally Embedded or Comprehensively Marginalised?' (2002) 10 Feminist Legal Studies 213.

51 Clare Wenham et al., 'COVID-19: The Gendered Impacts of the Outbreak' (2020) The Lancet 846; World Bank (WB), 'Gender Dimensions of the COVID-19 Pandemic' (2020) Policy Note; World Economic Forum (WEF), 'Why We Need Women's Leadership in the COVID-19 Response' (2020).

segregation in the labour market, and the unequal distribution of unpaid work that already existed within households before the pandemic, have made the impact of the crisis very different for men and women. While, in many ways, women seem to have paid a higher social and economic price, new opportunities to achieve a better work–life balance for both genders have emerged. Although still far from being complete, the growing evidence base helps to evaluate the early concerns about the possible damage that COVID-19 can do to gender equality in Europe as well as the hope of moving current normative frameworks towards making proposals for equal gender norms. Blasko focuses on the crisis-enforced changes in households and by looking at findings from COVID-19 surveys (national and comparative ones), her account helps to better understand some of the main developments in gender equality in Europe one year after the outbreak of the crisis.

Martucci, Minello, and Manzo's chapter 'The Unequal Ivory Tower: The Effects of COVID-19 on Academic Mothers' complements Blasko's chapter by zooming in on how the COVID-19 lockdown exacerbated gender inequality in heterosexual families, as well as in women's workplaces. With the shift to remote work for professionals in spring 2020, mothers took on more of the burdens of childcare and other domestic tasks, compared with their male partners. Within academia, gender inequality in the home and in the workplace interacted to create a significant impact on mothers' careers.[52] The closure of childcare services and universities led to a conflict between domestic duties and extremely demanding careers, and many mothers had to delay less time-sensitive work tasks like research and writing. Martucci, Minello, and Manzo show how academic mothers feared that the interruption caused by COVID-19 would affect their career trajectories in the long term. The only women in their sample who consistently felt successful as academics and mothers during the lockdown were the ones who had access to childcare from family, partners, babysitters, or nannies – the ones for whom a more 'sustainable' version of life persisted. Based on their findings, Martucci, Minello, and Manzo propose policy recommendations that take into account the 'motherhood gap' and alternative ways to evaluate academic careers.

This final chapter of Part 2, by Harvey and Cristani 'Women and Financial Equality: Rewriting the Rules' investigates financial equality and financial literacy to identify a new narrative that can empower girls and women to participate in the financial economy. Harvey and Cristani argue that without a new narrative, it will be hard to expedite the path towards economic gender

---

52 Alessandra Minello, 'The Pandemic and the Female Academic' (2020) Nature.

equality. It will also be difficult to influence gendered structures that embrace the distributions of economic resources, such as earning, negotiating, and investing.[53] After a preliminary overview of the theoretical and legal framework of financial equality, they illustrate the salient elements of the new narrative needed to achieve financial inclusion and to overcome the barriers that women are still facing in the financial sector. Harvey and Cristani advocate for strengthening financial education, starting at an early age, as a powerful tool to achieve financial equality.

They go on to suggest a gender-reinterpretation of social and economic structures to facilitate women's full enjoyment of equal access to material resources and opportunities.[54] This chapter provides a fresh articulation that directly connects the interdependence of persons and the power relations they face, or generate, with central aspects of contemporary economic and social practice.[55]

4.3 *Women's Participation at the International Level and Institutional Encounters*

The last part of the volume concentrates on the gendered dimensions of participation at international level.[56] The limited participation of women is becoming an increasing concern with respect to international representation.[57] According to the GQUAL campaign 'women are underrepresented in virtually every international body responsible for adjudicating, monitoring, and developing international law'.[58] To address this situation, this part of the book takes up the very challenging task of understanding how to improve

53 The review by Larking confirms that 'women are frequently excluded from access on equal terms to financial markets and services' Larking (n 48) 308.

54 Guimei Bai, 'Women's Rights are Human Rights. A Response to Hilary Charlesworth and Christine Chinkin from a Chinese Perspective' in Fassbender and Traisbach (eds) (n 25).

55 As suggested by Larking 'given the structural power imbalances and deepening material inequalities within the marketplace, incorporating more women within it will not miraculously ensure an improvement in their economic and social status. Moreover, it will undermine women's capacity to structure their lives according to alternative social understanding and political economies' Larking (n 48) 322.

56 Steans and Tepe-Belfrage (n 12).

57 UN Human Rights Council, A/HRC/47/51, 'Current Levels of Representation of Women in Human Rights Organs and Mechanisms: Ensuring Gender Balance' (21 May 2021) Report of the Human Rights Advisory Committee; Freya Baetens (ed), *Identity and Diversity on the International Bench, Who is the Judge?* (OUP 2020).

58 Claudia Martin, 'Article 8 of the Convention to Eliminate All Forms of Discrimination against Women (CEDAW): A Stepping Stone in Ensuring Gender Parity in International Organs and Tribunals' (2016) INTLAWGRRLS.

women's participation by describing formal and informal mechanisms that influence gender divides.[59] While the UN Secretary-General has achieved gender parity at the top management level of the UN, a wide gender gap remains in other bodies.[60] The International Law Commission (ILC) offers a significant example. The ILC was established by the General Assembly in 1947 to implement article 13 (1a) of the UN Charter, which states that the General Assembly 'should initiate studies and make recommendations for the purpose of promoting co-operation in the political field and encouraging the progressive development of international law and its codifications'.[61] The ILC is mostly composed of men. During the 70th anniversary celebration of the ILC, held in New York in May 2018, a side event entitled '7 Women in 70 Years: Achieving Gender Parity in the ILC' was organised and 'the title by itself spoke volumes'.[62] In seventy years, only seven members out of the total 229 members elected to the ILC have been women, with the first woman elected in 2001.[63] In 2021, for the first time in its history, four women out of a total of thirty-four members of the Commission are serving at the same time.[64] The new ILC members were elected in November 2021 and five women will start their mandate in 2023.[65] The imbalance of representation was highlighted by representatives of regional groups before the elections.[66] Pinto, a former member of the ILC, recently stressed the need to 'encourage states to reach parity

59 Gulay Caglar et al., 'Gender in International Governance' in Steans and Tepe-Belfrage (n 12); Anne-Marie Slaughter and Hilary Charlesworth, 'The Gender of International Institutions. Proceedings of the Annual Meeting' (5–8 April 1995) American Society of International Law, 89 Structures of World Order 79.

60 UN Human Rights Council (n 49).

61 UN General Assembly Resolution 174 (11) (21 November 1947).

62 Miguel de Serpa Soares, 'Seven Women in Seventy Years: A Roundtable Discussion on Achieving Gender Parity at the International Law Commission' (2018) Statement, United Nations Office of Legal Affairs; Oral Nilufer, 'Gender Equality in the United Nations System: A Closer Look at the International Law Commission' in Gender Lecture Series 'Talking Gender, Equality and Diversity' organized by Fornalé, World Trade Institute, 29 May 2019.

63 Monica Pinto, 'The Authority and the Membership of the Commission in the Future' in The United Nations, *Seventy Years of the International Law Commission. Drawing Balance for the Future* (Brill 2021).

64 See the website of the International Law Commission <https://legal.un.org/ilc/ilcmembe .shtml> accessed 29 November 2021.

65 See outcome of the elections 2021. Women elected include: Ms Okowa Phoebe (Kenya), Ms Mangklatanakul Vilawan (Thailand), Ms Galvao Teles Patricia (Portugal), Ms Oral Nilufer (Turkey), Ms Ridings Penelope (New Zealand) <https://legal.un.org/ilc/elections/ 2021election_outcome.shtml> accessed 29 November 2021.

66 In the list of candidates out of 42 candidates, only 8 were women.

when proposing candidates'.[67] The 'glass ceiling' ('the invisible barriers, created by attitudinal and organisational prejudices, to block women from senior executive position')[68] has been a significant obstacle for women working at the UN, which has been likened to 'the world's largest men's club'.[69]

Kessedjian's chapter 'Gender Equality in the Judiciary – with an Emphasis on International Judiciary' offers fresh insights into the historical and current participation of women in the international judiciary to advance the existing literature on this topic.[70] In recent years, this research area has attracted increasing interest,[71] especially in the context of international law,[72] and it

67 See for instance 'to conclude my remarks, allow me to make a brief but important reflection on the composition of the International Law Commission from a gender perspective. As other delegations have already pointed out, we cannot fail to draw attention to the fact that the ILC includes a small number of women among its members (4 at present) and that the number of women candidates in the current electoral process is also very small (only 8 candidates). It is obvious that the composition of the Commission does not reflect the reality of the group of jurists specialized in international law and we can only express our wish that this inadequacy be progressively reduced'. Agustin Santos Maraver, at the Sixth Committee of the 76th Session of the General Assembly, Agenda Item 82: 'Report of the International Law Commission on the Work of its Seventy-Second Session' Cluster II, Statement, Spain, 1 November 2021. 'I would like to close by briefly addressing the upcoming ILC election. Simply put, the ILC historically and currently lacks anything close to gender balance. The statistics are well known – in the 72 years of its existence, the ILC has had just seven female members. In its current composition, the ILC has just four women out of 34 members. Prior to those four, only three women had ever served on the ILC. There is an opportunity this year to move the ILC in the right direction, so that its membership comes a little closer to reflecting the global community. There are eight women running in this year's election, all well qualified in their own right. This includes the U.S. candidate, Professor Evelyn Aswad, who, if elected, would bring to the commission a valuable combination of government, multilateral, and academic experience. Even if all eight of these candidates are elected, women would still constitute less than a quarter – 8 out of 34 seats – of the membership on the ILC. We can and must do better. In the meantime, the United States expresses its appreciation to the governments nominating or otherwise supporting female candidates for the ILC this year. We also thank and congratulate the seven women who previously served on the ILC, who helped blaze the trail'. Richard Visek, Statement at the 76th Session General Assembly Sixth Committee Agenda Item 82: 'Report on International Law Commission on the Work of its 72nd Session' United States Department of State, October 26, 2021.

68 Kirsten Haack, 'Breaking Barriers? Women's Leadership and Representation at the United Nations' (2014) 20 Global Governance 37.

69 Gayle Kirshenbaum, 'Inside the World's Largest Men's Club' (1992) MS 16.

70 Françoise Tulkens, 'Parity on the Bench: Why? Why not?' (2014) 6 EHRLR 587–595.

71 Stephanie Hennette Vauchez, 'More Women – But Which Women? The Rule and the Politics of Gender Balance at European Court of Human Rights' (2015) 26 (1) European Journal of International Law 195.

72 Françoise Tulkens, 'More Women – But Which Women? A Reply to Stéphanie Hennette Vauchez' (2015) 26 (1) European Journal of International Law 223.

constantly raises questions related to the legitimacy of the judiciary. The chapter provides an empirical analysis of the process by which judges are recruited and appointed in the international judiciary and the dynamics and barriers to be overcome by women.

The final chapter by Germano and Fornalé reflects on the whole process of institutionalisation during the lockdown that has seen only a very small proportion of women occupying positions in international and domestic institutions, such as the 'technoscientific' ones, created by Member States to respond to the pandemic.[73] Germano and Fornalé offer a historical overview of the role of participatory rights guaranteed by the CEDAW Convention (article 7 and article 8). The CEDAW was the first international instrument to clearly address (in article 8) the issue of equal participation and representation at the international level, calling upon states to ensure women's presence 'as delegates and representatives of their own countries at international level and to participate in the work of international organizations'.[74] While substantial scholarship has focused on gender parity and quota mechanisms at domestic level,[75] much less attention has been paid to the international domain and how the dynamics of women's representation in international institutions mirrors the weaknesses of the domestic domain.[76]

The point made is that we 'should not assume too early' that participation at the international level will sort itself out as a direct outcome of the domestic struggle; instead, we need to engage critically with the informal and discretionary mechanisms that may increase the inclusion of women at the international level.[77] The chapter's major aim is to conduct an in-depth investigation of the creation of these institutional mechanisms at international level (e.g. WHO) and at domestic level (e.g. Italy) to understand how they interfere

73 Lena Felton, 'The Consequences of a Coronavirus Task Force Made Almost Entirely of Men' (2 March 2020) <https://www.thelily.com/the-consequences-of-a-coronavirus-task-force-made-almost-entirely-of-men/?> accessed 29 November 2021.

74 Committee on the Elimination of Discrimination against Women (CEDAW Committee), CEDAW/C/1994/4, 'Implementation of Article 21 of the Convention on the Elimination of All Forms of Discrimination Against Women, Analysis of Articles 7 and 8 of the Convention' (1993) Report by the Secretariat 22.

75 Eléonore Lépinard and Ruth Rubio-Marín (eds), *Transforming Gender Citizenship. The Irresistible Rise of Gender Quotas in Europe* (CUP 2018); Drude Dahlerup, 'Gender Quotas in Politics' in L Sandy Maisel (ed), *Oxford Bibliographies in Political Science* (OUP 2020); Drude Dahlerup, *Has Democracy failed Women?* (Polity Press 2017).

76 Charlesworth and Chinkin (n 1).

77 Pippa Norris (n 12).

with the exercise of 'participatory rights' guaranteed by the CEDAW (article 7 and article 8).[78] To this end, Germano and Fornalé use this emergency-led development as a 'reality check' to explore the normative implications of the concept of 'representation' at institutional level (the so-called 'gendering' of institutional bodies at all levels) to understand the ways in which it is possible to intervene both formally and informally in the mechanisms that contribute to hinder women's access.

5 Background Information

This book originates from the Gender Lecture Series 'Know the GAP! Talking Gender, Equality and Diversity', which took place from September 2019 to May 2022.[79] This is the first English-language series open to the full university and to the general public, featuring prominent individuals in academia, private sector and international organisations and focused on both research and actual experience with gender balance and policy. Inaugurated in 2019, this lecture series has so far involved twenty-five leading speakers from around the world to address pressing gender issues, including: gender equality and human rights; gender equality and women's empowerment; power and representation during the pandemic.[80] Our authors are women who have successfully broken through the 'glass ceiling' and their personal accounts provide insights about the meaning given to gender based on choices, roles, social interactions and experiences in real life. With this publication, we aim to transform their original contributions into a new format that will contribute to the advancement of

78 Sarah Wittkopp, 'Article 7' in Marsha Freeman et al. (eds), The UN Convention on the Elimination of all Forms of Discrimination Against Women (OUP 2012); Sarah Wittkopp, 'Article 8' in Marsha Freeman et al., *The UN Convention on the Elimination of all Forms of Discrimination Against Women* (OUP 2012); Ruth Rubio-Marín and Will Kymlicka (eds), *Gender Parity and Multicultural Feminism: Towards a New Synthesis* (OUP 2018).

79 After the adoption of the Gender Action Plan (GAP) in 2018, the World Trade Institute created its own Gender Team (*Know the GAP! Team*). Since then, the team has been led by SNSF Prof. Elisa Fornalé, acting as gender coordinator. She has been supported by Ms Sophia Thompson (in charge of administrative activities), Mr Francesco De Fino (in charge of communication activities), Mr Pablo Das (in charge of social media tools), Ms Susan Kaplan (coaching) and Dr Aylin Yildiz (in charge of ensuring peer-to-peer engagement).

80 All podcasts are available online <https://www.wti.org/institute/equality/#open-92959-podcasts> accessed 29 November 2021.

gender equality. To this end, papers have been selected and tailored to create a coherent manuscript that sheds new light on the socio-economic and political conceptual dimensions behind the inequality we face today.

References

Adami R, *Women and the Universal Declaration of Human Rights* (Routledge 2019).

Adami R and Plesch D (eds), *Women and the UN: A New History of Women's International Human Rights* (Routledge 2022).

Allotey P et al., 'Doing Gender Better: Can the UN Step Up?' (2019) 393 The Lancet 2371.

Anderson E, *The Imperative of Integration* (Princeton University Press 2010).

Anderson E, *Social Movements, Experiments in Living and Moral Progress: Case Studies from Britain's Abolition of Slavery* (University of Kansas 2014).

Baetens F (ed), *Identity and Diversity on the International Bench, Who is the Judge?* (OUP 2020).

Banda F, 'The Limits of Law' in Fassbender B and Traisbach K (eds), *The Limits of Human Rights* (OUP 2019).

Byrnes AC, 'The "Other" Human rights Treaty Body: The Work of the Committee on the Elimination of Discrimination against Women' (1989) 14 (1) Yale Journal of International Law 1–67.

Brooks T (ed), *The Oxford Handbook of Global Justice* (OUP 2020).

Buss D and Manji A (eds), *International Law: Modern Feminist Approach* (Hart Publishing 2005).

Cairns I, 'The Costs of (Partial) Inclusion: The Evolution, Limits and Biases of Principal Feminist Challenges to International Law', in Jänterä-Jareborg M and Tigroudja H (eds), *Women's Human Rights and the Elimination of Discrimination* (Hague Academy of International Law, Brill 2015).

Charlesworth H and Chinkin C, *The Boundaries of International Law: A Feminist Analysis* (Manchester University Press 2000).

Charlesworth H and Chinkin C, 'Between the Margins and the Mainstream' in Fassbender B and Traisbach K (eds), *The Limits of Human Rights* (OUP 2019).

Chinkin C, 'Gender and Economic, Social, and Cultural Rights' in Riedel E et al. (eds), *Economic, Social and Cultural Rights in International Law* (OUP 2014).

Collins P, *Black Feminist Thought: Knowledge, Consciousness, and the Politics of Empowerment* (Routledge 2008).

Dahlerup D, 'Representing Women: Defining Substantive Representation of Women' in Escobar-Lemmon MC and Taylor-Robinson MM (eds), *Representation. The Case of Women* (OUP 2014).

Dahlerup D, 'The Critical Mass Theory in Public and Scholarly Debates' in Campbell R and Childs S (eds), *Deeds and Words: Gendering Politics after Joni Lovenduski* (ECPR Press 2014).

Dahlerup D, *Has Democracy failed Women?* (Polity Press 2018).

Dahlerup D, 'Gender Quotas in Politics' in Maisel S (ed), *Oxford Bibliographies in Political Science* (Oxford 2020).

de Burca G, *Reframing Human Rights in a Turbulent Era* (OUP 2021).

D'Ignazio C and Klein L, *Data Feminism* (MIT 2020).

Franceschet S and Krook ML (eds), *The Palgrave Handbook of Women's Political Rights* (Palgrave Macmillan 2019).

Haack K, 'Breaking Barriers? Women's Leadership and Representation at the United Nations' (2014) 20 Global Governance 37.

Heyward C and Roser D (eds), *Climate Justice in a Non-Ideal World* (OUP 2016).

Herten-Crabb A and Davies S, 'Why WHO Needs a Feminist Economic Agenda' (2020) 28 The Lancet 1018–1020.

Hellum A and Aasen HS (eds), *Women's Human Rights, CEDAW in International, Regional and National Law* (CUP 2013).

Htun M and Weldon SL, *The Logics of Gender Justice State Action on Women's Rights Around the World* (CUP 2018).

Knop K (ed), *Gender and Human Rights* (OUP 2004).

Krisch N, 'International Law in Times of Hegemony: Unequal Power and the Shaping of the International Legal Order' (2005) 16 European Journal of International Law 369.

Kuovo S, 'The United Nations and Gender Mainstreaming: Limits and Possibilities' in Buss D and Manji A (eds). *International Law: Modern Feminist Approaches* (Hart 2005) 237.

Lépinard E and Rubio-Marín R (eds), *Transforming Gender Citizenship. The Irresistible Rise of Gender Quotas in Europe* (Cambridge 2018).

Luhmann N, *Trust and Power* (Polity Press 2017).

Magar V et al., 'Gender Mainstreaming within WHO: Not without Equity and Human Rights' (2019) 393 (10182) The Lancet 1678.

MacKinnon AC, *Feminism Unmodified Discourses on Life and Law* (Harvard University Press 1987).

Ni Aolain F, 'More Women – But Which Women? A Reply to Stéphanie Hennette Vauchez' (2015) 26 (1) European Journal of International Law 229.

Nivedita C and Deshpande M, 'Role of Feminist Movements in Gender Mainstreaming Policies: The Case of UN' (2019) 6 (1) International Journal of Research and Analytical Reviews (IJRAR) 26.

Nussbaum M, 'Women's Progress and Women's Human Rights' in Fassbender B and Traisbach K (eds), *The Limits of Human Rights* (OUP 2019).

Nussbaum M, *Women and Human Development: The Capabilities Approach* (CUP 2000).

Otto D, 'The Exile of Inclusion: Reflections on Gender Issues in International Law Over the Last Decade' (2009) 10 (1) *Melbourne Journal of International Law*, 11–26.

Otto D (ed), *Gender Issues and Human Rights* (Edward Elgar 2013).

Patel G, *Women and International Human Rights Law* (Routledge 2019).

Peters A, *Women, Quotas, and Constitutions: A Comparative Study of Affirmative Action for Women under American, German, EC, and International Law* (Kluwer Law International 1999).

Ravindran T and Kelkar-Khambete A, 'Gender Mainstreaming in Health: Looking Back, Looking Forward' (2008) 3(Suppl 1) Global Public Health 121–142.

Rimmer H and Ogg K (eds), *Research Handbook on Feminist Engagement with International Law* (Edward Elgar 2019).

Robertson E et al., 'Best Practices for Election of Members to International and Regional Treaty Bodies' (2019) Women at Table https://www.skadden.com/-/media/files/publications/2018/10/womenthetablereportoct2018.pdf.

Rubio-Marín R and Kymlicka W (eds), *Gender Parity and Multicultural Feminism: Towards and New Synthesis* (OUP 2018).

Phillips A, *Engendering Democracy* (The Pennsylvania State University Press 1991).

Pinto M, 'The Authority and the Membership of the Commission in the Future' in The United Nations, *Seventy Years of the International Law Commission. Drawing Balance for the Future* (Brill 2021).

Pitkin HF, *The Concept of Representation* (University of California Press 1967).

Schachter O and Joyner CC (eds), *United Nations Legal Order* (2 vols.) (Cambridge University Press 1995).

Schoop-Schilling HB and Flinterman C (eds), *The Circle of Empowerment: Twenty Five Years of the UN Committee on the Elimination of Discrimination Against Women* (The Feminist Press at the City University of New York 2007).

Shaw J, 'The European Union and Gender Mainstreaming: Constitutionally Embedded or Comprehensively Marginalised' (2002) 10 (3) Feminist Legal Studies 213.

Sikkink K, *Evidence for Hope: Making Human Rights Work in the 21st Century* (Princeton University Press 2017).

Sluga G and James C (eds), *Women, Diplomacy and International Politics since 1500* (Routledge 2015).

Steans J and Tepe-Belfrage D (eds), *Handbook on Gender in World Politics* (Edward Elgar 2013).

Tulkens F, 'Parity on the Bench: Why? Why not?' (2014) 6 EHRLR 587.

Tulkens F, 'More Women – But Which Women? A Reply to Stéphanie Hennette Vauchez' (2015) 26 (1) EJIL 223.

Vauchez SH, 'More Women – But Which Women? The Rule and the Politics of Gender Balance at European Court of Human Rights' (2015) 26 (1) EJIL 195.

Walby S, 'The European Union and Gender Equality: Emergent Varieties of Gender Regimes' (2004) 11 (1) Social Politics 4.

PART 1

Women and Resilient Inequalities

CHAPTER 1

Progress in and Challenges to the Rights of Women to Non-discrimination and Gender Equality

Patricia Schulz

1 Introduction

As is well documented, the recognition of women's rights to non-discrimination based on sex and/or gender and to gender equality is a lengthy process, marked by obstacles and sometimes backlash.[1] Indeed, the evolution that took place in the field of the law reflected the evolution in the power relationships between women and men, marked by the 'public man, private woman' divide,[2] a binary and hierarchical division of human beings, based on their biological sex. On the basis of this patriarchal construct, group characteristics have been attributed to human beings, such as intellect to men and feelings to women. Gender stereotypes and gender stereotyping have helped to maintain the power divide based on sex and gender.[3] This has had numerous consequences for access

1 See among others, Gita Sen and Marina Durano (eds), *The Remaking of Social Contracts, Feminists in a Fierce New World* (Zed books 2014); Albie Sachs and Joan Hoff Wilson, *Sexism and the Law. A Study of Male Belief and Judicial Bias* (M. Robertson 1978). See for a wealth of data, United Nations, 'The World's Women 2020. Trends and Statistics' <https://worlds-women-2020-data-undesa.hub.arcgis.com/> accessed 29 November 2021; UN Women, <https://www.unwomen.org/en> accessed 17 June 2021; The World Bank gender portal, The World Bank, 'The World Bank in Gender' <https://www.worldbank.org/en/topic/gender> accessed 29 November 2021; the SDG's UNDP gender portal, UNDP, 'Goal 5: Gender Equality' <https://www.undp.org/sustainable-development-goals#gender-equality> accessed 29 November 2021; and its COVID-19 Response tracker, UNDP, 'COVID-19 Global Gender Response Tracker' <https://data.undp.org/gendertracker/> accessed 17 June 2021; the Inter Parliamentary Union, IPU, 'Gender Equality' <https://www.ipu.org/our-impact/gender-equality> accessed 29 November 2021; the International Labour Organization, ILO, 'Gender, Equality, Diversity and Inclusion Branch (GEDI)' <https://www.ilo.org/gender/lang--en/index.htm> accessed 29 November; and Observatory on the Universality of Rights, OURS, 'Trends Report 2017' <https://www.oursplatform.org/> accessed 29 November 2021, and 'Trends Report 2021' <https://www.oursplatform.org/resource/rights-at-risk-time-for-action/> accessed 29 November 2021.

2 Jean B Elshtain, *Public Man, Private Woman* (Princeton University Press 1981).

3 Rebecca J Cook and Simone Cusack, *Gender Stereotyping. Transnational Legal Perspectives* (University of Pennsylvania Press 2010); See also Simone Cusack, 'The CEDAW as a Legal Framework for Transnational Discourses on Gender Stereotyping' in Anne Hellum and

to property including land, inheritance, work, education, health care, justice, decision-making positions in politics, science, and the economy,[4] among others. As Virginia Woolf exposed brilliantly, women have had to fight for the right to think, work, access education, and the right to autonomy, and this fight is ongoing,[5] with the pandemic having disrupted or destroyed some of the progress made in the past 20 years.

The evolution of rights and their implementation occur at the local, national, regional and international levels. Most often, change in the legal system occurs because of civil society engagement and sometimes also as a response to situations, such as conflicts and/or socio-economic crises.

At the national level, constitutions, laws and ordinances, and court cases can be the source of the legal basis for the recognition of women's rights. Programmes and strategies can support change. At the international level, a number of UN documents, adopted by the UN General Assembly or other organs play a huge role. Some have a normative nature and are legally binding for the States that ratify them. Others have a declaratory nature: without binding force, they are political declarations that often serve as an important tool for advocacy. The Universal Declaration of Human Rights is the main UN Declaration.[6] Together with the two covenants, one on civil and political rights[7] and the other on economic, social and cultural rights,[8] it forms the International Bill of Rights. They all contain the principle of sex and gender equality and non-discrimination based on sex. Other thematic

Henriette Sinding Aasen (eds), *Women's Human Rights. CEDAW in International, Regional and National Law* (Cambridge University Press 2013).

4 For an analysis of these numerous consequences in various fields, see Caroline Criado Perez, *Invisible Women. Exposing Data Bias in a World Designed for Men* (Vintage 2019).

5 Virginia Woolf, *Three Guineas* (First published by the Hogarth Press 1938, Penguin Books, 1979); UN Women, 'Turning Promises into Action: Gender Equality in the 2030 Agenda for Sustainable Development' (2018); e.g. in 2020, the Commission on the Status of Women (CSW) expressed concern that 'that major gaps remain and that obstacles, including structural barriers, discriminatory practices and the feminization of poverty, persist' and recognized 'that 25 years after the Fourth World Conference on Women, no country has fully achieved gender equality and the empowerment of women and girls'. Political Declaration on the occasion of the twenty-fifth anniversary of the Fourth World Conference on Women, ECOSOC, UN Doc E/2020/27 (E/CN.6/2020/10) 6/33, 'Report of the Commission on the Status of Women. Report on the Sixty-fourth Session' (2020) para 6.

6 Universal Declaration of Human Rights (10 December 1948), Article 2.

7 International Covenant on Civil and Political Rights (16 December 1966), Article 2 para 1, Articles 3 and 26.

8 International Covenant on Economic, Social and Cultural Rights (16 December 1966), Article 2 para 2 and Article 3.

treaties (Convention on the Elimination of All Forms of Discrimination Against Women, Convention Against Torture, Convention on the Rights of the Child, Convention on the Elimination of Racial Discrimination),[9] also play a crucial role, even though some of these texts contain no reference to women's rights. The interpretation of these conventions by the treaty bodies[10] (i.e. experts' committees) tasked with monitoring their implementation by States has generally filled this void when there was a void in the text. Their interpretation has also expanded the meaning and content of rights contained in the conventions or that could be derived from them.[11] In addition, the State parties to specialised UN agencies such as the International Labour Organization (ILO) and United Nations Educational, Scientific and Cultural Organization (UNESCO), have adopted conventions, some of which are central to women's rights to non-discrimination and gender equality.[12] Various regional treaties adopted in Europe,[13] the Americas[14] and Africa[15] including on gender-based violence against women and girls[16] and the jurisprudence from courts and commissions

---

9 Office of the High Commissioner for Human Rights (OHCHR), 'Universal Human Rights Instruments' <https://www.ohchr.org/EN/ProfessionalInterest/Pages/UniversalHumanRightsInstruments.aspx> accessed 17 June 2021.

10 OHCHR, 'Human Rights Treaty Bodies' <https://www.ohchr.org/EN/HRBodies/Pages/TreatyBodies.aspx> accessed 17 June 2021; Committee on the Elimination of Discrimination against Women (CEDAW Committee); Human Rights Committee; Committee on Economic, Social and Cultural Rights; Committee on the Rights of the Child; Committee on the Elimination of Racial Discrimination; Committee on Migrant Workers; Committee on the Rights of Persons with Disabilities; Committee on Enforced Disappearances; Committee Against Torture; Sub-Committee on the Prevention of Torture.

11 For instance, the CEDAW Committee has performed pioneering work in considering violence against women as a form of discrimination defined in Article 1 of the CEDAW Convention and prohibited in Article 2, in its General Recommendation 19 of 1997, updated by General Recommendation 35 in 2018. This was the basis for further developments in the fight against violence against women and girls, including at the regional level.

12 See International Labour Organization (ILO), 'Violence and Harassment Convention' (2019) No. 190; See also the internet portal of ILO regarding Care economy. ILO, 'The Care Economy' <https://www.ilo.org/global/topics/care-economy/lang--en/index.htm> accessed 17 June 2021; and the UNESCO's Convention against Discrimination in Education adopted in 1960.

13 European Convention on Human Rights (4 November 1950).

14 Organization of American States, 'Basic Documents in the Inter-American System' <http://www.oas.org/en/iachr/mandate/basic_documents.asp> accessed 29 November 2021.

15 African Charter on Human and Peoples' Rights (1 June 1981), Article 2.

16 For Europe, Istanbul Convention Action against Violence against Women and Domestic Violence (11 May 2011); for the Americas, Inter-American Convention on the Prevention, Punishment and Eradication of Violence against Women (Belém do Parà); for Africa,

created by these treaties are also a normative source for gender equality and non-discrimination based on sex and gender. A political tool that is important in this field has existed since 2015, namely, the 17 Sustainable Development Goals, adopted by all UN Member States.[17]

2 Progress in the Rights of Women: Legal Concepts

2.1 *From Formal to Substantive Equality*

Recognition of the rights of women has occurred through the progressive development of legal concepts, influenced by the lasting efforts of women to ensure their rights.

The first step was the recognition of the same, formal rights as men to the same treatment by the laws, in one field after another. For instance, in the political sphere, women were finally recognised as citizens and granted the right to vote that had previously only been held by men, and to be elected to functions such as parliament or the executive.[18] There were no longer any legal obstacles preventing them from co-defining the policies of their country or community at the local or provincial level. The same process of extending to women the rights that were only held by men also occurred in other fields, such as in the laws on marriage, divorce, inheritance, education, work and social security.

However, formal gender equality did not eradicate the inequality and differences of treatment in practice that women were and still are exposed to. Indeed, in a world marked by the division of labour based on sex, women still do not benefit from an equal situation with men in all fields. Most notably, women are still expected to undertake most of the domestic and care activities, and they do so.[19] Gender stereotypes still convey (explicitly or implicitly) that women are more devoted (or should be) to these tasks than to their

---

Protocol to the African Charter on Human and Peoples' Rights on the Rights of Women in Africa (1 June 2003).

17 General Assembly Resolution A/RES/70/1 and United Nations Development Programme (UNDP), 'The SDGs in Action' <https://www.undp.org/content/undp/en/home/sustainable-development-goals.html> accessed 17 June 2021; United Nations, 'The 17 Goals' <https://sdgs.un.org/goals> accessed 29 November 2021.

18 The granting of the right to vote started in 1893 in New Zealand (although women did not get the right to be elected to Parliament until 1919) and the fight for this right is ongoing as women in some countries still cannot vote, or be elected, as men can.

19 United Nations, 'Time Spent in Unpaid Work; Total Work Burden; and Work Life in Balance' <https://worlds-women-2020-data-undesa.hub.arcgis.com/app/6f02cbbfb8d34cb7806d21f4bd14e826> accessed 29 November 2021.

professional activities, whereas men are made for the public sphere and the exercise of power.

The insufficient progress towards gender equality is the reason why the concept of substantive equality[20] was developed, as a way to overcome the perpetuation of gender inequality and discrimination in practice. Substantive equality is now a standard for all treaty bodies and for many courts that agree that a different treatment may be needed to overcome inequality. Possible measures include quotas for hiring and promoting women, study grants for girls or women, and reduction of transport costs for schoolgirls, in order to overcome discrimination in the labour market or in access to education. Substantive equality aims to remedy the structural obstacles to gender equality[21] and achieve the transformation of society.

2.2 *Forms of Discrimination*

Progressively, what had been conceived as the "natural order" between the sexes marked by a hierarchy between men – the superior beings – and women – the inferior ones – came to be seen as discrimination against women. Different forms of discrimination were identified and prohibited. The first to be recognised was direct discrimination, that is discrimination against women just because they are women, on the sole basis of their being women and not men. The refusal to grant women the right to vote is an example of such direct discrimination. Other examples included the lack of access to higher education or to certain professions, as was frequent even in the 1950s or 1960s in many industrialised countries.[22] Such direct discrimination has largely been eradicated from many legal systems; however, the legal subordination of women

20 See Andrew Byrnes and Puja Kapai Paryani, 'Article 1' in Patricia Schulz et al. (eds), *The UN Convention on the Elimination of All Forms of Discrimination Against Women and its Optional Protocol*, (2nd edn, forthcoming OUP 2022); See also, for an account of the four dimensions of substantive equality, Sandra Fredman, 'Substantive Equality Revisited' (2016) 14 International Journal of Constitutional Law 712.

21 See Andrew Byrnes and Meghan Campbell, 'Article 2' in Schulz et al. (eds), *The UN Convention on the Elimination of All Forms of Discrimination Against Women and its Optional Protocol*, (2nd edn, forthcoming OUP 2022).

22 Nancy Weiss Malkiel, *"Keep the Damned Women Out": The Struggle for Coeducation* (Princeton University Press 2016), showing that it took from 1969 to 1974 to see the top US universities accept women students, and for a brief presentation, 'When Women Were Admitted to Ivy League Schools, the Complaints Sounded a lot Like a Trump Tweet' *Los Angeles Times* (Los Angeles, 21 October 2016) <https://www.latimes.com/opinion/op-ed/la-oe-malziel-when-women-claim-male-roles-20161021-snap-story.html> accessed 1 November 2021. For the medical profession in the United Kingdom, Laura Jefferson et al., 'Women in Medicine: Historical Perspectives and Recent Trends' (2015) 114 British Medical Bulletin 5.

to their husbands, often grounded in custom or religion, is still seen in some countries, especially those with a pluralist legal system.[23]

However, the second, more subtle form of discrimination, that is indirect discrimination, plays a huge role and is far more difficult to detect and overcome. Indirect discrimination occurs where a seemingly gender-neutral norm in practice discriminates against women, without an objective justification. The CEDAW Committee noted that 'Moreover, indirect discrimination can exacerbate existing inequalities owing to a failure to recognise structural and historical patterns of discrimination and unequal power relationships between women and men'.[24] For instance, if jobs (or high-level jobs) in the civil service or private sector are being advertised and offered only as full-time posts, this will affect a much larger number of women than men. Women will be excluded from these opportunities as many of them tend to work part-time, whether willingly or not, because of unequal sharing of household and care responsibilities, insufficiency or lack of childcare facilities and care facilities for invalids or other family members in need of care.

The third form of discrimination is intersectional discrimination.[25] It occurs when a woman is discriminated against not only on the basis of her sex but also because of other criteria characterising her identity or situation, such as being a foreigner, a migrant woman, a woman with a disability, or belonging to a religious, ethnic or sexual minority.[26] Fighting against indirect and intersectional

23 CEDAW Committee's General Recommendation 33 on Women's Access to Justice; See the Concluding Observations and Recommendations (CO) of the CEDAW Committee to different countries: CO Qatar, CEDAW/C/QAT/CO/2 (2019) para 49(b); CO Singapore, CEDAW/C/SGP/CO/5 (2017) para 44; CO United Arab Emirates, CEDAW/C/ARE/CO/2-3 (2015) paras 45–6; CO Brunei Darussalam, CEDAW/C/BRN/CO/1-2 (2014) paras 38–9; CO Algeria, CEDAW/C/DZA/CO/3-4 (2012) paras 46–47; See also Zainah Anwar (ed), *Wanted: Equality and Justice in the Muslim Family* (Musawah, Sisters in Islam 2009).

24 CEDAW Committee's General Recommendation 28 on the core obligations of States parties under Article 2 of the Convention on the Elimination of All Forms of Discrimination against Women, paras 9, 16 and 35; Christa Tobler, *Indirect Discrimination. A Case Study into the Development of the Legal Concept of Indirect Discrimination under EC Law* (Intersentia 2005).

25 See Byrnes and Paryani (n 20); see also Dimitrina Petrova (ed), 'Special Focus: Intersectionality' (2016) 16 The Equal Rights Review 5.

26 CEDAW Committee's General Recommendation 28 (n 24) para 18, 'The discrimination against women based on sex and gender is inextricably linked with other factors that affect women, such as race, ethnicity, religion or belief, health, status, age, class, caste and sexual orientation and gender identity. Discrimination on the basis of sex or gender may affect women belonging to such groups to a different degree or in different ways to men. States parties must legally recognize such intersecting forms of discrimination and their compounded negative impact on the women concerned and prohibit them'.

discrimination is still very difficult. This is because (most) people, including employers, educators, judges, and social services, among others are not aware of their own biases. Furthermore, most justice systems are not (yet) capable of dealing in a gender-competent way with the complexity of these issues. The present legal order and procedural rules often force women who are discriminated against to choose to fight either racial or sexist discrimination but not both at the same time, in one legal case. Legal avenues, rules of procedure, sanctions and reparation often differ depending on the grounds for discrimination invoked, with no recognition of their intersectionality.

2.3 *Sex and Gender*

Historically, one spoke of equality between the sexes, and discrimination based on sex was prohibited, based on the biological characteristics of women compared with men. But this categorisation does not reflect the reality of power relations between the sexes and their dynamics. Therefore, the concept of gender was developed, referring to the socio-economic characteristics and role assumption markers linked to being a male or female human being. For instance, although it is women who bear children (biological sex) this does not mean that men cannot play an equal role in raising children (gender). These issues were dealt with extensively in the 1995 Beijing Declaration and Platform for Action adopted by States in 1995 and which, 26 years later, remains a visionary document, encapsulating the political commitments made by all States towards "Gender Equality, Peace and Development".[27] In General Recommendation 28, the Committee stated that:

> Although the Convention only refers to sex-based discrimination, interpreting article 1 together with articles 2 (f) and 5 (a) indicates that the Convention covers gender-based discrimination against women. The term "sex" here refers to biological differences between men and women. The term "gender" refers to socially constructed identities, attributes and roles for women and men and society's social and cultural meaning for these biological differences resulting in hierarchical relationships between women and men and in the distribution of power and rights favouring men and disadvantaging women. This social positioning of women and men is affected by political, economic, cultural, social,

27 The Fourth World Conference on Women, UN Doc A/CONF.177/20, 'Beijing Declaration and Platform for Action' (15 September 1995) paras 19, 24, 38; and Platform for Action: about 160 mentions of gender, gender-sensitive policies and programmes, mainstreaming a gender perspective, in the 12 Chapters.

religious, ideological and environmental factors and can be changed by culture, society and community. The application of the Convention to gender-based discrimination is made clear by the definition of discrimination contained in article 1. This definition points out that any distinction, exclusion or restriction which has the effect or purpose of impairing or nullifying the recognition, enjoyment or exercise by women of human rights and fundamental freedoms is discrimination, even where discrimination was not intended. This would mean that identical or neutral treatment of women and men might constitute discrimination against women if such treatment resulted in or had the effect of women being denied the exercise of a right because there was no recognition of the pre-existing gender-based disadvantage and inequality that women face'.[28]

Treaty bodies and many courts state that discrimination based on sex includes discrimination based on gender, including gender identity and/or sexual orientation and falls under the anti-gender discrimination prohibition.[29]

3 Progress in the Rights of Women

3.1 *Equal Participation, Representation and Decision-making Positions: Economic and Political Participation*

Formal equality is now being considered insufficient in many countries in the context of political rights. Indeed, decades after being granted political rights, women are still generally under-represented in most political institutions, with the average proportion of women in the lower chamber of parliament being 25% and few countries having a woman as head of government or head of State.[30] The same situation is seen in the judiciary,[31] the civil service, the

28 CEDAW Committee's General Recommendation 28 (n 24) para 5.

29 CEDAW Committee's General Recommendation 28 (n 24) para 18.

30 See women's participation in national parliaments, Inter-Parliamentary Union (IPU), 'Monthly Ranking of Women in National Parliaments' <https://data.ipu.org/women-ranking?month=1&year=2021> accessed 17 June 2021; and for an infographic showing women in the executive, women heads of State or government, women speakers of parliament and women ministers, Inter-Parliamentary Union (IPU), 'Women in Politics: 2021' <https://www.ipu.org/women-in-politics-2021> accessed 29 November 2021.

31 For instance, International Development Law Organization (IDLO), 'Women Judges in Kenya: Closer to Parity, Far From Meaningful Equality' (11 March 2020) <https://www.idlo.int/news/women-judges-kenya-closer-parity-far-meaningful-equality> accessed 29 November 2021.

private sector, and in research and tertiary education, where men in high-level positions are still over-represented. Therefore, the need for specific action has become more and more acceptable – although there is still considerable debate on the pros and cons of quotas or parity. More than half the countries in the world have some sort of quota for parliaments, at the national, regional or local levels and/or for various institutions such as commissions (e.g., water commission, forestry commission). The latest evolution concerns parity, i.e. the same representation of women as for men. The countries that have experienced a notable increase in the participation of women in parliament – and the executive – are those that have adopted rules.[32] Quotas and parity can be achieved thanks to their integration in the country's Constitution, and/or at the legislative level. A modification of the electoral system is generally needed to enable the envisaged quota or the principle of parity to become reality. At present, the International Parliamentary Union and the Council of Europe advocate for parity as an integral part of a democratic system and not "only" to ensure gender equality.[33]

The number of women in decision-making positions in the economy, including in the private sector is also increasing, often thanks to measures being taken, either temporary or long-term. Nevertheless, the glass ceiling remains a reality in most countries, unless they have taken implementable temporary or permanent measures to ensure substantive equality. For instance, imposing a quota of 40% women on corporate boards has been efficient. Diversity is being advocated as a good governance tool as it has been proven that mixed teams are more efficient.[34]

32 See IPU, 'Women in Parliament in 2020, the Year in Review' https://www.ipu.org/women-in-parliament-2020 accessed 29 November 2021. 'Of the 57 countries that held elections in 2020, 25 implemented legislated quotas (either reserved seats or candidate quotas). On average, parliaments with legislated quotas elected 11.8 per cent more women to single and lower chambers than parliaments with no legal quotas (27.4 per cent v. 15.6 per cent), and 7.4 per cent more women to upper chambers (25.6 percent v. 18.2 per cent)'.

33 Council of Europe, 'Achieving Balanced Participation of Women and Men in Political and Public Decision-Making: a Gender Equality and Democratic Requirement' <https://rm.coe.int/participation-femmes-et-hommes-brochure-en-a5/168078549f> accessed 29 November 2021; IPU, 'Gender Equality' <https://www.ipu.org/our-impact/gender-equality> accessed 29 November 2021.

34 CATALYST, 'Women on Corporate Board (Quick Take)' (13 March 2020) <https://www.catalyst.org/research/women-on-corporate-boards/> accessed 29 November 2021.

3.2 *Marriage, Unions and Families*

Progress is being made regarding the economic consequences of dissolution marriages or of *de facto* unions (unions of people who are not married or are not in registered partnerships). This has led to fairer sharing of the economic responsibilities for the children the partners had together, and also to better financial protection for the parent who cared for them full-time at home or had a part-time professional activity. The subrogation of the debtor of child maintenance by the State (or the institution tasked with this) means that women no longer have to fight in court themselves, sometimes for years, to get the financial support decided by the court in the divorce judgement or in the divorce agreement. A number of countries have introduced some kind of subrogation, that is State support, that can effectively prevent poverty of mothers and their children.[35] The sharing of assets accumulated during the marriage or partnership, including future pensions, is now becoming more equal in many countries. The whole of the occupational pensions linked to professional activity often went to the ex-husband, and the ex-wife who had stayed at home or reduced her professional activity and thus supported her husband's career by taking care of all domestic chores, was exposed to a high risk of poverty. Revisions of the relevant laws have been made to ensure that couples who lived a number of years together and had to accumulate forced savings in these pension funds during this time, will receive an equal share of these amounts.[36] These legislative changes tend to decrease the attractiveness of the traditional division of labour, when men realise that they will have to forgo half of their (future) pension!

The issue of gender-based violence has started to be taken seriously in certain countries in court decisions regarding the custody of the children. Whereas previously it was thought that children had to have contact with both parents and male partners or husbands were entitled to joint custody of their children, even when they had been violent towards the mother of the children,[37] court decisions (and sometimes also the legislation itself) are changing

---

35 UN Women, 'Gender Equality and Women's Rights in the Context of Child Custody and Child Maintenance. An International and Comparative Analysis' (2019) 30 Discussion Paper.

36 The Swiss legislation was progressively adapted, the last time in 2017: according to article 122 of the Swiss Civil Code, occupational pensions assets accrued during marriage until the introduction of divorce proceedings are shared between the ex-spouses. The principle of equal sharing can be replaced by equitable sharing, see articles 122 to 124 (e).

37 For an example of this approach, see the individual communication González Carreño v Spain case, CEDAW/C/58/D/47/2012: the Committee found Spain had violated the Convention by not protecting the daughter of Ms González Carreño against the violence of her father. He enjoyed unsupervised visitation rights although his ex-wife had invoked

this.[38] Violence towards the mother of the children can be a reason to grant her sole custody. It can also limit the visitation rights of fathers or impose conditions on their exercise, even if the men did not exert direct violence against the children themselves. Police or courts can also issue restraining or protection orders against violent partners and husbands, ordering them to stay away from the home and not to contact their wives or partners. The 34 States (as of 29/06/2021) that have ratified the Council of Europe Convention on Preventing and Combating Violence against Women and Domestic Violence (Istanbul Convention) "shall take the necessary legislative or other measures to ensure that, in the determination of custody and visitation rights of children, incidents of violence covered by the scope of this Convention are taken into account" and that "the exercise of any visitation or custody rights does not jeopardize the rights and safety of the victim or children" (Article 31). Thus, the best interests of the child must be paramount.[39]

Progress is also being made in tax law for households. In many countries, the couple continues to be considered as the tax unit, with the husband as its head. The income of the wife, considered as a secondary income, is added to the income of the husband. This means that their income reaches a higher level of taxation than if they were each taxed separately. This discourages the professional activity of women[40] and tends to support traditional role models,

his violence against her in the divorce proceedings and had on numerous occasions alerted the social services and civil courts about the danger he presented to her daughter, whom he finally killed before committing suicide.

38 To "take the necessary legislative or other measures to ensure that, in the determination of custody and visitation rights of children, incidents of violence covered by the scope of this Convention are taken into account" and that "the exercise of any visitation or custody rights does not jeopardize the rights and safety of the victim or children". The expert body monitoring the implementation of the Convention's standards (GREVIO), has found evidence of gender bias towards women in custody decisions and lack of attention paid by courts to patterns of abuse by fathers in all 10 States parties monitored so far.

39 Council of Europe Convention on Preventing and Combating Violence against Women and Domestic Violence (Istanbul Convention).

40 Alastair Tomas and Pierce O'Reilly, 'The Impact of Tax and Benefit Systems on the Workforce Participation Incentives of Women' (2016) Organisation of Economic Co-operation and Development (OECD) Taxation Working Paper No. 29; this is still the situation in Switzerland, although efforts to introduce individual taxation (or at least another system that would not discriminate unfairly between married couples and non-married ones) have been ongoing for years, see Administration Fédérale des Contributions, 'Imposition du Couple et de la Famille' <https://www.estv.admin.ch/estv/fr/home/allgemein/steuerpolitik/fachinformationen/botschaften/ehepaar-familienbesteuerung.html> accessed 29 November 2021; and The Swiss Parliament, 'Imposition Commune avec Splitting Intégral, et Imposition Individuelle. Evaluer les Deux Modèles Dans une

whereas separate taxation of each member of the couple respects the choices people make.[41]

A wide variety of measures exist to facilitate reconciliation of family and work responsibilities such as paternity or parental leave, efforts to increase the availability of good-quality, affordable nurseries and kindergartens, and harmonisation of school schedules with the work schedules of the parents.[42]

3.3 *Labour and Social Laws*

Labour laws and preventive measures are increasingly dealing with harassment in the workplace and specifically sexual harassment in the workplace. The adoption of ILO Convention No. 190 and Recommendation No. 206 "recognizes the right of everyone to a world of work free from violence and harassment, including gender-based violence and harassment".[43] Statistical and other methods have been developed to ensure the respect of the principle of equal pay for equal work or work of equal value. The idea of a universal basic income is the subject of a lively discussion.[44] The introduction of minimum wages is an efficient tool to improve the situation of women, as they generally account for most of the workers in the lower wage category.[45]

In the field of social laws, many European countries are trying to overcome the negative consequences for women of the linkage of social protection to the traditional division of labour, with men as breadwinners and women as

---

Perspective Libérale, d'Egalité des Sexes et de Politique' <https://www.parlament.ch/en/ratsbetrieb/suche-curia-vista/geschaeft?AffairId=20213190> accessed 29 November 2021.

41 See the proposal to modify the Swiss Constitution to introduce individual taxation of married spouses, Initiative Populaire pour l'Imposition Individuelle, 'De Quoi s'Agit-Il?' <https://www.individualbesteuerung.ch/um-was-geht-s> accessed 29 November 2021.

42 ILO, 'Work-Life Balance' <https://www.ilo.org/global/topics/working-time/wl-balance/lang--en/index.htm> accessed 29 November 2021.

43 ILO, 'Eliminating Violence in the World of Work' <https://www.ilo.org/global/topics/violence-harassment/lang--en/index.htm> accessed 29 November 2021.

44 BIEN, 'About Basic Income' <https://basicincome.org/about-basic-income/> accessed 17 June 2021; ILO, 'Universal Basic Income' <https://www.ilo.org/Search5/search.do?sitelang=en&locale=en_EN&consumercode=ILOHQ_STELLENT_PUBLIC&searchWhat=universal+basic+income&searchLanguage=en> accessed 29 November 2021.

45 See for the discussion in the USA, Courtney Connley, '59% of Workers Who Would Benefit From a $15 Minimum Wage Are Women – Here's How It Would Affect the Pay Gap' *CNBC* (03 February 2021) <https://www.cnbc.com/2021/02/03/what-15-minimum-wage-could-mean-for-women-and-the-pay-gap.html> accessed 29 November 2021; See also ILO information on the gender pay gap and the role of minimum wages to reduce it, ILO, 'Chapter 7: Monitoring the Effects of Minimum Wages' <https://www.ilo.org/global/topics/wages/minimum-wages/monitoring/WCMS_473657/lang--en/index.htm> accessed 29 November 2021.

homemakers. This division continues to have serious consequences for women. These include the lack of or insufficient social protection of women, as it previously seemed normal that their social protection depended on the continuation of their relationship with a man. Social protection floors,[46] implemented in a number of emerging economies where women are mainly active in the informal sector, ensure that women who have not paid into the social security system set up for workers in the formal economy will nonetheless benefit from old age pensions and other benefits, such as basic health care.[47]

3.4 *Education*

In most but still not in all countries, all formal obstacles to the access of girls to primary, secondary and (not always) tertiary education have been removed.[48] However, practical obstacles remain, such as the costs of transportation, school uniforms or materials, and lack of water, sanitation and menstrual hygiene facilities in schools. In addition, school-related gender-based violence plays a huge negative role. Thus, millions of girls may still be deprived of schooling,[49] mainly at the secondary and tertiary levels. Yet, completion of secondary school has been proven to be one of the most efficient measures to ensure national development and limit the number of early and child marriages, teenage pregnancies and of children per woman.

46 See ILO Recommendation 202, 'Social Protection Floors' (2012) para 2, 'social protection floors are nationally defined sets of basic social security guarantees which secure protection aimed at preventing or alleviating poverty, vulnerability and social exclusion'. Paras 4 and 5 define them, including essential health care, basic income security for children, basic income security, in particular in cases of sickness, unemployment, maternity, disability and old age.

47 ILO, 'Social Protection Floor' <https://www.ilo.org/secsoc/areas-of-work/policy-development-and-applied-research/social-protection-floor/lang--en/index.htm> accessed 17 June 2021; and United Nations Development Group, 'The UN Social Protection Floor Initiative (SPF-I)' <https://www.social-protection.org/gimi/gess/ShowProject.action?id=2767> accessed 29 November 2021.

48 In some countries, girls who are pregnant or have given birth are not allowed to continue their education or to come back to school, see Committee on the Elimination of Discrimination Against Women, General Recommendation No. 36 (2017) on the right of girls and women to education, para 24 (g); 'Concluding Observations on the Combined Initial to Third Periodic Reports of Solomon Islands' (2014) CEDAW/C/SLB/CO/1-3 para 32 (f) and 'Concluding Observations on the eighth periodic report of Australia (2018)', CEDAW/C/AUS/CO/8, para 41 (bn) and 42 (b).

49 UNESDOC, 'From Access to Empowerment: UNESCO Strategy for Gender Equality in and Through Education 2019–2025' <https://unesdoc.unesco.org/ark:/48223/pf0000369000> accessed 17 June 2021; and UNESCO, 'Over 11 Million Girls May Not Go Back to School after the COVID-19 Crisis' <https://en.unesco.org/covid19/educationresponse/girlseducation> accessed 29 November 2021.

Measures to ensure equal access for girls and women to all levels of education include special courses, scholarships, and endeavour to increase the number of women teachers and professors.[50] Efforts are being made to better balance the proportion of women and men at all levels of the education system. In Switzerland,[51] for example, all cantonal universities, universities of applied sciences and arts, universities for teacher education and the two federal institutes of technology have adopted measures to increase the representation of women in the fields where they are under-represented as students, or as teaching personnel or administrators. The Swiss National Science Foundation has its own programme to ensure gender equality in research.[52]

3.5 *Gender-based Violence against Women*

Gender-based violence against women is increasingly being recognised as a widespread issue threatening social peace and development,[53] all the more so in the context of the COVID 19 pandemic. Many countries have revised their definition of rape and other sexual crimes, putting the issue of consent or rather lack of consent at the centre. This is what Article 36 of the Istanbul Convention stipulates for sexual violence, including rape, 'Consent must be given voluntarily as the result of the person's free will assessed in the context of the surrounding circumstances'.[54] States also introduce legislation on marital rape, abandoning the traditional conception that by the celebration of marriage, a woman has agreed to all future sexual acts requested by her husband,

---

50 For an analysis at the international level dealing with all aspects of girls' and women's education, see Barbara Bailey and Hilary Gbedemah, 'Article 10' in Schulz et al. (eds), *The UN Convention on the Elimination of All Forms of Discrimination Against Women and its Optional Protocol*, (2nd edn, forthcoming OUP 2022).

51 Swissuniversities, 'Equal Opportunities & Diversity' <https://www.swissuniversities.ch/en/topics/equal-opportunities-and-diversity> accessed 29 November 2021.

52 Swiss National Science Foundation, 'Gender Equality' <http://www.snf.ch/en/theSNSF/research-policies/gender-equality/Pages/default.aspx> accessed 29 November 2021.

53 The World Bank, 'Gender-Based Violence (Violence against Women and Girls)' (25 September 2019) <https://www.worldbank.org/en/topic/socialsustainability/brief/violence-against-women-and-girls> accessed 29 November 2021; UN Women has called gender-based violence in the context of COVID-19 the Shadow Pandemic, and has launched the Shadow Pandemic Campaign, see UN Women, 'The Shadow Pandemic: Violence against Women during COVID-19' <https://www.unwomen.org/en/news/in-focus/in-focus-gender-equality-in-covid-19-response/violence-against-women-during-covid-19> accessed 29 November 2021.

54 Council of Europe, 'Complete List of the Council of Europe's Treaties' <https://www.coe.int/en/web/conventions/full-list/-/conventions/rms/090000168008482e> accessed 29 November 2021; See the criticism of the draft bill for the revision of the Swiss Penal Code by Amnesty International, 'Révision du Droit Pénal Sexuel, un Projet Décevant en Phase

thus respecting Article 36 of the Istanbul Convention, which includes 'acts committed against former or current spouses or partners as recognised by internal law'. Legislation and practical measures also address sexual harassment in the workplace, educational settings and public spaces generally.[55]

3.6 *Sexual and Reproductive Health and Rights*

Important changes have occurred in the field of sexual and reproductive health and rights. There is a tendency towards safe and legal abortion, covered by the national health system, information on and access to modern contraceptives, as well as comprehensive sexual education in schools.[56] Maternal mortality has also been decreasing, but with very different patterns depending on the region. The maternal mortality rate in 2017 varied from 11 per 100 000 live births in high-income countries to 462 per 100 000 live births in low-income countries.[57]

3.7 *Increased Awareness and Renewal/Revival of Feminism*

The revelations of massive violations of women's human rights during conflicts and the scandalous exploitation of women in the film and media industry, have triggered a widespread reaction. Awareness of the negative consequences of gender inequality and discrimination against women for individuals, communities, nations and the world has risen, together with the development of a

---

de Consultation' <https://www.amnesty.ch/fr/themes/droits-des-femmes/docs/2021/revision-droit-penal-sexuel-projet-decevant> accessed 29 November 2021.

55 UN Women, 'Facts and figures: Ending Violence against Women' <https://www.unwomen.org/en/what-we-do/ending-violence-against-women/facts-and-figures> accessed 29 November 2021.

56 Rebecca J Cook and Verónica Undurraga, 'Article 12' in Schulz et al. (eds), *The UN Convention on the Elimination of All Forms of Discrimination Against Women and its Optional Protocol*, (2nd edn, forthcoming OUP 2022).

57 WHO, 'Maternal Mortality' <https://www.who.int/news-room/fact-sheets/detail/maternal-mortality> accessed 12 July 2021: 'About 295 000 women died during and following pregnancy and childbirth in 2017. The vast majority of these deaths (94%) occurred in low-resource settings, and most could have been prevented. (...) Sub-Saharan Africa and Southern Asia accounted for approximately 86% (254 000) of the estimated global maternal deaths in 2017. Sub-Saharan Africa alone accounted for roughly two-thirds (196 000) of maternal deaths, while Southern Asia accounted for nearly one-fifth (58 000)'.; See also for an in-depth presentation, Rebecca J Cook et al., *Abortion Law in Transnational Perspective. Cases and Controversies* (University of Pennsylvania Press 2014); and for an analysis of a State's obligation to provide non-discriminatory access to safe abortion, See the report of the Committee on the Elimination on Discrimination against Women, CEDAW/C/OP.8/GBR/1, 'Inquiry Concerning the United Kingdom of Great Britain and Northern Ireland Under Article 8 of the Optional Protocol to the Convention on the Elimination of All Forms of Discrimination against Women' (2018).

new wave of feminism, which is active on many continents. More women have come forward to denounce the abuse and exploitation they experience(d) at the workplace, in the film and media industry, in sports and in educational settings, among others. Young women are finding innovative tools in the fight against sex- and gender-based discrimination and gender-based violence, making astute use of social media and technology. Global feminist networks are also very active. They enable the sharing of experiences between women's non-governmental organisations (NGOs) on different continents. Movements such as #MeToo and BlackLivesMatter show the potential for change that the sharing of painful experiences of abuse, both sexual and racial, has. Grassroots feminist initiatives are active in many fields,[58] with (young) women working directly for the world they want to have.[59] The side-events organised during the sessions of various international and regional institutions such as the Commission on the Status of Women, the Human Rights Council, the Joint United Nations Programme on HIV/AIDS (UNAIDS) and many others are opportunities for advocacy, exchanges and networking. For instance, more than 5,000 NGOs from over 150 countries participated in the more than 700 side-events at the 65th Commission on the Status of Women (CSW) session, which had more than 27,000 attendees.[60]

4 A Political Tool: The SDGs, Agenda 2030

A recent political instrument, the Sustainable Development Goals (SDGs), was adopted in 2015.[61] Also called Agenda 2030, the SDGs play an important role

58 Grassroot initiatives can cover many issues, such as agricultural development and/or environmental protection, See Maria Fides F Bagasao, 'Why Organized Grassroots Women Matter in the Sustainable Development of Rural Communities' <https://www.un.org/en/chronicle/article/why-organized-grassroots-women-matter-sustainable-development-rural-communities> accessed 29 November 2021. Regarding sexual and reproductive health and rights, see Women and Earth Initiative, <https://arrow.org.my/project/innovative-advocacy-programmes-on-srhr-and-climate-change-environmental-sustainability/> accessed 12 July 2021; and sex workers networks such as The Global Network of Sex Work Projects (NSWP), <https://www.nswp.org> accessed 29 November 2021.

59 See The Association for Women's Rights in Development (AWID), and its support to young activists, <https://www.awid.org/topics/young-feminist-organizing> accessed 29 November 2021; and UN Women's youth and gender strategy, and the Generation Equality forum.

60 UN Women, CSW 65th session, 15–26 March 2021, <https://www.unwomen.org/en/csw/csw65-2021> accessed 29 November 2021.

61 General Assembly Resolution (n 17); United Nations (n 17).

in the present discussions on gender equality and non-discrimination. States devoted a specific goal to gender equality (Goal 5, also covering gender-based violence against women), and it is also incorporated in other goals, expressly or implicitly. Most, if not all of the SDGs are based on legally binding human rights' instruments. There is consensus, at least at the level of discourse, that gender equality is a precondition for the attainment of the SDGs, including eradication of poverty (Goal 1), of hunger (Goal 2), achieving health and well-being (Goal 3), education (Goal 4), clean water and sanitation (Goal 6), peace, justice and strong institutions (Goal 16), among others.[62]

5 Challenges to the Rights of Women

5.1 *The COVID-19 Pandemic and the SDGs*

Even before the COVID-19 pandemic, it was evident that (most of) the SDGs that should have been reached by 2030 would not be reached for lack of sufficient will, action, and financing. The pandemic has increased gender inequality and gender-based violence, as it has disrupted economies, devastated employment, health, social and education systems, locked down people, in both rich and emerging economies, impacting women disproportionally.[63] The reduction of inequality within and among countries as embodied by Goal 10 has been halted by the pandemic as "the most vulnerable groups are being hit the hardest by the pandemic"[64] and this means women first and foremost.

62 UNDP, 'Gender Equality as an Accelerator for Achieving the SDGs' (4 February 2019) <https://www.undp.org/content/undp/en/home/librarypage/womens-empowerment/gender-equality-as-an-accelerator-for-achieving-the-sdgs.html> accessed 29 November 2021; and UNDP, 'What Does Equality Have to Do with the SDGs?' <https://www.undp.org/content/undp/en/home/blog/2019/what-does-equality-have-to-do-with-the-sdgs-.html> accessed 29 November 2021; UN Women, 'Turning Promises into Action: Gender Equality in the 2030 Agenda for Sustainable Development' <https://www.unwomen.org/en/digital-library/publications/2018/2/gender-equality-in-the-2030-agenda-for-sustainable-development-2018> accessed 29 November 2021.

63 United Nations (n 17). It is well worth reading the various goals and their detailed presentation, for instance on education, United Nations, 'Ensure Inclusive and Equitable Quality Education and Promote Lifelong Learning Opportunities for All' <https://sdgs.un.org/goals/goal4> accessed 29 November 2021: over 200 million children will still be out of school in 2030, and the impact of COVID 19 is described, including its consequences for girls in United Nations, 'Amid the Coronavirus Pandemic, the SDGs Are Even More Relevant Today than Ever Before' <https://www.un.org/sustainabledevelopment/blog/2020/04/coronavirus-sdgs-more-relevant-than-ever-before/> accessed 29 November 2021.

64 United Nations, 'Goal 10. Reduce Inequality Within and Among Countries' <https://sdgs.un.org/goals/goal10> accessed 29 November 2021.

Estimates suggest that 47 million more women and girls will fall into extreme poverty, increasing their number to 435 million.[65] Many girls will not be able to go back to school.[66] Financing for education is in danger. 'For low income countries and lower-middle-income countries, for instance, that gap had reached a staggering [US]$148 billion annually and it could now increase by up to one-third', according to the UN.[67]

Women are starkly under-represented in decision-making bodies dealing with the recovery measures, and the fear is that "Without women in decision-making roles, COVID-19 measures taken by governments are more likely to ignore women's needs and it could further exacerbate the unequal recovery opportunities from the pandemic, which is already threatening to reverse decades of progress on gender equality".[68] Far too few measures[69] address the mid- and long-term needs of women and will be able to effectively fight issues such as poverty, gender-based violence, and lack of economic opportunities. And yet there are measures that could help secure better outcomes, as shown by the gender tracker of UNDP and UN Women[70] and UNESCO's summary of gender-sensitive measures regarding education in the context of COVID-19.[71]

65 UN Women, 'From Insights to Action: Gender Equality in the Wake of COVID-19' <https://www.unwomen.org/en/digital-library/publications/2020/09/gender-equality-in-the-wake-of-covid-19> accessed 29 November 2021.

66 UNESCO, 'Over 11 Million Girls May Not Go Back to School after the COVID-19 Crisis' <https://en.unesco.org/covid19/educationresponse/girlseducation> accessed 29 November 2021.

67 UNESCO, 'Global Education Coalition. COVID-19 School Closures around the World Will Hit Girls Hardest' (31 March 2020) <https://en.unesco.org/news/covid-19-school-closures-around-world-will-hit-girls-hardest> accessed 29 November 2021; And United Nations, 'Policy Brief: Education during COVID-19 and beyond' (August 2020) <https://www.un.org/development/desa/dspd/wp-content/uploads/sites/22/2020/08/sg_policy_brief_covid-19_and_education_august_2020.pdf> accessed 29 November 2021.

68 UNDP, 'Women's Absence from COVID-19 Task Forces Will Perpetuate Gender Divide, Says UNDP, UN Women' <https://www.undp.org/content/undp/en/home/news-centre/news/2021/Womens_absence_COVID-19_task_forces_perpetuate_gender_divide_UNDP_UNWomen.html> accessed 29 November 2021.

69 UN Women, 'Global Gender Response Tracker: Monitoring How Women's Needs are Being Met by Pandemic Responses' <https://data.unwomen.org/resources/women-have-been-hit-hard-pandemic-how-government-response-measuring> accessed 29 November 2021.

70 UN Women, 'Expert's Take: Five Steps to Make the COVID-19 Social Protection and Jobs Response Work Better for Women' <https://www.unwomen.org/en/news/stories/2021/1/experts-take-constanza-tabbush> accessed 29 November 2021.

71 UNESCO, '#HerEducationOurFuture: Keeping Girls in the Picture during and after the COVID-19 Crisis. The Latest Facts on Gender Equality in Education' (2021) <https://unesdoc.unesco.org/ark:/48223/pf0000375707> accessed 29 November 2021; UNESCO, 'One Year into COVID: Prioritizing Education Recovery to Avoid a Generational Catastrophe'.

COVID-19 recovery measures are linked to the implementation of the SDGs and face the same obstacles: i.e. lack of will, knowledge, awareness and financing.

5.2 *Neo-Liberalism*

Neo-liberalism,[72] in the various forms it has taken since the 1970s, has brought increased gender inequality and poverty for most women, while opening up economic opportunities for some women. The reduction of the welfare State through budgetary cuts, privatisation and flexibilisation of the labour market have impacted women disproportionally. These impacts affect women as beneficiaries of State measures, workers employed in large numbers in the health, education and social services and as workers, often in the lowest income groups, who are also tasked with caring responsibilities.[73] Millions of women in industrialised countries are trapped in on-call work with zero-hour contracts, and have no protection under labour or social law. Structural adjustment programmes imposed on developing countries have increased their incapacity to ensure basic services for their populations, as austerity measures did in more developed economies.[74]

The privatisation of public services and/or reduction of public budgets for childcare, health care, education, water distribution, and transportation has increased unpaid care and household workloads for women, thus increasing the gender care gap. Women find themselves in an ever more disadvantaged position on the labour market. Women-headed households are particularly

(2021) <https://unesdoc.unesco.org/ark:/48223/pf0000376984> accessed 29 November 2021: 'According to the joint Education Finance Watch Study with the World Bank, 65% of low-income countries are cutting education budgets while education only accounts for 2% allocation in stimulus packages of 56 countries'.

72 Seen as giving priority to freedom of markets and capital, reducing the role of the State, government being seen as "the problem and not the solution" as Ronald Reagan said at his inaugural address in 1981; Richard Meagher, 'Neoliberal Language Lessons. How Right-Wing Power Along With Free Market Ideas Shifted from Conservative Christians to the Tea Party' (Political Research Associates, 30 October 2014) <https://www.politicalresearch.org/2014/10/30/neoliberal-language-lessons> accessed 21 June 2021; Elisabeth Prügl, 'Neoliberalism with a Feminist Face: Crafting a New Hegemony at the World Bank' (2017) 23 Feminist Economics 30.

73 Rahila Gupta, 'Has Neoliberalism Knocked Feminism Sideways?' (2012) <https://www.opendemocracy.net/en/5050/has-neoliberalism-knocked-feminism-sideways/> accessed 29 November 2021; Guy Standing, 'The Precariat: Today's Transformative Class?' (2018) <https://greattransition.org/publication/precariat-transformative-class> accessed 29 November 2021.

74 For an *a contrario* argumentation of what the economy and the States should deliver, see Amartya Sen, *Development as Freedom* (Anchor Books 2000); and Naomi Klein, *The Shock Doctrine. The Rise of disaster Capitalism* (Penguin Books 2007).

vulnerable to these policies. As mentioned above, measures to relaunch economies after the pandemic do not tackle gender inequality nor gender poverty in any meaningful way.[75]

5.3 *Increased Gender-based Violence against Women*

In countries in conflict, physical and sexual violence has been used against women and girls as a weapon of war as well as to impose a renewed masculine domination, and its use is increasing.[76] Child marriages increase as a response to poverty, exposing girls to unending sexual violence perpetrated by their husband and other forms of violence by members of his family. They are also at risk from early pregnancies, which are dangerous for their health and education, because they have to drop out of school.

In all countries, regardless of whether they are in conflict or not, gender-based violence has been proven to have increased during the pandemic, and the lockdown has exacerbated domestic violence,[77] including against women refugees in camps.[78] School-related gender-based violence is increasing as well. There is increased concern about gender-based violence in the public sphere as well as in cyberspace, which is also affecting girls and women disproportionately. Women in politics are exposed to several forms of violence – physical, sexual and psychological – often from their colleagues. They are also far more likely to be the targets of sexist and hate speech, and threats of violence in cyberspace than men, including death threats and threats of sexual violence.[79]

75 See UNESCO (n 67) and UNDP (n 68).

76 Jamey Keaten, 'Rights Experts Flag Violations of Rape, Sex Abuse in Yemen' *AP News* (3 September 2019) <https://apnews.com/article/ac80c7d3107e4af180638b2a75859ab9> accessed 29 November 2021.

77 UNDP, 'Gender-Based Violence and COVID-19' (11 May 2020) <https://www.undp.org/content/undp/en/home/librarypage/womens-empowerment/gender-based-violence-and-covid-19.html> accessed 29 November 2021.

78 UNCHR, 'Gender-Based Violence on the Rise during Lockdowns' (25 November 2020) <https://www.unhcr.org/news/stories/2020/11/5fbd2e774/gender-based-violence-rise-during-lockdowns.html> accessed 29 November 2021.

79 IPU, 'The Shadow Pandemic: Violence Against Women in Politics' (08 December 2020) <https://www.ipu.org/news/news-in-brief/2020-12/shadow-pandemic-violence-against-women-in-politics> accessed 29 November 2021; IPU, 'Report With IPU Data on Violence Against Women in Politics Presented at UNGA' <https://www.ipu.org/news/news-in-brief/2018-10/report-with-ipu-data-violence-against-women-in-politics-presented-unga> accessed 29 November 2021; General Assembly of the United Nations, 'Violence Against Women in Politics' (6 August 2018) <https://www.ohchr.org/EN/Issues/Women/SRWomen/Pages/ViolenceAgainstWomeninPolitics.aspx> accessed 29 November 2021.

Recently, violence against women in health care systems, specifically against pregnant women, women giving birth or women having an abortion, has been denounced.[80]

Migrant women are exposed to even greater risks than women who are citizens of a country because of their status as migrants, and also because of other characteristics (for example, level of education, mastery of language). In particular, if they are undocumented migrants, the risk of exposure to violence is high and they are unable to defend themselves for fear of deportation should they denounce the crimes committed against them to the police or social services.[81] Yet, women are migrating in increasing numbers, in search of a better life, and/or to flee poverty and conflicts as well as the degradation of their environment and living conditions due to climate change. Being trafficked into all sorts of forms of labour exploitation, in industry, agriculture, and the sex industry is the culmination of gender-based violence and abuse against women and girls.[82]

---

80 UN General Assembly, A/74/137, 'Report of the Special Rapporteur on Violence against Women, its Causes and Consequences on a Human Rights-based Approach to Mistreatment and Violence against Women in Reproductive Health Services with a Focus on Childbirth and Obstetric Violence' (11 July 2019); and for further information see the OHCHR page of the Special Rapporteur on Violence against Women, <https://www.ohchr.org/EN/Issues/Women/SRWomen/Pages/Mistreatment.aspx> accessed 29 November 2021; Ana Flavia Pires et al, 'Violence against Women in Health-Care Institutions: an Emerging Problem' (2002) 359 (9318) The Lancet 1681; OHCHR (n 79); See also the CEDAW Committee Concluding observations on the combined sixth and seventh periodic reports of Ireland, CEDAW/C/IRL/CO/6-7, paras 14–15.

81 UN General Assembly, Resolution A/RES/72/140, 'Violence against Women Migrant Workers' (2017).

82 See General Recommendation 35 on Gender-Based Violence, updating General Recommendation 19 of the CEDAW Committee for an analysis of violence as a continuum; See also Christine Chinkin, 'Violence Against Women: The International Legal Response' (1995) 3 (2) Gender and Development 23, and Janie Chuang and Sulini Sarugaser-Hug, 'Article 6' in Schulz et al.(eds) (n 20). For exploitation of women in the agricultural sector, see for instance a European Union study on the situation in Italy and Spain, Letizia Palumbo and Alessandra Sciurba, 'The Vulnerability to Exploitation of Women Migrant Workers in Agriculture in the EU: the Need for a Human Right and Gender Based Approach' (May 2018) <https://www.europarl.europa.eu/RegData/etudes/STUD/2018/604966/IPOL_STU(2018)604966_EN.pdf> accessed 12 July 2021; for the fishing industry, see a short article, Juno Fitzpatrick and Elena Finkbeiner, 'Symposium: Land and Sea: Gendered Nature of Labour and Sexual Exploitation in Fisheries' (19 March 2021) <https://delta87.org/2021/03/land-sea-gendered-nature-labour-sexual-exploitation-fisheries/?lang=fr> accessed 29 November 2021.

5.4 *Gender Stereotypes*

Despite more progressive laws and programmes in many fields, as well as national and international norms, resolutions, and plans of action, in practice, the situation changes very slowly. Women are still excluded or underrepresented in decision-making positions in politics and the economy, and they are still being underpaid, overworked and overexposed to men's violence. Persistent stereotypes[83] regarding masculine and feminine roles and tasks maintain the division of labour, restricting the fields and activities that are open to women and girls, and limiting their access to power, economic and personal autonomy. Stereotypes perpetuate, for instance, the very unequal sharing of care and domestic work[84] and the dominance of men in the public sphere. They also condition access to and quality of healthcare.[85] Numerous religious organisations (Catholic, Protestant, Russian Orthodox, Muslim) and some States are promoting a regressive view of "the family" recognising only the legal marriage between a man and a woman, opposing divorce, single parenthood, same sex unions, and abortion, among others, thus cementing the division of labour under a religiously based argumentation, and contesting women's economic autonomy.[86]

5.5 *The Slow Pace of Change*

Laws and practical programmes and measures are a necessary tool but are not sufficient to overcome the deeply ingrained discrimination and gender-unequal basis and organisation of societies. Progress is slow. In developing countries, many women remain stuck in the informal labour market because

83 Cook and Cusack (n 3).

84 Commission on the Status of Women, Sixty-first session, 13–24 March 2017, 'Women's Economic Empowerment in the Changing World of Work, Report of the Secretary-General', E/CN.6/2017/3, in particular paras 25–27; ILO 'Care Work and Care Jobs for The Future of Decent Work' (2018) <https://www.ilo.org/global/publications/books/WCMS_633135/lang--en/index.htm> accessed 29 November 2021.

85 Lori Heise et al., 'Gender Inequality and Restrictive Gender Norms: Framing the Challenges to Health' (2019) 393 (10189) The Lancet 2440.

86 Karolina Wigura and Jaroslaw Kuisz, 'Poland's Abortion Ban is a Cynical Attempt to Exploit Religion by a Failing Leader' *The Guardian* (London, 28 October 2020) <https://www.theguardian.com/commentisfree/2020/oct/28/poland-abortion-ban-kaczynski-catholic-church-protests> accessed 29 November 2021; John P Burgess, 'The Unexpected Relationship Between U.S. Evangelicals and Russian Orthodox' (2018) <https://www.christiancentury.org/article/features/unexpected-relationship-between-us-evangelicals-and-russian-orthodox> accessed 29 November 2021. Naureen Shameem (ed), 'Rights at Risk: Time for Action' (2021) <https://www.oursplatform.org/wp-content/uploads/RightAtRisk_TimeForAction_June2021.pdf> accessed 12 July 2021, see below 5.6.

they receive too little or no support to develop their incomes and diversify their activities, and little or no social protection,[87] limited access to adequate health care and sometimes to education. In industrialised countries, horizonal and vertical segregation of the labour market remains very much alive. Even when women achieve a good level of education, this does not translate easily into better chances in the labour market in industrialised or in developing countries. Men with primary or secondary education often hold better jobs than women with tertiary degrees. The more senior the position, the fewer women there are and the bigger the pay gap is between these women and their male colleagues.[88]

In addition, women's ignorance of their rights and ignorance – if not refusal by State officials to implement women's rights, in the education, justice, social and health sectors for instance, and by employers and religious leaders, among others – play an important role in the perpetuation of unequal relationships, gender inequality and discrimination. The negative impact of sexism on individuals and societies is still not sufficiently acknowledged. Too little, too late could be a summary of the situation up to now, to which one should add the danger arising from organised movements of masculinist men, some of whom absolutely hate women and have a very active "manosphere".[89]

5.6 *Backlash against Human Rights and Multilateralism*

A backlash against human rights and multilateralism is evident, with women's rights being singled out.[90] Attacks against freedom of speech, association, assembly, against the universalism, the indivisibility, interdependence and inter-relation of all human rights are seen daily, within the UN system

87 Rebecca Homes and Nicola Jones, *Gender and Social Protection in the Developing World: Beyond Mothers and Safety Nets* (Zed Books 2013).

88 ILO, 'Gender Pay Gap Widens for Higher-earning Women' <https://www.ilo.org/global/about-the-ilo/newsroom/news/WCMS_324651/lang--en/index.htm> accessed 29 November 2021.

89 Laura Bates, 'Men Going Their Own Way: The Rise of a Toxic Male Separatist Movement' *The Guardian* (London, 23 August 2020) <https://www.theguardian.com/lifeandstyle/2020/aug/26/men-going-their-own-way-the-toxic-male-separatist-movement-that-is-now-mainstream> accessed 29 November 2021; Steven Poole, 'Men Who Hate Women by Laura Bates Review Fierce and Eye-Opening' *The Guardian* (London, 2 September 2020) <https://www.theguardian.com/books/2020/sep/02/men-who-hate-women-by-laura-bates-review-fierce-and-eye-opening> accessed 29 November 2021.

90 The Observatory on the Universality of Rights (OURs), 'Rights at Risks: OURs Trends Report 2017' <https://www.oursplatform.org/resource/rights-risk-trends-report-2017/> accessed 29 November 2021.

and in other fora.[91] Attacks or threats against and criminalisation of human rights defenders are also on the increase, with women human rights defenders exposed to particular risks.[92]

Alliances of various States that do not share the values of democracy and rule of law erode the protection of human rights and attempt to reduce their role and importance. One way to do this is to under-finance the international mechanisms tasked with their monitoring. The role of the treaty bodies[93] and of some of the regional human rights commissions in monitoring violations of human rights is threatened because the lack of adequate resources prevents them from doing their work properly and meeting their deadlines.[94]

5.7 *Misusing the Language of Human Rights and Attacks on "Gender Ideology"*

The language of human rights is being used by opponents to undermine their significance. Attacks on so-called "gender ideology"[95] and anti-gender equality, anti-abortion and anti-LGBTI campaigns[96] have been conducted by

91 OURS, 'The Observatory on the Universality of Rights Trends Report 2021' and its 2017 report, 'Rights at Risk: Key Impacts on the Human Rights System' <https://www.oursplatform.org/resource/rights-risk-key-impacts-human-rights-system/> accessed 21 June 2021; Ximena Soley and Silvia Steininger, 'Parting Ways or Lashing Back? Withdrawals, Backlash and the Inter-American Court of Human Rights' (2018) 14 International Journal of Law in Context 237; Peter Geoghegan, 'Dark Money, Dirty Politics & the Backlash Against Human Rights' (22 August 2020) <https://www.indepthnews.info/index.php/opinion/3788-dark-money-dirty-politics-the-backlash-against-human-rights> accessed 29 November 2021.

92 International Service for Human Rights (ISHR), 'UN Adopts Landmark Resolution on Protecting Women Human Rights Defenders' <http://www.ishr.ch/news/un-adopts-landmark-resolution-protecting-women-human-rights-defenders> accessed 21 June 2021; OHCHR, 'Women Human Rights Defenders' <https://www.ohchr.org/EN/Issues/Women/WRGS/Pages/HRDefenders.aspx> accessed 29 November 2021.

93 Christen Broecker and Michael O'Flaherty, 'The Outcome of the General Assembly's Treaty Body Strengthening Process: an Important Milestone on a Longer Journey' (2014) Policy Brief.

94 Basak Cali and Alexandre Skander Galand, 'Strengthening and Enhancing the Effective Functioning of the UN Human Rights Treaty Body System Individual Complaint Mechanisms' (February 2020) <https://menarights.org/sites/default/files/2020-02/Recommendation_policy_report_17_February.pdf> accessed 29 November 2021; Ineke Boerefijn and Julie Fraser, 'Article 17' in Schulz et al. (eds), *The UN Convention on the Elimination of All Forms of Discrimination Against Women and its Optional Protocol*, (2nd edn, forthcoming OUP 2022).

95 Heron Greenesmith, 'Gender Ideology Yesterday, Today, and Tomorrow' *Political Research Associates* (26 March 2020) <https://www.politicalresearch.org/2020/03/26/gender-ideology-yesterday-today-and-tomorrow> accessed 29 November 2021.

96 As an example of one organization promoting only one form of family and opposing rights of LGBTQ persons, Peter Sprigg, 'Why "Sexual Orientation" and "Gender Identity" Should Never be Specially Protected Categories under the Law' (2018) Family Research Council.

sometimes strange coalitions[97] of States known for grave violations of human rights, such as Iran, Saudi Arabia, China, Venezuela, Russia, with strong, well-financed catholic and evangelical organisations[98] and Churches, the Holy See, Russian Orthodox Church, the US Christian right, the Organization of Islamic Cooperation.[99] They have a strong influence on national politics[100] and international negotiations.[101]

6 Conclusion

Coordinated action to prevent the continuation of existing and the development of new forms of violations of women's human rights is urgently needed,

---

97 For instance, the adoption of a resolution on "the family" at the Human Rights Council, ISHR, 'States Silence Debate on Family Diversity at Human Rights Council' (2014) <http://www.ishr.ch/news/states-silence-debate-family-diversity-human-rights-council> accessed 29 November 2021.

98 Human Life International, 'About Us' <https://www.hli.org/about-us/our-mission/> accessed 29 November 2021.

99 Marie Juul Petersen and Turan Kayaoglu (eds), *The Organization of Islamic Cooperation and Human Rights* (University of Pennsylvania Press 2019).

100 See the influence of churches on debates on sexual and reproductive health and rights for instance in Poland: so far the Catholic Church's links with the conservative government have imposed more restrictions to an already restrictive legislation, but there might be a change in public opinion, 'The Guardian View on Poland's Catholics: Losing Faith in their Church' *The Guardian* (London, 2 December 2020) <https://www.theguardian.com/commentisfree/2020/dec/02/the-guardian-view-on-polands-catholics-losing-faith-in-their-church> accessed 29 November 2021; Ireland and Argentina offer recent examples of the Catholic Church losing its grip on the issue, as abortion has been decriminalized in both countries, by referendum in Ireland, by Parliament in Argentina, but with new evangelical right wing groups becoming more active, Eduardo Campos Lima, 'The Catholic Church in Latin America is Losing Control of the Pro-Life Movement. Can It Win It Back?' *America Magazine* (5 October 2020) <https://www.americamagazine.org/politics-society/2020/10/02/catholic-church-latin-american-pro-life-abortion> accessed 29 November 2021; See also a Pew Research Center survey on the morality of eight behaviours in Latin America, showing that Protestants are systematically more conservative than Catholics, Pew Research Center, 'Religion and Morality in Latin America' (13 November 2014) <https://www.pewforum.org/interactives/latin-america-morality-by-religion/> accessed 29 November 2021. See also an analysis of the influence of Orthodox Church in central and eastern Europe, Michael Lipka and Neha Sahgal, '9 Key findings about Religion and Politics in Central and Eastern Europe' *Pew Research Center* (10 May 2017) <https://www.pewresearch.org/fact-tank/2017/05/10/9-key-findings-about-religion-and-politics-in-central-and-eastern-europe/> accessed 29 November 2021.

101 Graduate Institute of International and Development Studies, 'Inequality and Gender' (2021) <https://globalchallenges.ch/issue/9/inequality-and-gender/> accessed 22 June 2021; see (n 90) and (n 91) above.

especially given the worsening of women's rights and situations brought about by COVID-19. For this, States, intergovernmental organisations (universal UN/ regional AU, EU), and civil society organisations need to work competently and often in cooperation, at the local, regional, national and international levels. There is also a need for strong and competent mechanisms for the control and implementation of women's human rights at all levels. What makes me optimistic is to see new forms of activism and more collaboration between various actors. More and more people, sometimes very young, both women and men, are engaged in classical and new forms of politics and social movements, with a feminist, environmental, economic and social justice agenda. Many grassroots initiatives are bringing innovative ideas and ways of living, calling power relations based on sex and gender into question. These issues are being connected with others such as discrimination based on race and ethnicity, disability, sexual orientation or gender identity, or religion. They have a participative, inclusive and diverse agenda that is often shared across continents. Movements such as #metoo or Black Lives Matter have highlighted the extent of sexism, racism, sexual and racial abuse, which has shocked many people and, hopefully, this raised awareness will provoke change. However, social media have also been denounced for the ease with which they enable sexist, racist, homophobic and religiously based attacks, and the dissemination of hate speech.

With the urgent need for social justice and a redefinition of values and the role of States, the coronavirus pandemic might be an opportunity for a new global world order in which gender equality and the prohibition of discrimination based on sex and gender are a reality, with respect for nature and for all of us human beings. Beyond talk, we need a much more energetic commitment and actions by all stakeholders towards the full implementation of the principles of gender equality and prohibition of discrimination against women and girls, as part of a global agenda of environmental, climate and social justice.

References

Anwar Z (ed), *Wanted: Equality and Justice in the Muslim Family* (Musawah, Sisters in Islam 2009).

Bailey B and Gbedemah H, 'Article 10' in Schulz P et al. (eds), *The UN Convention on the Elimination of All Forms of Discrimination Against Women and its Optional Protocol: A Commentary.* Second Edition. (2nd edn, OUP forthcoming 2022).

Boerefijn I and Fraser J, 'Article 17' in Schulz P et al. (eds), *The UN Convention on the Elimination of All Forms of Discrimination Against Women and its Optional Protocol: A Commentary.* Second Edition. (2nd edn, OUP forthcoming 2022).

Byrnes A and Paryani PK, 'Article 1' in Schulz P et al. (eds), *The UN Convention on the Elimination of All Forms of Discrimination Against Women and its Optional Protocol: A Commentary.* Second Edition. (2nd edn, OUP forthcoming 2022).

Byrnes A and Campbell M, 'Article 2' in Schulz P et al. (eds), *The UN Convention on the Elimination of All Forms of Discrimination Against Women and its Optional Protocol: A Commentary.* Second Edition. (2nd edn, OUP forthcoming 2022).

Bunch C, 'Women's Rights and Gender Integration', Weiss TG and Daws S (eds), *The Oxford Handbook on the United Nations* (OUP 2018).

Celorio R, *Women and International Human Rights in Modern Times* (Edward Publishing 2022).

Charlesworth H, 'Women' in Chesteraman S et al. (eds), *The Oxford Handbook of United Nations Treaties* (OUP 2019).

Charlesworth H, 'Gender and International Law', in Steans J and Tepe-Belfrage D (eds) *Handbook on Gender in World Politics* (Edward Elgar Publishing 2016).

Chinkin C, 'Violence Against Women: The International Legal Response' (1995) 3 (2) Gender and Development 23.

Chinkin C, Violence Against Women, in Schulz P et al. (eds), *The UN Convention on the Elimination of All Forms of Discrimination Against Women and its Optional Protocol: A Commentary*. Second Edition. (2nd edn, OUP forthcoming 2022).

Chuang J and Sarugaser-Hug S, 'Article 6' in Schulz P et al. (eds), *The UN Convention on the Elimination of All Forms of Discrimination Against Women and its Optional Protocol: A Commentary*. Second Edition. (2nd edn, OUP forthcoming 2022).

Cook RJ and Undurraga V, 'Article 12' in Schulz P et al. (eds), *The UN Convention on the Elimination of All Forms of Discrimination Against Women and its Optional Protocol: A Commentary.* Second Edition. (2nd edn, OUP forthcoming 2022).

Cook RJ and Cusack S, *Gender Stereotyping. Transnational Legal Perspectives* (University of Pennsylvania Press 2010).

Cusack S, 'The CEDAW as a Legal Framework for Transnational Discourses on Gender Stereotyping' in Hellum A and Aasen SH (eds), *Women's Human Rights. CEDAW in International, Regional and National Law* (Cambridge University Press 2013).

Cusack S and Pusey L 'CEDAW and the Rights to Non-Discrimination and Equality' (2013) 14 Melbourne Journal of International Law 1.

Elkayam-Levy C, 'Path to Transformation: Asking 'the Women Question' in International Law 42' (2021) 42 (3) Michigan Journal on International Law 429.

Elshtain BJ, *Public Man, Private Woman* (Princeton University Press 1981).

Fredman S, 'Substantive Equality Revisited' (2016) 14 International Journal of Constitutional Law 712.

Homes R and Jones N, *Gender and Social Protection in the Developing World. Beyond Mothers and Safety Nets* (Zed Books 2013).

Jefferson L et al., 'Women in Medicine: Historical Perspectives and Recent Trends' (2015) 114 British Medical Bulletin 5.

Klein N, *The Shock Doctrine. The Rise of Disaster Capitalism* (Penguin Books 2007).
Malkiel WN, *"Keep the Damned Women Out": The Struggle for Coeducation* (Princeton University Press 2016).
Nijman J E, Marked Absences: Locating Gender and Race in International Legal History, 31 (2020) The European Journal of International Law 1025.
Patel G, *Women and International Human Rights* (Routledge 2020).
Perez CC, *Invisible Women. Exposing Data Bias in a World Designed for Men* (Vintage 2019).
Petersen MJ and Kayaoglu T (eds), *The Organization of Islamic Cooperation and Human Rights* (University of Pennsylvania Press 2019).
Petrova D (ed), 'Special Focus: Intersectionality' (2016) 16 The Equal Rights Review 5.
Prügl E, 'Neoliberalism with a Feminist Face: Crafting a New Hegemony at the World Bank' (2017) 23 Feminist Economics 30.
Sachs A and Wilson JH, *Sexism and the Law. A Study of Male Belief and Judicial Bias* (M. Robertson 1978).
Schulz P et al. (eds), *The UN Convention on the Elimination of All Forms of Discrimination Against Women and its Optional Protocol: A Commentary.* Second Edition. (2nd edn, OUP forthcoming 2022).
Sen A, *Development as Freedom* (Anchor Books 2000).
Sen G and Durano M (eds), *The Remaking of Social Contracts, Feminists in a Fierce New World* (Zed books 2014).
Soley X and Steininger S, 'Parting Ways or Lashing Back? Withdrawals, Backlash and the Inter-American Court of Human Rights' (2018) 14 International Journal of Law in Context 237.
Tobler C, *Indirect Discrimination. A Case Study into the Development of the Legal Concept of Indirect Discrimination under EC Law* (Intersentia 2005).
Woolf V, *Three Guineas* (First published by the Hogarth Press 1938, Penguin Books, 1979).
Zwingel S, *Translating International Women's Rights. The CEDAW Convention in Context* (Palgrave 2016).

CHAPTER 2

The Urgency of a Quantum Leap for Gender Equality in the World of Work

Valentina Beghini, Umberto Cattaneo, and Emanuela Pozzan

1 Introduction[1]

In the past century, laws and justice have played a crucial role in advancing gender equality in the world of work. However, despite recent progress in equality legislation and in women's educational attainment, the dividends of such progress have not fully translated into substantial closing of longstanding gender gaps at work. This is evident in the gender gaps relating to key labour market indicators, which have not narrowed in any meaningful way for more than 20 years. Such gender gaps further widen when gender intersects with other personal characteristics, such as race, ethnicity, nationality, sexual identity, age, disability or HIV status.[2] This chapter provides an overview of longstanding structural barriers that have confined women to playing a supporting role in economies and labour markets designed by and for men. It examines how the COVID-19 pandemic has exacerbated an already inequitable situation reversing, perhaps for many years to come, some of the progress towards gender equality. It gives an account of how women have historically fared in the world of work, highlighting the role played by the International Labour Organization (ILO) in shaping a rights agenda for women at work. It concludes with a call for a quantum leap for gender equality in the world of work through concrete policy recommendations.

2 Endemic Gender Gaps in the Labour Market: Before the COVID-19 Pandemic

Over the past 27 years, the gender employment gap has shrunk by less than two percentage points. Both women's and men's employment rates have declined

1 This Chapter draws upon the report published by the International Labour Organization in 2019 (International Labour Organization (ILO), 'A Quantum Leap for Gender Equality – For a Better Future of Work for All' 2019).

2 ILO (n 1).

globally, but men's have declined at a faster rate. In 2018, 1.3 billion women were in employment compared to 2.0 billion men, which means that there were still more than 700 million fewer women in employment than men. In other words, women were still 26.0 percentage points less likely to be employed than men. This is despite the fact that gross enrolment ratios for secondary and tertiary education have increased for both women and men and gender gaps in enrolment rates had almost closed in 2017. However, 21.2 per cent of youth are neither in employment nor in education or training, and a high proportion of those (69.1 per cent) are women.[3]

Despite improvements in female educational attainment, occupational and sectoral segregation remains deeply entrenched globally, with women still clustered in low-paid jobs, with poor working conditions and limited prospects for career advancement. Although the expansion of new sectors, such as technology and renewable energy, provides an opportunity to increase women's employment in male-dominated areas, increased participation in the labour force does not automatically result in equal opportunities and treatment for women. The persistence of occupational segregation stems from a combination of factors including gender differences in the fields of study, training and experience; multiple and intersecting forms of discrimination; deeply rooted social norms; and the unequal distribution of unpaid care and domestic work with women performing most of it. Stereotypes about gender roles and perceived differences in aptitudes also contribute to occupational segregation.[4]

Women are more exposed than men to informal employment in over 90 per cent of sub-Saharan African countries, 89 per cent of countries in Southern Asia and almost 75 per cent of Latin American countries.[5] In addition, women are often found in the occupations that are the most vulnerable to decent work deficits, such as domestic work and other home-based occupations. Such occupations are frequently undervalued because they mirror work that has traditionally been carried out by women in the home without pay, or simply because it is work mainly performed by women. Discrimination on grounds that intersect with sex or gender, further exacerbates the likelihood of women experiencing unfavourable working conditions and might

3 ibid.
4 United Nations (UN), 'Women's Human Rights in the Changing World of Work', A/HRC/44/51 (2020).
5 ILO, 'Women and Men in the Informal Economy: A Statistical Picture' (Third edition, 30 April 2018).

increase informality rates.[6] Overall, women are more likely to be employed in non-standard forms of employment or at the sharp end of the supply chain. While these arrangements may provide women with an opportunity to be in the labour market, job insecurity, low pay and lack of access to social protection continue to fuel economic insecurity and structural discrimination and abuse.[7]

Women are also under-represented in managerial and leadership positions. Globally, in 2020, only 28.3 per cent of managers and leaders were women, a figure that has changed very little over the past 27 years.[8] However, even though few women make it to the top, those who do, get there faster than men. Across the world, women managers and leaders are almost one year younger than men. Women managers are also more likely to have a higher level of education than men managers. Globally, 44.3 per cent of women managers have an advanced university degree compared with 38.3 per cent of men managers.[9]

Overall, women working in the same occupation as men are systematically paid less, even if their educational levels equal or exceed those of their male counterparts. The global gender wage gap is still an average of 20 per cent throughout the world.[10] Women experience further pay penalties when they belong to indigenous communities, ethnic minorities or racialised groups, are migrants or persons with disabilities.[11] Furthermore, women continue to perform the lion's share of unpaid care work. Worldwide, 606 million women of working age (or 21.7 per cent) are engaged full-time in unpaid care work, compared to 41 million men (or 1.5 per cent). Between 1997 and 2012, the time that women devoted to housework and caregiving diminished by only 15 minutes per day, whereas for men it increased by just eight minutes per day. At this pace, it is estimated that the gender gap in time spent doing unpaid care work will take many more generations to close.

---

6 ILO (n 1).

7 UN (n 4).

8 ILO, 'Building Forward Fairer: Women's Rights to Work and at Work at the Core of the COVID-19 Recovery', Policy Brief (2021).

9 ILO (n 1).

10 ILO, 'Global Wage Report 2018/2019' (2018).

11 ILO, 'Implementing the ILO Indigenous and Tribal Peoples Convention No. 169: Towards an Inclusive, Sustainable and Just Future' (2020); ILO, 'ILO Global Estimates on International Migrant Workers' (2021); ILO, 'The Migrant Pay Gap: Understanding Wage Differences between Migrants and Nationals' (2020); and the Centre for Social Justice (CSJ) Disability Commission, 'Now Is the Time' (2021).

Unpaid care work and a lack of social infrastructure is also one of the main reasons why women are outside the labour force, or do not progress in the labour market at the same pace as men do.[12] A positive development in this context is Resolution I, adopted in 2013 by the 19th International Conference of Labour Statisticians (ICLS). This resolution defines unpaid caregiving services and unpaid domestic services for household and family members as 'own-use provision of services'. It also makes it clear that work can be performed in any kind of economic unit, including households and communities, and can also include services that are not provided in the context of market transactions. In 2018, the 20th ICLS went one step further in its Resolution I by providing a new International Classification of Status at Work (ICSaW-18), which covers all jobs and work activities in all forms of work, including own-use provision of services.[13] Such progress makes the amount of unpaid care work performed by women and men visible and measurable. The 19th and 20th ICLS resolutions expand the boundaries of work beyond pure market transactions, recognising unpaid care work as work and opening the door to a future where social and economic progress is measured by more than just a country's gross domestic product (GDP).[14]

Critically important is the fact that mothers, particularly those with young children, experience systemic disadvantage in the workplace. This results in larger pay gaps and substantially lower retirement savings or pension contributions. For instance, working mothers are less likely to be in employment than women without children or fathers with young children. They are also less likely to reach managerial and leadership positions compared with their male counterparts. This is due to difficulties in balancing work and family responsibilities. However, where men share unpaid care work more equally with women, more women are found in managerial positions.[15]

Discriminatory laws restricting women's rights at work and discriminatory practices including pregnancy discrimination, unfair treatment, abuse, violence and harassment remain among the top challenges facing women in the world of work, especially young women and women from further marginalised

---

12 ILO, 'Care Work and Care Jobs for the Future of Decent Work' (2018).

13 ILO, 'Resolution I – Resolution Concerning Statistics of Work, Employment and Labour Underutilization' (2013), 19th International Conference of Labour Statisticians; and ILO, 'Resolution I – Resolution Concerning Statistics on Work Relationships', 20th International Conference of Labour Statisticians (2014).

14 ILO (n 1).

15 ibid.

populations.[16] Discrimination, violence and harassment at work have a detrimental impact on women's health and well-being, their participation in employment and the quality of their work. Tackling this issue is essential both from a human rights perspective and for a gender-equal future of work, with decent work for all. There is a growing number of laws addressing violence and harassment, including gender-based violence and harassment, but they are often limited in their coverage and application. Moreover, these laws often have not sufficiently taken into account new and emerging forms of ICT-facilitated violence and harassment against women in the workplace, or the impact of domestic violence in the world of work.[17]

3 The COVID-19 Pandemic: Undoing Already Too Slow Progress

Almost two years into the COVID-19 pandemic, there is no question that COVID-19 has dramatically widened existing gender inequalities relating to gender division of labour and economic stability. The accompanying social and economic crises have further exacerbated gender gaps in the labour market. Between 2019 and 2020, women's employment declined globally by 3.6 per cent, representing a decrease of 47 million jobs, whereas men's employment declined by 2.9 per cent, or 57 million jobs. Not all regions have been impacted in the same way. The region of the Americas experienced the greatest reduction in women's employment as a result of the pandemic (−8.9 per cent). The second biggest drop in the number of employed women was observed in Asia and the Pacific. Between 2019 and 2020, women's employment declined by 3.3 per cent and men's by 2.9 per cent.[18]

In 2021, the number of employed women globally was still 20 million less than in 2019, while the number of men in employment was 10 million less than in 2019.[19] Young people, especially young women, continue to face greater employment shortfall. This gap between women and men in the world of work is likely to persist into the near to medium term with young women being the

16 ILO-Gallup, 'Towards a Better Future for Women and Work: Voices of Women and Men' (2017).
17 ILO, 'Violence and Harassment in the World of Work: A Guide on Convention No. 190 and Recommendation No. 206' (2021).
18 ILO, Building Forward Fairer: Women's Rights to Work and at Work at the Core of the COVID-19 Recovery (2021).
19 ibid.

most affected and facing the biggest shortfall relative to the pre-crisis situation in 2019.[20]

The COVID-19 pandemic has also brought to the surface wide gender gaps in the quality of employment, mainly for the many women working in sectors and occupations with high proportions of women, and in the informal economy. Of the 740 million women working in the informal economy,[21] 42 per cent were in sectors at high risk of job-losses and reductions in working hours,[22] compared to 32 per cent of men.[23] On the other hand, during the pandemic, 96 million women have continued to do essential work in the health and social work sector as well as in other essential occupations, often putting their lives at risk and facing increased working hours at work and at home.[24] For most women and men employed either in high-risk sectors or in essential work, the COVID-19 pandemic has increased care demands within households on an unprecedented scale. New evidence confirms that women continue to shoulder most of the unpaid care work. This has led the women who remained in employment to cut down on paid working hours or to extend their total daily working hours (paid and unpaid) to unsustainable levels.[25]

The COVID-19 pandemic has hit those at the bottom of the wage scale harder than those at the top and women are disproportionately represented in low-paid jobs. COVID-19 has unsettled the livelihoods of women working in the informal economy, as many informal businesses were forced to close temporarily or permanently. This has led to severe loss of income for women without recourse to social security measures and an increased risk of falling further into poverty. Domestic workers, many of whom work informally, were even more exposed to significant decent work deficits in respect of working hours, wages, social security, occupational safety and health, including violence and harassment.[26]

20 ILO, 'ILO Monitor: COVID-19 and the World of Work' (8th edn, 2021).

21 ILO (n 5).

22 Such as accommodation and food services; real estate, business and administrative activities; manufacturing; and the wholesale/retail trade.

23 ILO, 'The COVID-19 Response: Getting Gender Equality Right for a better Future for Women at Work' (2020).

24 ibid.

25 European Institute for Gender Equality (EIGE), 'Gender Equality and the Socio-Economic Impact of the COVID-19 Pandemic' (2021) Research Note.

26 ILO (n 23).

4 More than a Century of Women's Rights at Work: But Still a Long Way to Go

Persisting gender gaps in the labour market and the regressing position of women in the world of work as a result of the COVID-19 pandemic prompt a reflection on the historical efforts made to advance gender equality at work over the past century. The situation also highlights the need to focus better and act faster to ensure a more equal world of work where women in all their diversity enjoy equal opportunities and treatment.

Undoubtedly, women's increased involvement in the paid economy was the one of the most significant changes in labour markets during the past century. The two World Wars, in particular the second one, were the major catalyst for women's increased entry into the labour market. However, for many women from less privileged socio-economic backgrounds, race, colour, national extraction or social origin, participation in the labour market was an economic imperative or a result of discriminatory practices that came much earlier than this, including in many parts of the world with still largely agrarian economies and societies. In all cases, women's role and participation in the world of work have been conceived according to a structure of the world of work designed by men for men, and women had to fit in.[27]

Historically, the treatment of women's rights at work revolved around the debate between 'protectionism' and 'equal rights for women'. Protectionists claimed that women workers required special measures to protect their health and safety and, most importantly, their reproductive health and their role as caregivers. On the other hand, proponents of equal rights contended that establishing special protective measures for women detracted from the overall aims of labour legislation to protect all workers, including men.[28]

In the first deliberations of the ILO,[29] adult women were protected against arduous working conditions on account of their reproductive role and traditional family responsibilities. The first Maternity Protection Convention,

27 ILO, 'The Women at Work Initiative: The Push for Equality', Report of the Director-General I (B) (2018).

28 Eileen Boris et al. (eds), *Women's ILO, Transnational Networks, Global Labour Standards and Gender Equity, 1919 to Present* (BRILL 2018).

29 The ILO was established in 1919, as part of the Treaty of Versailles that ended World War I, to reflect the belief that universal and lasting peace can be accomplished only if it is based on social justice. The ILO is the only tripartite United Nations agency, which brings together governments, employers, and workers of 187 Member States to set labour standards, develop policies and devise programmes promoting decent work for all women and men.

1919 (No. 3) and the Night Work (Women) Convention, 1919 (No. 4), are two examples.[30] These protective measures were adopted despite the opposition of certain factions of the women's movements, which deemed these measures discriminatory and called for a more general protection of workers' health, irrespective of their sex.[31]

It took some time for gender justice to prevail over the protectionist approach and the increasing activism of women's organisations was instrumental in achieving this result.[32] This shift was also reflected in the adoption of new international labour standards promoting equality and non-discrimination at work. Combating discrimination and ensuring equality of opportunity and treatment are essential to decent work, and success on this front has resonated well beyond the workplace. In 1951, the ILO adopted the Equal Remuneration Convention (No. 100), followed by the Discrimination (Employment and Occupation) Convention, 1958 (No. 111), aimed at preventing discrimination in employment and occupation on the grounds of race, colour, sex, religion, political opinion, national extraction or social origin, in both the public and private sectors. This Convention requires the elimination not only of direct discrimination based on one or more prohibited grounds, but also of more subtle and less visible forms of discrimination (indirect discrimination) and discriminatory-based harassment.[33] It also requires that the underlying causes of inequalities that result from deeply entrenched discrimination, complex social patterns, institutional structures, policies and legal constructs, be addressed, including through the implementation of proactive measures, with the aim of achieving substantive equality.[34] This can only be realised through the effective participation and involvement of women from all spheres and backgrounds.

In the same period, the ILO also adopted other relevant international labour standards for the promotion of women's employment, such as the Social Security Convention, 1952 (No. 102) and the Employment Policy Convention,

---

30 George P Politakis, 'Night Work of Women in Industry: Standards and Sensibility' (2001) 140 (4) International Labour Review 403.

31 Boris et al. (n 28).

32 Eileen Boris, *Making the Woman Worker. Precarious Labor and the Fight for Global Standards, 1919–2019* (OUP 2019); and Sandra Whitworth, 'Gender, International Relations and the Case of the ILO' (1994) 20 Review of International Studies 389.

33 Committee of Experts on the Application of Conventions and Recommendations (CEACR), 'General Observation on Discrimination (Employment and Occupation) Convention, 1958 (No. 111)' (2019).

34 CEACR, 'Giving Globalization a Human Face (General Survey on the Fundamental Conventions)' (2012).

1964 (No. 122), aimed at ensuring full and productive employment and freedom of choice of employment and the promotion of equality of opportunity for all workers.[35]

Alive to the demands of civil rights movements and women's liberation movements, the ILO adopted the Declaration on Equality of Opportunity and Treatment for Women Workers (1975).[36] This Declaration set forth a number of principles as targets to be achieved progressively in relation to the integration of women in economic life. The Declaration reflected the continuing shift away from protectionism. It acknowledged that women's status in the world of work cannot be changed without also changing the role of men in society and in the family and therefore reflecting on the different power relationships that perpetuate discrimination. It also recognised the need to enable women to exercise their right to gainful employment, regardless of family situation. It declared that 'all forms of discrimination on the grounds of sex which deny or restrict [equality of opportunity and treatment for all workers] are unacceptable and must be eliminated'. A reflection of the times during which it was adopted, but perhaps still relevant to some of the debates of today, the Declaration calls for particular attention to be devoted to 'the situation of women in countries under foreign domination or subject to the practices of apartheid'.[37]

From the 1980s onwards, the ILO adopted further standards to advance a gender-equal approach to work–family reconciliation. In particular, the Workers with Family Responsibilities Convention, 1981 (No. 156) finally recognised that family responsibilities not only lie on women's shoulders, but are shared with men and the state. The Convention requires governments to ensure that persons with family responsibilities are not subjected to discrimination on account of those responsibilities, including in access to or progression within employment. Governments are also required to develop provisions such as childcare and family services to facilitate a good work–life balance. The most recent ILO standard on maternity protection, the Maternity Protection Convention, 2000 (No. 183), has sought to prevent maternity-based discrimination by, *inter alia*, shifting the onus of financing income replacement for mothers away from employers to social insurance or general taxation, making this a collective responsibility for the society.[38]

35 ILO (n 1).

36 ILO, 'Declaration on Equality of Opportunity and Treatment for Women Workers' (25 June 1975).

37 Boris et al. (n 28).

38 ibid.

Although it recognises that gender-based occupational segregation is a form of discrimination, the ILO has also adopted standards to respond to the specific needs and situations of segments of the labour force that are female dominated.[39] These include the Home Work Convention, 1996 (No. 177) and the Domestic Workers Convention, 2011 (No. 189). These conventions afforded home-based and domestic workers equality of treatment in employment with other workers, including the right to organise and bargain collectively. Similarly, the Part-Time Work Convention, 1994 (No. 175) provides for equality of treatment for part-time workers.

Most recently, in 2019, the Violence and Harassment Convention (No. 190) and its accompanying Recommendation (No. 206) were adopted, addressing one of the most pernicious and persistent barriers preventing women from accessing, remaining and advancing in the labour market. The Convention represents a game changer in fighting against discrimination and inequality in the world of work, by making the invisible visible and acknowledging the pervasiveness and unacceptability of violence and harassment. For the first time, violence and harassment in the world of work, which includes gender-based violence and harassment, is defined, and a common framework for action is provided. The Convention acknowledges that to be able to fully prevent and eradicate gender-based violence and harassment in the world of work, it is necessary to address its underlying causes, such as multiple and intersecting forms of discrimination, gender stereotypes and unequal gender-based power relations.[40] In this regard, the Convention calls on governments to adopt legislation ensuring the right to equality and non-discrimination in employment and occupation for all, and to develop and implement an inclusive, integrated and gender-responsive approach for the prevention and elimination of violence and harassment in the world of work. Moreover, by requiring that workplace risk assessments should take into account factors such as social and cultural norms that increase the likelihood of gender-based violence and harassment, it provides a concrete and effective entry point to change attitudes. Finally, the Convention also recognises, for the first time, domestic violence as an element that affects employment, as well as the health and safety of everyone in the world of work and calls on governments to take measures to mitigate its effects at work.

All these achievements have undoubtedly contributed towards advancing gender equality at work. However, as we have seen, the current landscape of

39 See ILO, 'Convention on Discrimination (Employment and Occupation), 1958 (No. 111)' (4 June 1958).

40 ILO (n 17).

women's position in the labour market remains uneven and unsatisfactory, and it is imperative to accelerate action. Unless the present trajectory is changed and policy choices are made that put gender equality at their core, the situation is likely to deteriorate further as work becomes more fragmented and the future remains uncertain. A quantum leap for gender equality at work is urgently needed. This has been further reaffirmed in the 2019 ILO Centenary Declaration for the Future of Work and in the most recent 2021 Global call to action for a human-centred recovery from the COVID-19 crisis that is inclusive, sustainable and resilient.[41]

5 At the Crossroads of Gender Equality in the World of Work: The Right Path to Gender Equality

Sluggish progress, stagnation and even setbacks in women's employment outcomes should no longer be given room in the societies and economies of the present and the future. Economic transformation and growth must be equitably distributed, and be of equal benefit to women in all their diversity. The world of work is in the midst of profound and rapid changes. There is a need to recognise the full range of opportunities and risks of these changes and to have an explicit agenda for the achievement of equality and equity for all women and men.[42]

Cognisant of these persistent gaps in the labour market and of the new challenges, including digitalisation, migration, demographic shifts and climate change, the ILO has in recent years made it clear that immediate bolder actions are needed. 'If we fail to deliver on gender equality, the attainment of decent work for all will be illusory'.[43] The ILO Centenary Declaration for the Future of Work, adopted in 2019 on the occasion of the 100th anniversary of the ILO, specifically called for achieving gender equality at work through a transformative agenda. This includes the recognition and redistribution of care work, both paid and unpaid, as one of its key pillars as well as the need to ensure equal opportunities, equal participation and equal treatment for all women.[44]

41 ILO, 'ILO Centenary Declaration for the Future of Work, 2019' (2019); and ILO, 'Global Call to Action for a Human-Centred Recovery from the COVID-19 Crisis that is Inclusive, Sustainable and Resilient' (2021).

42 UN (n 4).

43 ILO (n 27).

44 ILO (n 41).

In 2021, in its Resolution concerning a global call to action for a human-centred recovery from the COVID-19 crisis that is inclusive, sustainable and resilient, the ILO re-asserted the need to bring gender equality to the core of the COVID-19 recovery effort.[45] Recognizing that women are not a homogeneous group, the ILO 2021 Resolution goes a step further and calls for the adoption of a transformative agenda for equality, diversity and inclusion to be executed across the public and private sectors. This agenda aims at eliminating violence and harassment in the world of work and discrimination on all grounds. It also takes into account the specific circumstances and vulnerabilities of migrants, indigenous and tribal peoples, people of African descent, ethnic minorities, older persons, persons with disabilities and persons living with HIV/AIDS.[46]

Rethinking the economy post-COVID-19 should be based on forward-looking gender-sound and transformative multi-systems decisions with adequate allocations in national budgets to respond to all women's needs and priorities. The allocations need to include women in the informal economy and those who face multiple or intersecting forms of discrimination, who are often left at the margins of the economy and our societies. Gender-responsive and social budgeting can be an important tool for more effectively prioritising gender equality and diversity in the overall set of national policies. Data disaggregated by sex and other characteristics, such as race, indigeneity, disability, and sexual orientation and gender identity status, will be essential to design policies and monitor outcomes to establish what works for women. Urgently needed interventions are discussed the following subsections.

5.1 *Double Investments in the Care Economy*

Current levels of public investments (proportionate to GDP) in the care sectors need to be doubled to ensure that gender equality stands a chance of being achieved, together with the creation of decent work for paid care workers. One hundred and twenty million more quality jobs in the care sectors (health, social work and education) and one hundred and forty-nine million indirect jobs in non-care sectors could be generated with the right investments.[47] Investing in the care economy is a win-win solution. It would offset job losses resulting from the economic fallout, while making health care systems more resilient to pandemic outbreaks. It would also increase educational opportunities for current and future generations. Creation of quality decent care jobs can help to accelerate progress in closing gender gaps in labour markets and disrupting

45 ILO (n 41).
46 ibid.
47 ILO (n 12).

entrenched gender-based occupational segregation. The potential growth of the care sector must appropriately value paid care work both economically and socially through decent wages and working conditions. This should go hand in hand with concluding the longstanding debate on rethinking GDP measurement to recognise the value of unpaid care work as well as to account for the value of the vast informal economy.[48]

5.2 *Promote Policies for Time and Care*

COVID-19 has led to an increase in care leave, availability of childcare services, and flexible working arrangements, including teleworking. However, latest ILO estimations show that the deficit in care leave policies and childcare services provision still results in a gap of 4.2 years between the end of paid care leave and the start of free and universal ECCE or primary education.[49] Such measures have long been called for to better balance the work–family equation for all workers and to promote women's participation in the labour force. In recovering from the COVID-19 crisis, such measures should be further advanced. Increased allocations of resources together with a comprehensive system of legislation providing for paid family and care leave for both women and men, whatever the form of their working arrangements or employment status, should be prioritised. This approach will ensure greater time sovereignty, allowing workers to exercise more choice and control over their working hours. In designing family leave and care policies, including flexible working arrangements, there should be no space for reinforcing traditional gender roles, avoiding the situation in which only women make use of them, while continuing to shoulder the majority of unpaid care work. Relevant ILO labour standards including the Maternity Protection Convention No. 183 and the Workers with Family Responsibilities No. 156 and their respective recommendations offer valuable policy guidance.

5.3 *Expand Social Protection for a Human-centred World of Work*

Public investment in social protection is required to overcome the COVID-19 crisis and build a solid base for systemic change. This is an opportunity to expand social protection to women in vulnerable working situations and to promote their transition from the informal to the formal economy in line with the ILO Recommendation No. 204. Efforts should also be directed towards providing universal access to comprehensive, adequate and sustainable social

48 UN, 'Our Common Agenda' (2021) Report of Secretary-General.

49 ILO, 'Care at Work: Investing in Care Leave and Services for a More Gender Equal World of Work' (2022).

protection for all, with a view to reducing the current gender gap in social protection coverage. These systems should also be financed in a sustainable and equitable way, usually by a combination of taxes and contributions. To this end, fiscal space must be expanded to promote investment in care provision, services and infrastructure. Creating fiscal space is feasible, even in low-income countries.

5.4 *Overcome Discrimination, Gender Stereotypes, Violence and Harassment*

Structural and systemic discrimination, including the persistence of stereotypes and expectations based on sex or gender, race or other grounds of discrimination, as well as violence and harassment, need to be specifically addressed. Otherwise, existing inequalities in the world of work will continue to be a barrier for women to enter, remain and succeed in the world of work. Discrimination is not only a persistent scourge that needs to be prevented and eliminated, but it also influences how, and in what ways, women are more vulnerable to violence and harassment both at home and at work. Laws to establish that women and men have equal rights are the basis for demanding and achieving substantive equality in practice. In this regard, ILO international labour standards, including Conventions Nos. 111 and 190, are more than ever an essential compass to guide the design and implementation of human-centred laws and policies for a future of work based on dignity and respect for all. Collective agreements and workplace measures can be important vehicles for ensuring and promoting equality, as well as for addressing violence and harassment in the world of work by improving the scope and coverage of existing legislation or by filling a gap when legislation is non-existent.[50]

Achieving gender equality in the world of work is possible if laws that discriminate against women and girls in employment and occupation, as well as prior to entry into the labour market are repealed. Lifting such barriers has been shown to have a positive effect on the participation of women in the labour market. Mainstreaming equality and other proactive measures would be particularly valuable since they imply initiatives aiming at identifying and targeting those who are disadvantaged in several different ways.[51] For instance, to rebalance occupational segregation, it is equally important to introduce incentives and measures to encourage women to take up jobs in male-dominated sectors as it is to encourage men to take up jobs in female-dominated sectors,

---

50 ILO (n 1).

51 ibid; Sandra Fredman, 'Intersectional Discrimination in EU Gender Equality and Non-Discrimination Law' (4 August 2016).

while simultaneously addressing the social and cultural norms that perpetuate gendered occupational segregation.[52]

5.5 *Lifelong Learning so that No One Is Left Behind*

The fast-changing pace at which the world of work is transforming requires an approach that allows workers to keep up with demands for new skills. Lifelong learning can be instrumental in helping to prevent people, women in particular, from being left behind during social and economic development. Proactive measures encouraging young women to study science, technology, engineering and mathematics (STEM) and occupational trajectories are increasing, as are training programmes aimed at facilitating the return to work for women and men either after childbirth, following a period of parental leave, or as a result of long-term unemployment due to unpaid family care responsibilities. Closing the digital gender divide must also be a focus of gender-responsive lifelong learning initiatives.

Without targeted intervention, existing patterns of segregation will be replicated in newly emerging sectors. Such interventions include temporary special measures to increase women's representation in high-growth sectors; the provision of education, skills development, on-the-job and lifelong learning for women to transition from jobs that are at risk of automation to high-growth areas; and incentives and interventions to increase women's representation in education and employment in STEM. In designing such measures, special attention should be given to women further disadvantaged because of additional layers of discrimination. Policy and regulatory frameworks can play an important role in creating obligations for employers to report on the gender composition of their enterprises or organisations by occupation, gender pay gap and women's representation in leadership.[53]

5.6 *Give Decision-making Power to Women*

Having more women in decision-making structures, including task forces appointed to plan the recovery from the impacts of COVID-19 will have a positive influence on the overall response to COVID-19 as well as on governance, identity and public image.[54] It can influence women's perceptions about the values of these organisations and incentivise them to participate. The presence of women in decision-making bodies is an important precondition for the pursuit of women's interests in the world of work.

52 ILO (n 1).

53 UN (n 4).

54 See Chapter 10.

In redesigning the economy, sound industrial relations and effective mechanisms for social dialogue will be essential to ensure good governance and inclusive economic growth and democracy. The participation of women, with all their diverse characteristics and backgrounds, in these processes is important to ensure democratic participation and equitable outcomes. The presence of women in the collective bargaining processes that will follow the post-COVID-19 order will be important to achieving outcomes that benefit women. In the case of informal workers, leveraging the capacities of women's organisations and associations of informal economy workers would be instrumental to a solid response to the needs of women in vulnerable situations.

6 Conclusions: A Quantum Leap for Gender Equality at Work and Beyond

The right path to equality at work for all women, irrespective of their personal characteristics, is in front of us, but only fair and forward-looking choices and actions will determine whether the world of work will be a more equal place for women and, as a consequence, for men too. This will require an ecosystem of reinforcing measures and an unwavering commitment to equality for all women, which definitely should encompass challenging and addressing the confluence of different power relationships which compound disadvantage.

To move from potential to reality, a human-centred agenda offers the best way to achieve the transformative and multi-systems changes needed in this new era. Women have always made an important contribution to the economy and to societies. All these contributions need to be acknowledged and valued, and solutions that will allow women to fully enjoy equal opportunities and treatment at work need to be consciously accelerated with women leading the way. COVID-19 has been a reminder that we must do better because humanity is at its best when gender equality is at its core. A giant leap for gender equality at work and at home is of benefit to all.

References

Boris E, *Making the Woman Worker. Precarious Labor and the Fight for Global Standards, 1919–2019* (OUP 2019).

Boris E et al. (eds), *Women's ILO, Transnational Networks, Global Labour Standards and Gender Equity, 1919 to Present* (Brill 2018).

Fredman S, 'Intersectional Discrimination in EU Gender Equality and Non-Discrimination Law' (4 August 2016) European Commission.

ILO, 'A Quantum Leap for Gender Equality – For a Better Future of Work for All' (2019).

ILO, 'Violence and harassment in the world of work: A Guide on Convention No. 190 and Recommendation No. 206' (2021).

ILO, 'Care at work: Investing in care leave and services for a more gender equal world of work. Geneva: International Labour Office' (2022).

Politakis PG, 'Night Work of Women in Industry: Standards and Sensibility' (2001) 140 (4) International Labour Review 403.

Whitworth S, 'Gender, International Relations and the Case of the ILO' (1994) 20 Review of International Studies 389.

CHAPTER 3

Gender Mainstreaming at the World Health Organization

Experience, Challenges, and Pitfalls in Global Health

Flavia Bustreo, Rachael Hinton, Anna Giulia Ponchia, and Cecilia Rocco

1 Introduction

Gender inequality is one of the biggest obstacles to realising the Sustainable Development Agenda by 2030. Gender mainstreaming offers a way to address gender discrimination and contribute to achieving Sustainable Development Goal (SDG) five, gender equality, and related SDGs including quality education, and good health and wellbeing. Despite global promotion of gender mainstreaming as a tool for meeting gender equality objectives, no country is set to achieve gender equality by 2030.[1] In this chapter we will reflect on what has worked and what more needs to be done for gender mainstreaming to deliver on its promise.[2] To illustrate this assessment, we will examine the pioneering experience of WHO in its effort to mainstream gender as a relational concept across the organisation and its programmes. The lessons learnt can help to inform the implementation of innovative mainstreaming strategies to tackle the structural causes of gender inequalities and to achieve real transformative social change.

2 What Is Gender Mainstreaming?

Within the UN, the concept of gender mainstreaming was first introduced in the 'Forward-Looking Strategies for the Advancement of Women' adopted at

1 The 2019 Sustainable Development Goal (SDG) Gender Index provides a snapshot of where the world stands, right now, linked to the vision of gender equality set out by the 2030 Agenda. It measures the state of gender equality aligned to 14 of the 17 SDGs in 129 countries in five regions and 51 issues ranging from health, gender-based violence, and climate change, to decent work and others. Overall, the index shows that, across all the goals and indicators studied, no country has fully achieved gender equality <https://data.em2030.org/2019-sdg-gender-index/explore-the-2019-index-data/> accessed 2 July 2021.

2 Emanuela Lombardo and Petra Meier, 'Gender Mainstreaming in the EU? Incorporating a Feminist Reading?' (2005) 13 (2) European Journal of Women's Studies 151.

DOI:10.1163/9789004467682_005

the Third UN World Conference on Women, in Nairobi in 1985.[3] The strategies outlined measures for achieving gender equality at the national level to promote women's participation in peace and development efforts.

A decade later, the Beijing Declaration and Platform for Action, reaffirmed the principles of the Nairobi conference, and recognised gender mainstreaming as a fundamental tool for meeting gender equality commitments. More specifically, the Declaration states:

> It is essential to design, implement and monitor, with the full participation of women, effective, efficient and mutually reinforcing gender-sensitive policies and programmes, including development policies and programmes, at all levels that will foster the empowerment and advancement of women.[4]

---

3 UN Women, 'World Conferences on Women' (2021) <https://www.unwomen.org/en/how-we-work/intergovernmental-support/world-conferences-on-women> accessed 2 July 2021.

4 ibid; 'The Beijing Declaration and Platform for Action of 1995 is a visionary agenda for the empowerment of women. It remains to this day the most comprehensive global policy framework and blueprint for action and is a current source of guidance and inspiration to achieve gender equality and respect the human rights of women and girls, everywhere' (Introduction). The document covers twelve 'critical areas of concern': Women and poverty (A); Education and Training of Women (B); Women and Health (C); Violence Against Women (D); Women and Armed Conflict (E); Women and the economy (F); Women in Power and Decision-making (G); Institutional Mechanisms for the Advancement of Women (H); Human Rights of Women (I); Women and the Media (J); Women and the Environment (K); The Girl Child (L). 'For each critical area of concern, strategic objectives are identified, as well as a detailed catalogue of related actions to be taken by Governments and other stakeholders at national, regional, and international level' (Introduction). Gender mainstreaming was introduced as an official indicator to address the second strategic objective of area H on institutional mechanisms: integrate gender perspectives in legislation, public programmes, and projects. This encompasses a set of sub-objectives: 'a) Ensure that before policy decisions are taken, an analysis of their impact on women and men, respectively, is carried out; b) Regularly review national policies, programmes and projects, as well as their implementation, evaluating their impact in order to guarantee that women are direct beneficiaries of development and that their full contribution to development, both remunerated and unremunerated, is considered in economic policy and planning; c) Promote national goals and strategies for equality between women and men in order to eliminate obstacles to the exercise of women's rights and eradicate all forms of discrimination against women; d) Work with members of legislative bodies, as appropriate, to promote a gender perspective in all legislation and policies; e) Give all ministries the mandate to review policies and programmes from a gender perspective and place the responsibility for implementing that mandate at the highest possible level; and establish and/or strengthen an inter-ministerial coordination structure to carry out this mandate, monitor progress and network with relevant machineries' (Strategic

After the adoption of the Beijing Declaration, the term 'gender mainstreaming' began to be used in the international arena influencing the political debate. The verb 'to mainstream' means that ideas and opinions are thought to be *normal* because they are shared by most people. The purpose of gender mainstreaming was therefore to make gender issues 'main', or more precisely, *normal* and widely accepted. This concept contrasted with 'gender side streaming',[5] the idea of gender specialisation where specific agencies, such as gender-oriented organisations, are solely responsible for addressing gender issues. The need to change the nature of gender issues from *peripheral* to *central* was the driving force behind gender mainstreaming. However, while the *logic* behind the term is clear, there is no universal and homogeneous definition of gender mainstreaming. This renders the concept *fluid* and difficult to grasp, which has implications for how the concept of gender mainstreaming is translated into practice.

There is general agreement that the main goal of gender mainstreaming is to produce gender-equal policies and programmes. To counter gender bias in society and to challenge androcentric policy norms, gender mainstreaming is also promoted as a strategy to transform unequal gender roles and practice.[6] The definition of gender mainstreaming in the Beijing Declaration focused on policy planning and evaluation, recognising the role policies play in the gendered distribution of resources. As androcentric policy planning can become a potential multiplier of inequalities, the Declaration called for the integration of gender perspectives in the policy formulation process as well as legislation, public programmes, and projects.

Based on these considerations, in 1997, the UN Economic and Social Council (ECOSOC), in their agreed conclusions 1997/2, elaborated a broader definition of gender mainstreaming as:

> the process of assessing the implications for women and men of any planned action, including legislation, policies or programmes, in all areas

---

Objective H.2) (UN Women, 'Beijing Declaration and Platform for Action' (1995) and 'Beijing +5 Political Declaration' (2015) <https://www.unwomen.org/sites/default/files/Headquarters/Attachments/Sections/CSW/PFA_E_Final_WEB.pdf> accessed 24 June 2021; United Nations (UN), 'Report of the Fourth World Conference on Women' (A/CONF.177/20/REV.1., United Nations, 1996, chap. I, resolution 1, annex I).

5 Hilary Charlesworth, 'Not Waving but Drowning: Gender Mainstreaming and Human Rights in the United Nations' (2005) 18 Harvard Human Rights Journal 1.

6 Mieke Verloo, 'Displacement and Empowerment: Reflections on the Concept and Practice of the Council of Europe Approach to Gender Mainstreaming and Gender Equality' (2005) 12 (3) Social Politics: International Studies in Gender, State & Society 344.

> and at all levels. It is a strategy for making women's as well as men's concerns and experiences an integral dimension of the design, implementation, monitoring and evaluation of policies and programmes in all political, economic and societal spheres so that women and men benefit equally, and inequality is not perpetuated.[7]

The ECOSOC definition – on which most 'global commitments on gender mainstreaming' are based – is relevant for several reasons. First, it underlined the need to strengthen the accountability for gender mainstreaming. It also put further emphasis on mainstreaming gender in the different stages of policy making, such as policy design, implementation, monitoring, and evaluation. A focus on policy making was further expanded in the definition developed by the Council of Europe:

> The (re)organization, improvement, development and evaluation of policy processes, so that a gender equality perspective is incorporated in all policies at all levels and at all stages, by the actors normally involved in policymaking.[8]

---

7 ECOSOC Definition: 'A. Definition of the concept of gender mainstreaming: Mainstreaming a gender perspective is the process of assessing the implications for women and men of any planned action, including legislation, policies or programmes, in all areas and at all levels. It is a strategy for making women's as well as men's concerns and experiences an integral dimension of the design, implementation, monitoring and evaluation of policies and programmes in all political, economic, and societal spheres so that women and men benefit equally, and inequality is not perpetuated. The ultimate goal is to achieve gender equality. B. Principles for mainstreaming a gender perspective in the United Nations system: 1 Issues across all areas of activity should be defined in such a manner that gender differences can be diagnosed – that is, an assumption of gender-neutrality should not be made. 2 Responsibility for translating gender mainstreaming into practice is system-wide and rests at the highest levels. Accountability for outcomes needs to be monitored constantly. 3 Gender mainstreaming also requires that every effort be made to broaden women's participation at all levels of decision-making. 4 Gender mainstreaming must be institutionalized through concrete steps, mechanisms, and processes in all parts of the United Nations system. 5 Gender mainstreaming does not replace the need for targeted, women-specific policies and programmes or positive legislation, nor does it substitute for gender units or focal points. 6 Clear political will and the allocation of adequate and, if need be, additional human and financial resources for gender mainstreaming from all available funding sources are important for the successful translation of the concept into practice' (UN Economic and Social Council, 'Report of Economic and Social Council for 1997'. A/52/3, United Nations, 1997).

8 Council of Europe, 'Final Report of Activities of the Group of Specialists on Mainstreaming (EG-S-MS) – Gender Mainstreaming. Conceptual Framework, Methodology and Presentation of Good Practices' (1998). For a more comprehensive definition 'Gender

To incorporate a gender equality perspective in policy making, it is suggested that five policy shifts are needed.[9] First, it requires the formulation of a concept of gender equality that targets the multiple interconnecting causes of gender equality. It also requires the rearticulation of policy ends and means from a gender perspective and equal and diverse gender representation in politics. A 'shift in institutional and organisational cultures' towards gender equality also requires a change in policy processes, mechanisms and leadership support. Lastly, there needs to be greater diversity of the actors involved in policy making, including increased participation of civil society. These criteria could be used to assess the effectives of gender mainstreaming in bringing about institutional and policy change.

Although the ECOSOC definition is widely accepted and used among scholars and practitioners, it has been criticised for being too broad, contributing to confusion about what gender mainstreaming is and how it can be implemented.[10] However, the ECOSOC definition does highlight some fundamental principles of gender mainstreaming, including that it is a *process*. It is a concept *in fieri* – in progress – something that can shift and adapt to a changing context. As a result, gender mainstreaming should not be seen as an end in itself but as a means to achieve gender equality. Gender mainstreaming seeks to reposition gender issues at the centre of policies and programmes. The need to re-balance a world where norms presented as neutral are, in reality, male-centred, is the bedrock of gender mainstreaming.[11] From this perspective, gender mainstreaming is a political strategy that envisions the transformation of

---

mainstreaming means integrating a gender equality perspective at all stages and levels of policies, programmes and projects. Women and men have different needs and living conditions and circumstances, including unequal access to and control over power, resources, human rights and institutions, including the justice system. The situations of women and men also differ according to country, region, age, ethnic or social origin, or other factors. The aim of gender mainstreaming is to take into account these differences when designing, implementing, and evaluating policies, programmes and projects, so that they benefit both women and men and do not increase inequality but enhance gender equality. Gender mainstreaming aims to solve –sometimes hidden- gender inequalities. It is therefore a tool for achieving gender equality' <https://www.coe.int/en/web/genderequality/what-is-gender-mainstreaming> accessed 24 June 2021.

9 Emanuela Lombardo, 'Integrating or Setting the Agenda? Gender Mainstreaming in the European Constitution-Making Process' (2005) 12 (3) Social Politics: International Studies in Gender, State & Society 412; Lombardo (n 2).

10 Katharine Sarikakis, 'Power, Patriarchy, Profit: Barriers to Gender Mainstreaming in Media Policy' in UNESCO International Association for Media and Communication Research (eds), *Media and Gender: a Scholarly Agenda for the Global Alliance on Media and Gender* (2014).

11 Mary Hawkesworth, 'Policy Studies Within a Feminist Frame' (1994) 27 Policy Sciences 97.

existing unequal gender roles and practices through the adoption of specific policies and programmes built on measurable targets.

Gender mainstreaming can be seen as a transformative tool for addressing gendered power imbalances; however, scholars recognise that its implementation in practice has been uneven and somewhat limited in impact.[12] Indeed, questions have been raised about the achievements of gender mainstreaming, and whether it has 'failed' in terms of its original objectives.[13] Despite global endorsement of gender mainstreaming, the principles of gender equality remain marginalised in many countries and gender mainstreaming has not been transformative in terms of breaking down existing structures of power and privilege related to gender and other intersecting factors including education, disability, racism, harmful masculinity and male privilege among others.

3 Barriers to Gender Mainstreaming

To further unpack these critiques, in this section we examine three barriers to the effective implementation of gender mainstreaming in policies and programmes: addressing conceptual challenges, the need for leadership and commitment, and overcoming practical constraints.

3.1 *Addressing Conceptual Challenges*

A broad definition of gender mainstreaming has made it a particularly contested concept.[14] Its practical application has in turn been affected by this conceptual gap. The conceptual confusion is two-fold. First, as previously stated, the purpose of gender mainstreaming was to make gender issues 'main', or more

12 Mieke Verloo, 'Another Velvet Revolution? Gender Mainstreaming and the Politics of Implementation' (2001) Institute for Human Sciences (IWM) Working Paper 5/2001; Sonia Mazey, 'Gender Mainstreaming in the EU: Delivering on an Agenda?' (2002) 10 (3–4) Feminist Legal Studies 227; Teresa Rees, 'Reflections on the Uneven Development of Gender Mainstreaming in Europe' (2005) 7 (4) International Feminist Journal of Politics 555.

13 Mary Daly, 'Gender Mainstreaming in Theory and Practice' (2005) 12 (3) Social Politics: International Studies in Gender, State & Society 433; Tania Lyons et al., 'Developing Gender Mainstreaming and Gender Respect' (2004) 64 Development Bulletin 37; Caroline Moser, 'Has Gender Mainstreaming Failed? A Comment on International Development Agency Experiences in the South' (2005) 7 (4) International Feminist Journal of Politics 576.

14 Sylvia Walby, 'Gender Mainstreaming: Productive Tensions in Theory and Practice' (2005) 12 (3) Social Politics: International Studies in Gender, State & Society 321.

precisely, normal and widely accepted in contrast to 'gender side-streaming'.[15] However, the notion of 'mainstreaming', that is how to integrate gender at the different levels of the policy-making process, is not always well understood or implemented. In many cases 'mainstreaming' is at best operationalised as the need to add 'women's interests' to existing policies and programmes, rather than an approach to addressing unequal gendered power relations.

In addition, mainstreaming, in practice, often involves the layering of the concept onto a presumed immutable system. The existing system is very rarely challenged to ensure it is adaptable and fit for purpose to achieve the desired transformation.

Secondly, there is confusion about what 'gender' means, and why it is necessary to understand the critical dimensions of the impact of gender. Gender is still not always understood as the social construction of roles and power dynamics but believed to be primarily related to biological differences. This confusion in turn limits the development of local, national, regional, and international policies and approaches to addressing gender discrimination and inequality. This is particularly relevant to gender mainstreaming policies in health, as both biological factors, including reproductive, genetic, and hormonal differences, and socially constructed differences between women and men play a part in exposure to different diseases and in health experience.[16] What is more, more recent understandings of gender go beyond the dominant discourse of a gender binary, that is the classification of gender into two distinct, opposite forms of male and female, which stays static over time. Gender also intersects with other social determinants to shape people's experiences.

As a result, gender mainstreaming can be 'fuzzy' and contradictory in practice with a lack of tailored strategies and measurable targets. This conceptual gap has also contributed to gender mainstreaming being reduced to a technical exercise with a reliance on toolkits and guidance. Moving beyond a tick-box exercise requires high-level commitment and resources to gender mainstreaming and gender equality more broadly.

3.2 *Need for Strong Leadership and Commitment*

The decision to introduce and properly fund gender mainstreaming in policies and programmes depends on the commitment and willingness of organisational leadership. Gender mainstreaming measures need to be robust while

15 Charlesworth (n 5).

16 Sarah Payne, *The Health of Men and Women* (Polity 2006); Theresa Wizemann and Mary Lou Pardue (eds), *Exploring the Biological Contributions to Health: Does Sex Matter?* (National Academic Press 2001).

demanding discussion, rigour, adaptability, action, and accountability to incite change in organisations and on the ground. This is where leadership is critical and why we argue that gender mainstreaming cannot be left up to a designated 'gender lead' – effectively side-lining the gender issues.[17]

Central to effective mainstreaming is real buy-in within an organisation so that addressing gender is integral to every role, rather than being a silo or an add-on. Champions at different levels of the organisation, including women in leadership is critical.[18] Clear roles and responsibilities that are endorsed by senior leadership are also needed for implementing, monitoring, and overseeing gender equality and mainstreaming objectives.

3.3 *Overcoming Practical Constraints*

Pragmatic barriers reflect the level of resources required for successful implementation of gender equality policies.[19] Related to the conceptual gap, an important practical constraint is that in many countries gender mainstreaming is not regarded as a priority, and that 'more urgent' problems should be solved before gender equality is tackled. Or the integration of gender equality principles into legislation and policies is a response to international pressure and/or because of a domestic push from civil society. This in turn can affect the priority and investment given to gender mainstreaming in policies and programmes.[20]

---

17 For example, in a commentary published in *The Lancet* in 2017, Roopa Dhatt, Ilona Kickbusch, Kelly Thompson, and other experts suggested concrete action in order to enhance female leadership in WHO, in particular '1 proposing reforms to the WHO secretariat that will institute specific measures to achieve gender parity in their top leadership; 2 ensuring equal representation of both women and men in our delegations to the World Health Assembly and WHO Executive Board meetings and regional governance meetings; and 4 maintaining gender parity in the organization of all panels and events that we convene during the WHA and other high level international and regional global health events', Roopa Dhatt et al., 'Act Now: a Call to Action for Gender Equality in Global Health' (2017) 389 (10069) Lancet 602.

18 'How Gender Mainstreaming Can Help "Build Back Better" from COVID-19' (Apolitical, 5 August 2020) <https://apolitical.co/solution-articles/en/gender-mainstreaming-build-back-better-from-covid-19> accessed 2 July 2021.

19 Sally Theobald et al., 'Engendering the Bureaucracy? Challenges and Opportunities for Mainstreaming Gender in Ministries of Health under Sector-Wide Approaches' (2005) 20 (3) Health Policy and Planning 141.

20 An example is the Gender Equality Duty, that was introduced in the United Kingdom in 2007. 'The UK policy agenda has not been completely devoid of a focus on gender. However, gender mainstreaming has not been well understood. [Indeed] it has been hard to discern the mainstreaming of gendered perspectives into general policy-making and gender has not yet been effectively mainstreamed into the work of local planning authorities in the UK. The Gender Equality Duty presents an opportunity for gender to be

Other practical constraints on gender mainstreaming include the lack of appropriate, regular, and accurate data disaggregated by sex and other relevant characteristics in programmes and health information systems. This limits the effectiveness of decision-making on policies, especially in relation to service access and coverage. Moreover, policies and programmes cannot be evaluated without specific gender information and indicators. Institutional capacities to analyse the health and development situation with a focus on gender and other determinants of inequality, such as socioeconomic status, disability, or experiences of racism is also weak in many contexts. This is partly because many activities aimed at addressing gender inequalities neglect to examine the multifaceted determinants that intersect with gender to cause inequalities.[21]

4 What Can We Learn from Mainstreaming Gender, Equity, and Rights within the World Health Organization

The links between gender inequality, health and development were reinforced in the Beijing Platform for Action and, in response, many organisations including within the UN started to develop initiatives to address gender in policies and programmes. In this section we reflect on WHO's experience of mainstreaming gender, drawing on published literature and the personal expertise of authors (FB) and illuminate the lessons learnt for policy and practice. We focus on the formative years that coincide with the leadership of Director-General Dr Margaret Chan (2007–2017).

Following the 1995 Beijing Declaration, WHO began to operationalise programmes on gender and human rights, initially focusing on reproductive health and, later, on sexual health and reproductive rights. In 2000, WHO also created the Department of Gender and Women's Health (later renamed

considered in policy making. This new legislation required public authorities involved in planning and regeneration to take gender into account. Fundamentally, the duty requires more than equal treatment for men and women (Equal Opportunities Commission, 2007). Public bodies must promote and take action to bring about gender equality. This involves looking at gender equality issues for men and women, understanding why inequalities exist and how to overcome them and creating effective service provision for all, so that everyone can access services that meet their needs;' Gemma Burgess, 'Planning and the Gender Equality Duty – Why Does Gender Matter?' (RICS 2009).

21 Aliu Monday, 'Practical and Theoretical Limitations of Inclusion of Gender Mainstreaming Strategy in Development Activities of Agencies' (2018) 9 Mediterranean Journal of Social Sciences 37.

Department of Gender, Women and Health).[22] WHO's Executive Board, at its 116th session in 2006, requested the Director-General to prepare a 'draft strategy and plan of action for bringing gender into the mainstream of WHO's work'.[23] Responding to this request, the Secretariat submitted a draft strategy through the Executive Board to the World Health Assembly for its consideration. Subsequently, the Sixtieth World Health Assembly in 2007 adopted resolution WHA 60.25: 'Strategy for integrating gender analysis and actions into the work of WHO', which focused on disaggregation of data, gender analysis, and strengthening accountability mechanisms.[24]

The 2007 World Health Assembly urged Member States to formulate national strategies for addressing gender issues in health policies, programmes, research, and planning processes. It also pressed Member States to ensure that a gender equality perspective be incorporated at all levels of health care delivery and services. In addition, the resolution requested the Director-General to ensure the full implementation of the strategy. The purpose of the strategy was to 'enhance, expand, and institutionalise WHO's capacity to analyse the role of gender and sex in health, and to monitor and address systemic and avoidable gender-based inequalities in health'.[25] The strategy was consistent with the UN system-wide policy on gender equality and the strategy on gender mainstreaming. It included four strategic directions:

i. building WHO's capacity for gender analysis and planning;
ii. bringing gender into the mainstream of WHO's management;
iii. promoting use of sex-disaggregated data and gender analysis; and
iv. establishing accountability.[26]

5 Moving the Strategy Forward

In 2008 a baseline assessment was conducted as part of the monitoring and evaluation of the WHO strategy for integrating gender analysis and actions

22 Veronica Magar et al., 'Gender Mainstreaming within WHO: Not without Equity and Human Rights' (2019) 393 (10182) Lancet 1678 <http://www.thelancet.com/article/S0140673619307639/fulltext> accessed 28 September 2021.

23 World Health Organization (WHO), 'Integrating Gender Analysis and Actions into the Work of the WHO: Draft Strategy', Sixtieth World Health Assembly (A60/19, 29 March 2007).

24 World Health Organization (WHO), 'Strategy for Integrating Gender Analysis and Actions into the Work of WHO' (WHO/FCH/GWH/08.1, World Health Organization, 2008).

25 WHO (n 24).

26 WHO (n 24).

into it work. The results of the baseline assessment presented the status of gender mainstreaming in WHO as well as the gaps and actions required for implementing the strategy. Findings were presented for 17 indicators that corresponded to the four strategic directions.[27]

The results showed that although WHO staff had high levels of knowledge of gender issues, application of gender analysis skills and institutional support for gender mainstreaming was weak. Staff identified collaboration with and technical support from gender focal points and units as a facilitating factor for building awareness and knowledge, and the lack of an enabling institutional environment for mainstreaming was identified as a barrier. Much more needed to be done to mainstream gender into the operational planning, programme implementation, and monitoring and evaluation cycle as well as to promote the use of sex-disaggregated data in programmes. There was a need for advocacy to increase institutional commitment to gender equality at the senior management level as well as with Member States to reflect gender in country cooperation strategies and plans.

At this time the small department of Gender, Women and Health was based within the cluster of Family, Women and Children's Health. As well as a focus on gender, the department had small teams made up of 2 or 3 people working on the intersecting areas of equity and human rights. Although junior, these teams created a small island of excellence, building strong networks beyond WHO, including with civil society. However, compared to other priorities within the organisation, these efforts attracted limited support and attention from the organisational leadership and within the organisation more generally.

Furthermore, because gender mainstreaming had been criticised for its exclusive focus on women and for overlooking the multiple and intersecting drivers of inequality, a new approach was designed to support all WHO staff members to integrate the core values of gender, equity, and human rights in their work. Central to this strategy was the creation of a new unit reporting to the WHO Director-General, through the office of the Assistant Director-General, Family, Women's and Children's Health. The unit was positioned to work across the organisation headquarters, headed by a senior staff, with competences on gender, human rights, and equity. In 2013, WHO's governing bodies requested an effective and integrated approach to mainstreaming, whereby

27 World Health Organization (WHO), *Gender Mainstreaming in WHO: Where are We Now? Report of the Baseline Assessment of the WHO Gender Strategy* (World Health Organization, 2011).

WHO's Gender, Equity and Human Rights (GER) team was established.[28] Its aim was to integrate gender, equity, and human rights into health programmes and policies across the different programme areas that make up WHO. As well as headquarters, all six WHO regional offices have dedicated GER staff as do some WHO country offices.

The GER team are expected to work with staff at all levels of WHO to catalyse, support, and coordinate the 'mainstreaming of gender, equity, and human rights approaches in health'. Thus, GER provides the infrastructure for mainstreaming across the organisation, which operates through a range of activities and publications aimed to:

1. Support the review of national health programmes to leave no one behind, which includes the development of the technical handbook 'Innov8'[29] for reviewing national health programmes and country case studies of its application.
2. Address barriers to equitable health systems for everyone, which includes the development of the handbook for conducting an adolescent health services barriers assessment (AHSBA)[30] and country assessments and reports.
3. Advance gender, equity, and human rights in programmes and policies including with the WHO Equity, Gender and Human Rights Country Support package for leaving no one behind.

---

28 WHO's Gender, Equity and Human Rights team (GER) 'The GER team leads the performance assessment of the organization's actions to mainstream gender, equity and human rights into programmes and workplans. The team manages the implementation and monitoring of WHO's achievements in the United Nations System-wide Action Plan for Gender Equality and the Empowerment of Women (UN SWAP). The team also leads the development of technical and normative guidance to mainstream and support WHO's commitment to "leave no one behind" towards achieving the Sustainable Development Goals (SDGs); particularly SDG 3: *Ensure healthy lives and promote well-being for all at all ages*, SDG 5: *Achieve gender equality and empower all women and girls*, SDG10: *Reduce inequality within and among countries*, and SDG16: *Promote just, peaceful and inclusive societies'* <https://www.who.int/teams/gender-equity-and-human-rights/about>.

Placed within the Director-General's Office to underscore its high priority for the Organization, the GER Team operates under the leadership of the Assistant Director-General for Strategic Priorities, Dr Princess Nothemba Simelela. The Team at headquarters works in close cooperation with the Global GER Network of Regional Focal Points'. For more information see <https://www.who.int/teams/gender-equity-and-human-rights/about> accessed 21 July 2021.

29 Magar et al. (n 22); <https://www.who.int/life-course/partners/innov8/innov8-informative-brochure-171106.pdf?ua=1> accessed 21 July 2021.

30 ibid.

6 Impact of WHO's Gender Mainstreaming Work on the Ground

WHO can be seen as a pioneer within the UN in its approach towards 'mainstreaming gender as a relational concept that intersects with other drivers of inequalities' to impact on people's health and wellbeing.[31] We provide below some examples of the GER approach in practice.

6.1 *Integrating a GER Analysis in Sexual and Reproductive Health Assessments*

WHO provides its staff at headquarters and country level with capacity building and a package of tools and resources aligned with the GER criteria aimed at increasing impact at the country level. It also provides technical support to Member States via its country offices. For example, WHO supported the Government of Nepal to apply Innov8 – a methodology for reorienting health programmes towards equity – for the identification of barriers to access to sexual and reproductive health services faced by adolescents.[32] The analysis revealed challenges facing Nepalese adolescent girls, including early marriage, higher school dropout rates, gender-based violence, heavy workload, restricted mobility in rural areas, and limited household autonomy, as outlined in the case study below (see Box 1 below).[33] [34] [35] [36]

Case Study Nepal

The *Innov8* approach was implemented in Nepal by a diverse team of experts, including representatives from national and subnational authorities, civil society, and research institutes. Its aim was to identify inequities

31 Flavia Bustreo et al., 'Strengthening the Transformative Potential of Gender Mainstreaming in Global Health' (2021) 34 EClinicalMedicine <https://pubmed.ncbi.nlm.nih.gov/33937728/> accessed 2 July 2021.

32 Magar et al. (n 22).

33 Pan American Health Organization (PAHO) and World Health Organization (WHO), 'Policy on Ethnicity and Health' (Pan American Health Organization, 2017).

34 ibid.

35 'National Adolescent Development and Health Strategy 2075' (Public Health Update, 6 August 2020) <https://publichealthupdate.com/national-adolescent-development-and-health-strategy-2075/> accessed 1 November 2021.

36 Please see WHO 'Finding the gaps in meeting adolescent health needs in Nepal' <https://www.who.int/news-room/feature-stories/detail/finding-the-gaps-in-meeting-adolescent-health-needs-in-nepal> accessed 21 July 2021.

in adolescents' access to sexual and reproductive health (SRH) services and improve the overall health of adolescents by addressing diverse gendered barriers. It was born out of a need to fill the gaps left by Nepal's original adolescent SRH programme, which did not take into account specific barriers to SRH access, such as distance and cost of travel, opening times, lack of privacy and confidentiality, and harmful gender norms.

Informed by the *Innov8* approach, adolescent-friendly and gender-responsive services were introduced and communities were engaged in the programme to reach remote and disadvantaged populations. Adolescents also participated in local decision-making processes concerning adolescent-friendly services. The use of an intersectionality approach also enabled the SRH programme to engage with other sectors, including education and social protection, to tackle issues such as early marriage, pregnancy, and harmful and stigmatising social norms. A new adolescent health strategy was created in 2020 to support the redesign and implementation of SRH programmes. Legislative measures such as outlawing early marriage and promoting greater access to SRH services were also introduced.

6.2 *Examining the Role of Power Relations in Access to Care*

Understanding the influence of gender norms and adopting an intersectionality approach is especially important for addressing gendered barriers to access to health services.[37] WHO works closely with national authorities to improve access to health care using the gender, equity, and human rights approach. This enables a better understanding of the impact of power relations and gender norms on people's health and wellbeing throughout the life course.

For example, a gender, equity, and rights lens were used to assess the barriers faced by adolescents in accessing health services in Nigeria and the United Republic of Tanzania. A range of individual and systemic barriers were identified. The assessment showed that adolescent boys encountered negative attitudes of health staff and were often denied access to clinics due to their reported substance use.[38] In addition, because boys believed that services were exclusively for girls, they often chose to avoid health facilities. These

37 Julie Pulerwitz et al., 'Proposing a Conceptual Framework to Address Social Norms That Influence Adolescent Sexual and Reproductive Health' (2019) 64 Journal of Adolescent Health S7 <https://www.sciencedirect.com/science/article/pii/S1054139X19300564?via%3Dihub> accessed 21 July 2021.

38 Magar et al. (n 22).

perceptions and masculine norms resulted in a delay in health care seeking among adolescent boys. Girls, mostly from poor rural settings, were less likely than boys to purchase medicines and pay fees for health services and laboratory tests. Additionally, adolescent girls face stigma in care-seeking for maternal health services.[39] These findings are being analysed and the results used to reduce gender-related barriers to improve services and quality of care for adolescents.

6.3 *Working alongside Other Social Justice Agendas*

In 2017, the Pan American Health Organization, which functions as the WHO regional office for the Americas, adopted a Policy on Ethnicity and Health to address health inequalities among Indigenous peoples. This included addressing the high rates of maternal mortality in Indigenous women partly owed to 'culturally inappropriate health services, and stigma and discrimination based on both gender and ethnicity'.[40] The policy recognised the need to address the interconnection 'between ethnicity, gender, equity, and human rights if the health service barriers rooted in discrimination, racism, and exclusion' were to be addressed.[41] This approach, which examined health through the lens of power relations and gender norms, enabled the development of a concrete action agenda to both improve health equity outcomes and advance gender equality and women's empowerment.[42]

The Strategy and Plan of Action on Ethnicity and Health 2019–2025 promotes intercultural approaches to health and direct action to tackle the social determinants of health. With the participation of the groups involved, and incorporating a gender perspective, the plan of action seeks to produce evidence for decision-making on public health policies, promote policy action for universal access to health, strengthen social participation and strategic partnerships, recognise ancestral knowledge and traditional and complementary medicine, and build capacity to facilitate and foster intercultural action at all levels.[43]

---

39 ibid.

40 ibid; Pan American Health Organization (PAHO), 'Policy on Ethnicity and Health' (28 September 2017) <https://iris.paho.org/handle/10665.2/34447> accessed 21 July 2021.

41 Flavia Bustreo, Anna Giulia Ponchia, Cecilia Rocco, Rachael Hinton, 'Strengthening the Transformative Potential of Gender Mainstreaming in Global Health' (14 April 2021) 34 (100858) EClinicalMedicine.

42 Mary Manandhar et al., 'Gender, Health and the 2030 Agenda for Sustainable Development' (2018) 96 Bulletin of the World Health Organization 644 <http://www.who.int/bulletin/volumes/96/9/18-211607/en/> accessed 29 May 2021.

43 Pan American Health Organization (PAHO), 'Strategy and Plan of Action on Ethnicity and Health 2019–2025' (2019) <www.paho.org> accessed 2 July 2021.

WHO's approach to gender mainstreaming in countries has helped inform the design of actionable and measurable criteria for mainstreaming gender, equity, and human rights (the GER criteria) across the organisation, including in monitoring output achievement. The GER criteria set minimum standards for mainstreaming and offer aspirational goals such as changing global treaty monitoring processes to ensure that health measures are consistent with sustainable development goals.[44]

7 Reflections on WHO's Experience

There are important lessons to be learned from WHO's formative experience with mainstreaming GER across the organisation and its programmes. These lessons, which are focused around the three barriers to implementing gender mainstreaming – conceptual considerations, leadership, and practical constraints – have broader implications for how WHO and other such organisations can meaningfully address gender and intersecting inequalities in policies and programmes.

7.1 *Conceptual Considerations*

A more practical approach is seen as a way to move beyond the conceptual confusion surrounding gender mainstreaming. However, for GER such a 'practical approach' became equated with a sense of pressure to show success using a narrow technocratic, tick-box exercise. For example, a GER unit is established and a budget line is allocated, or new procedures, checklists, and guidelines for GER are produced. The challenge arises when a mainstreaming strategy is rolled out as a one-size-fits-all response across an institution that has departments that are very set in their ways of working. To take on gender, a cultural change is needed that goes deeper than purely undertaking a gender analysis and 'fixing' the identified gaps. 'Mainstreaming GER' should be part of a formula for both the structure and ethos of the institution, otherwise it will always be an add-on.

GER mainstreaming did not operate in a social and political vacuum. We found it was determined by the institutional context and the interplay of internal and external influences. GER mainstreaming focal points did face resistance to gender equality as well as attempts to disregard their work. However, the positive impact of GER mainstreaming also lies in the increasing number

44 World Health Organization (WHO), *Integrating Equity, Gender, Human Rights and Social Determinants into the Work of WHO Roadmap for Action* (World Health Organization 2015).

of potential and actual allies within WHO that had greater sensitivity and awareness of the issues and sought support for implementing GER in their own programme activities.

7.2 *The Role of Leadership*

Within WHO, gender mainstreaming is an organisation-related strategy of change that takes a top-down approach. High-level support and championing has been critical for driving the agenda to mainstream gender, equity, and rights. However, GER mainstreaming was also seen as a political imperative by Member States, reflected in the decisions of the Executive Board. This external push also included pressure from civil society groups, and the Director-General's (Dr Chan) engagement in leadership networks such as International Gender Champions,[45] that asked WHO to make specific commitments to gender mainstreaming. This in turn gave further impetus to making gender mainstreaming an organisational priority.

As a top-down approach, the responsibility for the process of GER mainstreaming is in the hands of WHO leadership as well as the entire staff. The issue of responsibility and accountability is important in gender mainstreaming because, as some suggest, when the responsibility for gender equality is given to all, it can become everybody's and nobody's responsibility.[46] However, gender mainstreaming cannot be 'the sole responsibility of a gender focal point' or GER unit as the impact would be limited and the potential for failure high.[47] It was GER's role to support staff to build the competencies needed to integrate GER-related issues in their work. There were, however, several practical constraints (see below).

7.3 *Practical Constraints*

Financing for gender mainstreaming is often a major constraint, as mainstreaming is not a cost- or 'resource-free process'.[48] For a large organisation

45 The International Gender Champions (IGC) is a leadership network that brings together female and male decision-makers determined to break down gender barriers and make gender equality a working reality in their spheres of influence. The initiative was co-founded by former UN Geneva Director-General Michael Møller, former US Ambassador to the UN in Geneva Pamela Hamamoto and Women@TheTable CEO/Founder Caitlin Kraft-Buchman in 2015. The network numbers more than 250 active Champions and 160 Alumni who are the heads of international organizations, permanent missions, and civil society organizations <https://genderchampions.com/about> accessed 24 June 2021.

46 Monday (n 21).

47 Bustreo et al. (n 31).

48 African Development Bank Group, 'Mainstreaming Gender Equality: A Road to Results or a Road to Nowhere?' An Evaluation Synthesis, Working Paper (May 2011).

such as WHO with established programmes and funding, it was not easy to fund a programme of work that cuts across different areas and structures of the organisation, especially when there can be some internal resistance to doing so. Such resistance can arise when sensitivity and awareness about mainstreaming issues at the senior management level are not well established.

In addition, donor organisations were more willing to support specific health programmes and initiatives than to devote sufficient resources to support mainstreaming gender equality across WHO's programmes. To encourage teams across the organisation to mainstream gender in their work, such as to develop gender-disaggregated programme data, financial incentives were also considered. Although small amounts of funding were provided to programmes through the GER budget, overall, funding for GER-related activities was a constraint.

This is illustrated by the 2014/2015 WHO programme budget where gender, equity, and human rights mainstreaming had the second-lowest approved funding across the entire organisation at US$13.9 million. Although this increased by 2.4% in the proposed 2016/2017 budget to US$16.3 million, gender, equity, and human rights mainstreaming remained the second-lowest budget item after ageing and health (US$ 9.5 million and US$ 13.5 million).[49] However, the proposed percentage budget increase of 4% for ageing and health was nearly double the increase of the GER budget.

Tools and analyses can be used to raise awareness, generate evidence and may even result in change in policy and practice, but there is not always sufficient knowledge, interest, or willingness to understand and examine the gender-differentiated impacts on health. For instance, without gender- and other disaggregated data one cannot establish that inequalities exist, which is why the adoption of a GER perspective, and the production of disaggregated statistics is needed in all WHO policy-making and programme processes. Yet the capacity and willingness to gather and use sex-disaggregated data (and other disaggregated data) was not always at hand. For some programmes the analysis of gender-disaggregated data, let alone markers of other disadvantages, such as disability status, or education, did not exist. People, funds and time are needed to support this work, but such activities go beyond the funding remit of GER mainstreaming and must be integrated within specific programme budgets.

49 World Health Organization (WHO), Sixty-Eighth World Health Assembly, 'Proposed Programme Budget 2016–2017' (World Health Organization 2015) <https://apps.who.int/gb/ebwha/pdf_files/WHA68/A68_7-en.pdf> accessed 2 July 2021.

8 Conclusions

Gender mainstreaming is often still seen as an end in itself and it is approached from a technical perspective. In practice, this means that the transformational aspects of gender mainstreaming can be side-lined, especially in large institutions like WHO, which are composed of many different departments with long-established working processes, history, and expertise.

The experience of mainstreaming within WHO clearly illustrates the main challenges – conceptual confusion, role of leadership, and practical constraints. We found that GER mainstreaming did not operate in a social and political vacuum. As such, addressing the conceptual challenges, which includes addressing the cultural change required, is paramount if GER mainstreaming is to become a way of working and more than an add-on. A commitment to gender mainstreaming is also one of the most effective ways that leadership, whether that be senior management within an organisation or public policy-makers, can support and promote gender equality. Any policy mandate for GER mainstreaming must be supported by leadership, financial investment, and technical expertise.

We found that political support by Member States was critical to GER mainstreaming and will remain an important factor in its success or failure. Further, only senior managers can direct a cross-cutting issue like GER mainstreaming, which intersects with management structures and different areas of an organisation. Organisational leadership plays a vital role in promoting and implementing gender equality commitments as it provides the enabling institutional environment and support for cooperation, consensus, and programming.

The principle for addressing gender inequality must be a shared responsibility for all staff within an organisation and it must not be just the job of the GER team or 'designated' gender lead. Senior managers must be clear about the priority given to gender equality and gender mainstreaming and support demands on staff for information, analysis, and measurement, such as in terms of gathering and using sex-disaggregated data. As described elsewhere, when such demands are not made or when staff are not held accountable for their efforts on issues of equality, there is little motivation for action.

Gender mainstreaming is not a panacea or the only modality for achieving gender equality. Instead, it should go hand in hand with other approaches to build women's empowerment, redefine masculinity, and address the interconnected drivers of inequalities. Gender mainstreaming can still be a useful strategy if adequate funding and high-level commitment are assured.

But the concept requires further thought to reflect current understandings of gender such as that 'women' includes lesbian, bisexual, asexual, transgender, and queer women; that 'gender' also includes the differing experiences of men and non-binary persons.[50] It requires far-reaching and transformative thinking and approaches to address the inequalities related to individuals' identities in addition to gender – e.g., ethnicity, age, sexual orientation, and socioeconomic status.

As seen with GER, this intersectionality enables us to understand how people are vulnerable to multiple marginalities. We may need different agendas to promote the specific needs of women, men, and people with non-conforming gender identities, but our common agenda is to promote policies, approaches, and investments to address gender inequalities and unequal power dynamics.[51]

Finally, to strengthen the transformative potential of gender mainstreaming, a feminist economic approach would help global health institutions such as WHO address the social, political, and commercial determinants of health care delivery, resourcing, and decision-making.[52] Such an approach would ensure gender equality becomes and remains a priority for all health and development decision-makers.

References

Allotey P and Remme M, 'Gender Equality Should Not Be about Competing Vulnerabilities' *The BMJ Opinion*, 17 April 2020.

Burgess G, 'Planning and the Gender Equality Duty – Why Does Gender Matter?' Findings in Built and Rural Environments (RICS 2009).

Bustreo F et al., 'Strengthening the Transformative Potential of Gender Mainstreaming in Global Health' (2021) 34 EclinicalMedicine 100858.

Charlesworth H, 'Not Waving but Drowning: Gender Mainstreaming and Human Rights in the United Nations' (2005) 18 Harvard Human Rights Journal 1.

Daly M, 'Gender Mainstreaming in Theory and Practice' (2005) 12 (3) Social Politics: International Studies in Gender, State & Society 433.

Dhatt R et al., 'Act Now: a Call to Action for Gender Equality in Global Health' (2017) 389 (10069) Lancet 602.

50 Katelyn Jones and Olivia Shinners, 'Opinion – It's Time to Redefine Gender Mainstreaming' (*E-International Relations*, 14 September 2020) <https://www.e-ir.info/2020/09/14/opinion-its-time-to-redefine-gender-mainstreaming/> accessed 2 July 2021.

51 Pascale Allotey and Michelle Remme, 'Gender Equality Should Not Be about Competing Vulnerabilities' *The BMJ Opinion*, 17 April 2020 <https://blogs.bmj.com/bmj/2020/04/17/gender-equality-should-not-be-about-competing-vulnerabilities/> accessed 2 July 2021.

52 Bustreo et al. (n 31).

Hawkesworth M, 'Policy Studies Within a Feminist Frame' (1994) 27 Policy Sciences 97.

Jones K et al., 'Opinion – It's Time to Redefine Gender Mainstreaming' (*E-International Relations*, 14 September 2020).

Lombardo E, 'Integrating or Setting the Agenda? Gender Mainstreaming in the European Constitution-Making Process' (2005) 12 (3) Social Politics: International Studies in Gender, State & Society 412.

Lombardo E et al., 'Gender Mainstreaming in the EU? Incorporating a Feminist Reading?' (2005) 13 (2) European Journal of Women's Studies 151.

Lyons T et al., 'Developing Gender Mainstreaming and "Gender Respect"' (2004) 64 Development Bulletin 37.

Magar V et al., 'Gender Mainstreaming within WHO: Not without Equity and Human Rights' (2019) 393 (10182) Lancet 1678.

Manandhar M et al., 'Gender, Health and the 2030 Agenda for Sustainable Development' (2018) 96 Bulletin of the World Health Organization 644.

Mazey S, 'Gender Mainstreaming in the EU: Delivering on an Agenda?' (2002) 10 (3–4) Feminist Legal Studies 227.

Monday A, 'Practical and Theoretical Limitations of Inclusion of Gender Mainstreaming Strategy in Development Activities of Agencies' (2018) 9 Mediterranean Journal of Social Sciences 37.

Moser C, 'Has Gender Mainstreaming Failed? A Comment on International Development Agency Experiences in the South' (2005) 7 (4) International Feminist Journal of Politics 576.

Payne S, *The Health of Men and Women* (Polity 2006).

Pulerwitz J et al., 'Proposing a Conceptual Framework to Address Social Norms That Influence Adolescent Sexual and Reproductive Health' (2019) 64 Journal of Adolescent Health S7.

Theobald S et al., 'Engendering the Bureaucracy? Challenges and Opportunities for Mainstreaming Gender in Ministries of Health under Sector-Wide Approaches' (2005) 20 (3) Health Policy and Planning 141.

Rees T, 'Reflections on the Uneven Development of Gender Mainstreaming in Europe' (2005) 7 (4) International Feminist Journal of Politics 555.

Sarikakis K, 'Power, Patriarchy, Profit: Barriers to Gender Mainstreaming in Media Policy' in International Association for Media and Communication Research (eds), *Media and Gender: a Scholarly Agenda for the Global Alliance on Media and Gender* (UNESCO 2014).

Verloo M, 'Another Velvet Revolution? Gender Mainstreaming and the Politics of Implementation' (2001) IWM Working Paper No. 5/2001.

Verloo M, 'Displacement and Empowerment: Reflections on the Concept and Practice of the Council of Europe Approach to Gender Mainstreaming and Gender Equality' (2005) 12 (3) Social Politics: International Studies in Gender, State & Society 344.

Walby S, 'Gender Mainstreaming: Productive Tensions in Theory and Practice' (2005) 12 (3) Social Politics: International Studies in Gender, State & Society 321.

Wizemann T et al. (eds), *Exploring the Biological Contributions to Health: Does Sex Matter?* (National Academic Press 2001).

PART 2

Women and Socio-economic Equality

CHAPTER 4

(En)gendering EU Citizenship

Sandra Mantu

1 Introduction

This chapter discusses EU citizenship and the right to free movement of persons from the perspective of mobile EU women in order to understand how EU law shapes their capacity to make use of EU citizenship. The question that underpins the chapter is whether EU citizenship is a gendered status and if so, what are the consequences for those who do not fit the normative ideals embodied by it. Two interrelated issues concerning the free movement rights of EU citizens are discussed: (a) the intersection of gender with EU worker status, and (b) EU women's access to the welfare state. The focus is on women who hold the nationality of an EU Member State. My interest in this specific group stems from the common assumption that EU citizens are privileged over non-EU migrants when it comes to their legal position and experience of mobility since they benefit from a different and more comprehensive set of rights than third-country nationals (TCNs). However, the case law of the European Court of Justice shows that different categories of EU citizens enjoy different positions within the EU free movement framework and that EU citizens' mobility depends largely on their capacity for self-sufficiency, which is attained through work or independent financial capability to support themselves. Since EU case law is silent on gender issues and implications thereof, my aim is to analyse some of this case law through a gender lens in order to understand better the hierarchies that ensue in relation to EU citizenship and, ultimately, how encompassing EU citizenship status is.

2 Law, (EU) Citizenship and Gender

EU citizenship is a legal status that is additional to state nationality without replacing it (Article 20 Treaty on the Functioning of the European Union; TFEU). It entitles its holders – the nationals of the Member States – to a set of rights (Articles 21–25 TFEU): the right to move and reside freely within the territory of the Member States, electoral rights, the right to diplomatic protection while outside the EU, the right to petition the European Parliament

DOI:10.1163/9789004467682_006

and the Ombudsman, the right to petition EU institutions, and the right to access EU documents. In addition, Article 18 TFEU establishes a right to non-discrimination on the basis of nationality. Due to the history of the EU and its pedigree as an economic project built around labour migration, from the panoply of EU citizenship rights listed above, the right to free movement remains the most valued and most prominent.[1] The introduction of EU citizenship by the Maastricht Treaty is seen as part of a process of expansion of the right to free movement to economically inactive persons. The process started in the early 1990s and was subsequently consolidated by the European Court of Justice in its interpretation of EU citizenship read from the perspective of the general principle prohibiting discrimination on the basis of nationality.

At the national level, citizenship has been characterised as involving a complex relationship between an inside and an outside, those who are part of us and those who are not, which is difficult to challenge while remaining within the discourse of citizenship itself.[2] While claiming equality as one of its organising principles, national citizenship has had a fraught relationship with gender: conventionally, the citizen as legal subject has been white, male and the owner of property.[3] The enduring consequences of the failure to treat women equally to men become evident when looking at statistics on women's incorporation into the labour market, the gender pay-gap or access to top positions across the globe.[4] In the EU context, the choice of the language of citizenship has been criticised, mainly in light of the conditional nature of the right to free movement that privileges economically active and self-sufficient individuals, and EU citizenship's limited personal scope that excludes TCNs irrespective of how long they have resided in an EU state. These are illustrations of the boundary making and closure practices associated with the category of citizenship, more generally. However, as this chapter seeks to argue, because EU

1 For example, see, EU Commission, 'EU Citizenship Report 2020: Empowering Citizens and Protecting Their Rights' (European Union 2020).

2 Sandra Mantu, 'The Boundaries of EU Citizenship: Reflections on Borders, Citizenship and Sovereignty' in Paul Minderhoud, Sandra Mantu and Karin Zwaan (eds), *Caught In Between Borders: Citizens, Migrants and Humans. Liber Amicorum in Honour of Prof. Dr. Elspeth Guild* (Wolf Legal Publishers 2019); Sandro Mezzadra, 'The Gaze of Autonomy – Capitalism, Migration and Social Struggles' in Vicky Squire (ed), *The Contested Politics of Mobility. Borderzones and Irregularity* (Routledge 2011).

3 Heidi Gottfried, 'Why Workers' Rights are not Women's Rights' (2015) 4 Laws 139.

4 Jill Rubery and Aristea Koukiadaki, 'Closing the Gender Pay Gap: A Review of the Issues, Policy Mechanisms and International Evidence' (International Labour Office 2016); International Labour Organization, 'Global Wage Report 2018/19: What Lies behind Gender Pay Gaps' (International Labour Office 2018).

citizenship is moulded in the image of national citizenship, we should add to such criticisms, questions about the extent to which EU citizenship reifies at the supranational level the closure and boundary making exercises implied by national citizenship in relation to gender.

Notwithstanding the presence of well-developed gender equality law and jurisprudence, gender is seemingly absent from EU citizenship and free movement provisions, and from their interpretation by the Court of Justice.[5] The presence of a general principle of equality in EU law has encouraged scholars to claim that gender mainstreaming, that is the integration of the gender perspective in all its policies, is constitutionally embedded in EU law.[6] EU efforts towards gender equality focus on legislation that facilitates women's equal access to employment, regulates working time to make it compatible with caring and family responsibilities, and develops and promotes social inclusion measures. From this perspective, any efforts that benefit women generally will benefit mobile women as well, without the need to address gender as an EU citizenship issue. However, the success of these regulatory efforts is debatable. Critics highlight that despite the promotion of an adult (read gender-neutral) worker model, EU policy and law continue to reinforce gendered stereotypes and fall short of achieving equal gender policies.[7] The 'Gender Equality Strategy 2020–2025' published by the European Commission in 2020[8] continues to propose a dual approach to the implementation of the EU's gender strategy. The approach is built on 'targeted measures to achieve gender equality, combined with strengthened gender mainstreaming', to which intersectionality is added as a cross-cutting principle of implementation.

For the time being, and gender mainstreaming notwithstanding, the absence of gender considerations in the formulation of EU citizenship law itself is

5 Heli Askola, 'Tale of Two Citizenships? Citizenship, Migration and Care in the European Union' (2012) 21 (3) Social & Legal Studies 341.

6 Jo Shaw, 'The European Union and Gender Mainstreaming: Constitutionally Embedded or Comprehensively Marginalised' (2002) 10 (3) Feminist Legal Studies 213; Joyce Mushaben and Gabriel Abels 'The Gender Politics of the EU' in Ulrike Liebert and Janna Wolff (eds), *Interdisziplinäire Europastudien* (Springer 2015).

7 Gottfried (n 3); Encarnation Gutiérrez-Rodríguez, 'The Precarity of Feminisation: On Domestic Work, Heteronormativity and the Coloniality of Labour' (2014) 27 International Journal of Politics, Culture and Society 191; Michelle Weldon-Johns, 'EU Work-Family Policies – Challenging Parental Roles or Reinforcing Gendered Stereotypes' (2013) 19 (2) European Law Journal 1.

8 EU Commission, 'Communication from the Commission to the European Parliament, the Council, the European Economic and Social Committee and the Committee of the Regions. A Union of Equality: Gender Equality Strategy 2020–2025' (European Commission 2020).

problematic. Acker's criticism of free movement as gendered illustrates this point well.[9] In light of the EU's historical development, the provisions on free movement of persons were initially understood to cover only workers and economically active persons. Women were assumed to migrate mainly as family dependants seeking to join a male breadwinner in the host state, who would be paid a living wage that covered his and his family's expenses. This gendered vision of labour mobility has transitioned naturally into the provisions on EU citizenship whose starting point take the EU citizen as a neutral subject of law who encounters a level playing field when exercising free movement rights. It is difficult to identify legal provisions that are specifically designed to address the right to move and reside from a mobile woman's perspective or that take a gender-sensitive approach to intra-EU mobility. The relevant primary and secondary legislation relies on a gender-neutral notion of 'national of a Member State' or 'EU citizen' to describe the beneficiaries of the right to free movement. The preamble to Directive 2004/38, which is the main piece of legislation detailing the conditions under which the right to free movement is to be exercised, provides that the Directive should be implemented without any discrimination between beneficiaries on grounds of 'sex, race, colour, ethnic or social origin, genetic characteristics, language, religion or beliefs, political or other opinion, membership of an ethnic minority, property, birth, disability or sexual orientation'.[10] Except for this provision, it is unclear if and how gender considerations were integrated in the legal categories and rights detailed by the Directive. For example, the Directive contains provisions to ensure that family members do not lose rights in the event of death, departure from the host state, divorce, annulment or termination of registered partnership of the EU citizen exercising the right of residence (Articles 11/2, 12 and 13). Yet these provisions do not consider fully the potentially circumscribed status of women affected by family breakdown or bereavement.[11]

9 Louise Ackers, *Shifting Spaces. Women, Migration and Citizenship in the European Union* (Policy Press 1998).

10 Directive 2004/38/EC of the European Parliament and of the Council of 29 April 2004 on the right of citizens of the Union and their family members to move and reside freely within the territory of the Member States amending Regulation (EEC) No 1612/68 and repealing Directives 64/221/EEC, 68/360/EEC, 72/194/EEC, 73/148/EEC, 75/34 [2004] OJ L 158, Recital 31.

11 Louise Ackers, 'Citizenship, Gender and Dependence in The European Union: Women and International Migration' (1996) 3 Social Politics: International Studies in Gender, State & Society 316.

3 Mobile Women and EU Worker Status

Economically active EU citizens enjoy a privileged position when it comes to free movement rights. Prior to the acquisition of the right to permanent residence, the mobility of economically inactive EU citizens is conditioned by them having sufficient resources not to become a burden on the social assistance system of the host state and comprehensive medical insurance. Exercising free movement rights as an EU worker offers a more secure residence status, which is coupled with equal treatment and access to the host state's welfare system. In the case of EU workers, claiming benefits from the host state to supplement income will have no impact on residence status. The opposite is true for economically inactive EU citizens. When claiming benefits, the latter risk being classed as not meeting the requirement of self-sufficiency or as posing an unreasonable burden on the host state's welfare system. In both cases, the right to reside can be terminated. Thus, generally speaking and for women, in particular, the legal category under which EU citizens exercise mobility is highly relevant for their legal treatment in the host state.

The way the notion of EU worker has been defined by the Court of Justice plays an important role in shaping women's exercise of free movement rights. The Court has declared that the notion of EU worker has an autonomous, 'Union' meaning. The definition must be based on objective criteria and 'the essential feature of an employment relationship is that for a certain period of time a person performs services for and under the direction of another person in return for which he receives remuneration'.[12] This definition was further refined to clarify that work implies an economic activity and that the services performed must be capable of being regarded as forming part of the normal labour market, in the sense that there is demand for and a supply of such services.[13] Remuneration takes the form of money. In the rare cases where it does not,[14] the Court emphasised that payment in kind must nonetheless have a link with the market, which would exclude exchanges taking places wholly within the private sphere from the scope of the notion of EU worker. Emphasising the link between activities that can be considered 'work' and the market has exclusionary consequences for women who engage in activities that are not considered as part of the 'normal labour market' because they are not assigned an

---

12 Case 66/85 *Lawrie v Blum* [1986] ECR 02121.

13 Case C-196/87 *Steymann v Staatssecretaris van Justitie* [1988] ECR 6159; Case C-287/05 *Hendrix Raad van Bestuur van het Uitvoeringsinstituut Werknemersverzekeringen* [2009] ECR 6907.

14 ibid.

economic or monetary value. Thus, activities that belong to the private sphere, such as care work or rearing children are excluded, and this lends support to the view that EU citizenship is built upon the model of a male breadwinner who has less trouble meeting the requirements of the definition of worker.

Whereas the public–private divide is ill-reflected by EU provisions on free movement, some aspects specific to women in the labour market are better integrated into the definition of EU worker status: part-time work and, subsequently, lower remuneration. In this sense, part-time, atypical work and lower remuneration levels are specific to female employment[15] and can have potentially negative consequences for classification as an EU worker. In its jurisprudence, the Court has affirmed that part-time work and even atypical work do lead to the acquisition of the status of EU worker if the work is real and genuine to the exclusion of activities that are purely ancillary.[16]

Levin is a case in point because it illustrates well the intersection between gender and the definition of work that the Court has developed along with the implications of successful integration via work in the internal market.[17] Ms Levin was a British national married to a TCN spouse with whom she resided in the Netherlands. In 1979 she applied for a residence permit in the Netherlands based on free movement rules for workers. The Dutch authorities argued that Ms Levin was not working at the time of her application and, although she had found employment after the application, she was working part-time and for remuneration that fell below the minimum wage. Moreover, it was argued that Ms Levin started work only in order to acquire a residence permit for her TCN spouse. The Dutch authorities questioned her actual desire to work and argued that a person who subjectively does not wish to work should not benefit from the free movement rules. The Court found that the reasons for which a person decides to take up employment in a different Member State are irrelevant for qualifying that person as a worker as long as the activities performed are genuine and sufficient to meet the remaining conditions for being defined as a worker.[18] The Court reiterated that free movement is meant, among other objectives, to promote a 'harmonious development of economic activities and a raising of the standard of living' and that 'part-time employment although it may provide an income lower than what is considered to be the minimum

15 Eurostat 'Women's Employment in the EU' (*Eurostat* 6 March 2020).

16 Case C-357/89 *Raulin v Minister van Onderwijs en Wetenschappen* [1992] ECR 1027; Case 139/85 *Kempf v Staatssecretaris van Justitie* [1986] ECR 1741; Case C-413/01 *Ninni-Orasche v Bundesminister für Wissenschaft* [2003] ECR 13187.

17 Case 53/81 *Levin v Staatssecretaris van Justitie* [1982] ECR 1085.

18 ibid para 16.

required for subsistence, constitutes for a large number of persons an effective means of improving their living conditions'.[19]

It is noteworthy that the Court's reasoning for opening up the notion of 'worker' to include those in part-time employment relies partly on the social implications of the rules of free movement. This can be read as an attempt to reconcile market forces with the social realities of work in a neoliberal economy that relies increasingly on flexible and insecure work arrangements. Nevertheless, the move is partial and mitigated by the fact that the Court underlines that the free movement of persons covers only those 'who pursue or are desirous of pursuing an economic activity'. Economic activities are defined as 'effective and genuine activities, to the exclusion of activities on such a small scale as to be regarded as purely marginal and ancillary'.[20] Where exactly the line is drawn beyond which activities become ancillary remains an open question that is approached on a case-by-case basis.

The emphasis on individual assessment can lead to positive results for women, but does not always do so. Gender considerations are not integrated into the Court's reasoning, nor do they seem to play a role. I will exemplify this with cases on Germany's policy that excluded persons in minor employment from the EU notion of 'worker' and from the legal treatment that comes with it. In *Genc*, the applicant worked 5.5 hours per week as a cleaner.[21] The Court stressed that the notion of 'worker' has an EU meaning. It argued that the number of hours worked and the level of remuneration are not the only relevant elements. The following facts were seen as indicating that the professional activity was real and genuine: the applicant was entitled to paid leave and to sickness payment, her contract was covered by the relevant collective agreement, and her contractual relationship with the same undertaking lasted for almost four years. For Mrs Genc, being treated as a worker was relevant for her residence rights. She had entered Germany as the spouse of a Turkish national and was initially given a residence permit as a spouse. Once the relationship ended, her residence rights were questioned. Being classed as a 'worker' within the EU meaning of the term entitled her to rights based on the EC–Turkey Agreement and Decision 1/80 implementing it.

The *Hartmann* and *Geven* cases were decided on the same day and concern the entitlement of EU workers who resided outside Germany to child-raising

19 ibid para 15.
20 ibid para 17.
21 Case C-561/14 *Genc v Integrationsministeriet* [2016] ECR 247.

allowances in Germany.[22] The relevant law excluded workers in minor employment who were resident abroad from receiving the child-raising allowance. Their link with German society was considered by the legislator not to be strong enough to justify equal treatment and access to social benefits. Ms Hartmann applied successfully for the benefit as the stay-at-home family member of a full-time EU worker and as such was an indirect beneficiary of equal treatment. Ms Geven applied unsuccessfully for the same benefit as an EU worker in minor employment. The Court argued that while she did meet the definition of an EU worker, her minor employment coupled with residence abroad entitled Germany to treat her differently. What is striking about these three cases is the absence of any questioning of the gender implications of the policy under discussion. Nor is there any acknowledgement that minor employment is typical of women's employment and may require extra attention in a free movement context. The conditions for being a EU worker and discrimination on the basis of nationality steer the Court's analysis, leaving no room for other elements.

4 Retaining EU Worker Status: Interruptions in Employment History

As discussed above, becoming anchored in the labour market as an EU worker entitles mobile women and men to a secure legal status and usually equal treatment with nationals from the welfare state of the host country.[23] However, for women, being able to retain worker status in case of interruptions to their professional activity has proven contentious, especially when they interrupt their work due to pregnancy or caring obligations. Directive 2004/38 does not take into consideration the scenario where a migrant EU woman gives up work to care for her child in the host state. The Directive only deals with the situation where the migrant woman goes back to her state of origin for a maximum of one year due to childbirth or pregnancy: this option does not compromise the acquisition of the right to permanent residence in the host state.[24] It is

22 Case C-213/05 *Geven v Land Nordrhein-Westfalen* [2007] ECR 6347; Case C-212/05 *Hartmann v Freistaat Bayern* [2007] ECR 6303.

23 Sandra Mantu and Paul Minderhoud, 'Exploring the Links between Residence and Social Rights for Economically Inactive EU citizens' (2019) 21 (3) European Journal of Migration and Law 313.

24 Article 16 of Directive 2004/38 sets out the general conditions for the acquisition of the right to permanent residence, namely legal residence for a continuous period of 5 years in the host EU state. Exceptions from the general rule are listed in paragraph 3 which reads as follows: 'Continuity of residence shall not be affected by temporary absences not

unclear why the legislator considered that a woman who has worked for, say, three years in a host state and who decides to return to her state of origin for one year should not lose her acquired rights, while a woman who decides to remain in the host state but gives up work to care for her child will lose her EU right to reside and compromise the acquisition of permanent residence if she is not self-sufficient during that one year.

The above issue is illustrated in *Dias*, where the applicant had resided in the United Kingdom (UK) for more than five years, but had been in and out of work.[25] Had Ms Dias resided legally and continuously for five years in the UK, she would have been a permanent resident entitled to equal treatment. The UK authorities rejected her application for income support since they did not consider her to enjoy EU rights because of her periods of unemployment. The Court of Justice struggled with a period of one year during which she took time off work to care for her child. The Court found that she was voluntarily unemployed during that year and did not retain worker status. Since she was unemployed and not complying with the self-sufficiency requirements attached to the exercise of free movement rights, as an economically inactive mobile EU citizen, the Court found that that period of residence did not meet the conditions of regular (legal) residence under the Directive. In the end, Ms Dias received the benefit she had applied for because the Court considered that she had acquired permanent residence prior to leaving the labour market to care for her child. On one hand, the *Dias* case illustrates the importance attached to paid employment as the most secure way to enjoy the full advantages of EU citizenship. On the other hand, it suggests that, in such a system, women will generally be disadvantaged as they are 'less likely to take up paid work or stay in paid work once they have children, even if they migrated as workers'.[26]

The redeeming power of work comes back time and time again in the Court's jurisprudence on mobile EU women claiming social benefits. Directive 2004/38 provides for several situations in which worker status will be retained although there is no employment relationship as such.[27] These include illness,

---

exceeding a total of six months a year, or by absences of a longer duration for compulsory military service, or by one absence of a maximum of twelve consecutive months for important reasons such as pregnancy and childbirth, serious illness, study or vocational training, or a posting in another Member State or a third country'.

25 Case C-325/09 *Dias v Secretary of State for Work and Pensions* [2011] ECR 6387.

26 Heli Askola, 'Tale of Two Citizenships? Citizenship, Migration and Care in the European Union' (2012) 21 (3) Social & Legal Studies 341.

27 Retention of worker status is dealt with in Article 7(3) of Directive 2004/38 and reads as follows: '3. For the purposes of paragraph 1(a), a Union citizen who is no longer a worker or self-employed person shall retain the status of worker or self-employed person in

accident, involuntary unemployment and, under specific conditions, embarking upon vocational training. As mentioned earlier, the Directive does not contain provisions that specifically address the situation of women who give up their job because of pregnancy or childbirth. The possibility for these women to retain worker status is incompatible with Article 7(3), which makes retention of worker status dependent on involuntary unemployment and the person being available for work and registered as a job-seeker.[28]

The *Saint Prix* case shows the limitations of such a legal framing.[29] The applicant was a French national living and working in the UK who due to being in the late stages of her pregnancy had to give up work. The UK authorities denied her income support on the grounds that she lacked a (EU) right to reside. In their view, she no longer held EU worker status since she was voluntarily unemployed and not looking for work. She could not claim rights as an economically inactive person either, since she did not meet self-sufficiency requirements as shown by her request for financial assistance. Three months after the premature birth of her daughter Ms Saint Prix returned to work. This is one of the few cases where the Court of Justice has taken a stand on gender and mobility, acknowledging that 'a Union citizen would be deterred from exercising her right to freedom of movement if, in the event that she was pregnant in the host state and gave up work as a result, if only for a short period, she risked losing her status as a worker in that State'.[30] The Court's solution was to interpret the notion of EU worker broadly so as to allow for the retention of EU worker status for women who give up work or give up seeking work due to the constraints of the late stages of pregnancy and aftermath of childbirth. In these circumstances, mobile EU women enjoy rights directly from the Treaty (Article

the following circumstances: (a) he/she is temporarily unable to work as the result of an illness or accident; / (b) he/she is in duly recorded involuntary unemployment after having been employed for more than one year and has registered as a job-seeker with the relevant employment office; / (c) he/she is in duly recorded involuntary unemployment after completing a fixed-term employment contract of less than a year or after having become involuntarily unemployed during the first twelve months and has registered as a job-seeker with the relevant employment office. In this case, the status of worker shall be retained for no less than six months; / (d) he/she embarks on vocational training. Unless he/she is involuntarily unemployed, the retention of the status of worker shall require the training to be related to the previous employment'.

28 Sandra Mantu, 'Protecting EU Workers in Case of Involuntary Unemployment. Retention of Worker Status' (2014) 7 Online Journal on Free Movement of Workers in the European Union 15.

29 Case C-507/12 *Saint Prix v Secretary of State for Work and Pensions* [2014] ECLI:EU:C:2014:2007.

30 ibid.

45 TFEU) since Directive 2004/38 is not applicable. Furthermore, retention of worker status is linked to the woman in question returning to work or finding another job within a reasonable period after the birth of her child.[31]

While in *Saint Prix* the specific situation of pregnant women and the legislator's failure to regulate it in Directive 2004/38 are acknowledged by the Court, the setting is nonetheless a purely economic one. As the *Dias* case shows, taking time off to care for children has implications for residence and equal treatment. Prior to acquiring permanent residence, it is something that women with sufficient resources can do without losing rights, either because they can fall back on a spouse who works or has financial means or because they themselves have sufficient resources.

5 EU Citizenship: a Fundamental Change for Mobile EU Women?

Mobile EU women who claim social rights as economically inactive mobile EU citizens as opposed to EU workers or persons retaining worker status enjoy a more precarious legal position. This is because, for economically inactive EU citizens, claiming benefits can have negative consequences for entitlement to benefits and residence status, including termination of residence and expulsion from the host EU state.[32] The first case in which the Court of Justice relied on EU citizenship combined with the principle of the prohibition of discrimination on the basis of nationality to enlarge the personal scope of EU citizenship and include economically inactive citizens centred around a Spanish woman in Germany. Ms Martinez Sala had lived in Germany since her childhood; she had a patchy employment history and had received welfare assistance, including for her first child.[33] The German authorities refused to grant her benefits for her second child on the grounds that she could not produce a valid residence permit. She had applied for such a permit but only managed to obtain proof of application. The Court of Justice decided that a European citizen legally resident in Germany was entitled to rely on Article 12 EC (now Article 18 TFEU), which prohibits any discrimination on grounds of nationality, in order to claim equal treatment with national citizens in relation to claiming the child benefit. The requirement to produce a residence permit to obtain the benefit was judged to be direct discrimination on the basis of nationality since German nationals were not required to produce one. Ms

31 ibid.

32 Mantu and Minderhoud (n 23).

33 Case C-86/96 *Martinez Sala v Freistaat Bayern* [1998] ECR 2691.

Martinez Sala's residence was deemed legal since she could not be expelled from Germany as she fell within the scope of the European Convention on Social and Medical Assistance (1953). *Martinez Sala* is seen as the cornerstone of the Court's EU citizenship jurisprudence since it established that EU citizenship has the potential to expand the economic reading of free movement of persons. However, from a gender perspective, the Court's obliviousness as to why Ms Martinez Sala had stopped working – children and care obligations – and the emphasis on regular residence are symptomatic of its treatment of mobile women.

Fast forward some 16 years to the *Dano* decision and gender is still missing from the Court's analysis. In *Dano*, the applicant was a Romanian Roma woman who lived with her son in Germany in the apartment of one of her sisters who was also responsible for their maintenance.[34] Ms Dano had no qualifications and had not worked in either Romania or Germany; neither was she looking for a job in Germany. She applied for benefits under the German basic provision, and was rejected because these benefits were reserved for jobseekers. The Court of Justice stated that mobile EU citizens are entitled to equal treatment with nationals of the host state in relation to benefits only when their residence in the host state meets the requirements of Directive 2004/38. Member States must have the possibility to refuse to award social benefits to an economically inactive EU citizen who, according to national law, has exercised her right to free movement with the sole aim of obtaining another state's social assistance.

The facts of the *Dano* case lend themselves to an intersectional analysis of discrimination (gender, ethnicity and social class) in the context of EU mobility rather than simply discrimination on the basis of nationality.[35] Yet the Court's analysis focused exclusively on the legality of residence. It did not discuss how exercising free movement rights to join a family member (a sister in this case) who partially covers one's expenses can be labelled under the provisions of EU citizenship law. Exchanges that occur outside the normal employment market and cannot be monetised, such as taking care of each other's children, cleaning for the person who gives you shelter or doing other household work cannot be relied on as a basis to claim rights as an EU citizen. The market framework of EU citizenship remains relevant and is its driving engine. EU citizenship rules, legal provisions on free movement and their jurisprudential interpretation fail to acknowledge that 'housework and care, as well as various forms of

34 Case C-333/13 *Dano v Jobcenter Leipzig* [2014] ECLI:EU:C 2358.

35 Charlotte O'Brien, 'Civis Capitalist Sum: Class as the New Guiding Principle of EU Free Movement Rights' (2016) 53 (4) Common Market Law Review 937.

other work outside the relations of the market … are not merely residual activities but an integral part of capitalist economies'.[36]

6 Conclusions

This chapter has taken a closer look at gender and EU citizenship in law and case law. The picture that emerges is that the legal categories and rules governing the exercise of free movement rights are not designed to take the issues that are specific to women into account. This deficiency affects how the Court of Justice interprets them: gender as a category of prohibited discrimination appears absent. The introduction of EU citizenship, which has been described by the Court of Justice as the fundamental status of the nationals of the Member States, has not changed matters much. Like mobile men, mobile women who bring themselves within the scope of the notion of EU worker and who manage to remain within its orbit enjoy equal treatment and secure residence status. Yet this legal neutrality hides some uncomfortable truths. Statistical data on EU labour mobility shows that in terms of economic integration mobile women are worse off than mobile men,[37] while the exercise of mobility rights continues to be informed by a 'traditional gender divide … with work being predominant for males, and family (or personal relationships) being predominant for women'.[38]

The legislator's and the Court's silence on gender in the context of free movement and EU citizenship law needs to be questioned. Does it stem from a failure to identify the gendered implications of EU law? Is it connected with the neutral language used in law? How can women's different choices and life trajectories in relation to children, family life and care obligations be articulated in legal terms? Clearly, there is a need for better, and perhaps different, legal tools and strategies to put gender on the agenda. The emphasis on nationality discrimination and equal treatment with nationals of the host EU state is no longer sufficient. Issues such as the value of care work, opting out of employment for family reasons, concentration in low-paid, short-term and

36 Linda McDowell, 'Gender, Work, Employment and Society: Feminist Reflections on Continuity and Change' (2014) 28 (5) Work, Employment and Society 825.

37 European Commission, '2017 Annual Report on Intra-EU Mobility' (European Commission 2018).

38 Veronika Fajth, 'Mobility in the European Union: What Don't we Know?' (*Reminder-Project.eu*, 19 April 2018) <https://www.reminder-project.eu/blog/mobility-in-the-european-union-what-dont-we-know/> accessed 30 July 2021.

insecure jobs, and interruptions to working life need to play a much bigger role in public, political and legal debates around EU mobility. But before entering into a dialogue on how gender intersects with EU mobility and what we can do to improve women's position, a first step would be to recognise the gendered nature of EU citizenship.

References

Ackers L, *Shifting Spaces. Women, Migration and Citizenship in the European Union* (Policy Press 1998).

Ackers L, 'Citizenship, Gender and Dependence in the European Union: Women and International Migration' (1996) 3 Social Politics: International Studies in Gender, State & Society 316.

Askola H, 'Tale of Two Citizenships? Citizenship, Migration and Care in the European Union' (2012) 21 (3) Social & Legal Studies 341.

Gottfried H, 'Why Workers' Rights are not Women's Rights' (2015) 4 Laws 139.

Gutiérrez-Rodríguez E, 'The Precarity of Feminisation: On Domestic Work, Heteronormativity and the Coloniality of Labour' (2014) 27 International Journal of Politics, Culture and Society 191.

Mantu S, 'The Boundaries of EU Citizenship: Reflections on Borders, Citizenship and Sovereignty', in Minderhoud P, Mantu S and Zwaan K (eds) *Caught in Between Borders: Citizens, Migrants and Humans. Liber Amicorum in Honour of Prof. Dr. Elspeth Guild* (Wolf Legal Publishers 2019).

Mantu S and Minderhoud PE, 'Exploring the Links between Residence and Social Rights for Economically Inactive EU Citizens' (2019) 21 (3) European Journal of Migration and Law 313.

Mantu S, 'Alternative Views on EU Citizenship' in Grutters C at al. (eds) *Migration on the Move – Essays on the Dynamics of Migration* (Brill Nijhoff 2017).

McDowell L, 'Gender, Work, Employment and Society: Feminist Reflections on Continuity and Change' (2014) 28 (5) Work, Employment and Society 825.

Mezzadra S, 'The Gaze of Autonomy – Capitalism, Migration and Social Struggles' in Squire V (ed), *The Contested Politics of Mobility. Borderzones and Irregularity* (Routledge 2011).

Mushaben JM (et al.), 'The Gender Politics of the EU' in Liebert U and Wolff J (eds) *Interdisziplinäire Europastudien* (Springer 2015).

O'Brien C, 'Civis Capitalist Sum: Class as the New Guiding Principle of EU Free Movement Rights' (2016) 53 (4) Common Market Law Review 937.

Shaw J, 'The European Union and Gender Mainstreaming: Constitutionally Embedded or Comprehensively Marginalised' (2002) 10 (3) Feminist Legal Studies 213.

Shaw J, 'Importing Gender: The Challenge of Feminism and the Analysis of the EU Legal Order' (2000) 7 (3) Journal of European Public Policy 406.

Walby S, 'The European Union and Gender Equality: Emergent Varieties of Gender Regime' (2004) 11 (1) Social Politics: International Studies in Gender, State and Society 4.

Weldon-Johns M, 'EU Work-Family Policies – Challenging Parental Roles or Reinforcing Gendered Stereotypes' (2013) 19 (2) European Law Journal 1.

CHAPTER 5

Gender Gaps in Migration Studies

Recent Developments and Prospects

Asuncion Fresnoza-Flot

1 Introduction

The field of migration studies focuses on spatial movements of people from one place, temporality, and social space to another, including their multi-faceted dimensions and underlying processes. Feminist scholars from different disciplines introduced gender perspectives in this research field and contributed to the burgeoning of what is known today as "gender and migration" scholarship.[1] More than four decades later several questions can be raised: what is the present state of broader migration studies? Are there still gender gaps in this field of research? How can we further advance migration studies?

In this chapter, "gender gaps" in specific epistemologies refer to lacunas in the extent to which scholarly focuses, methodologies, and analyses are gender inclusive, gender informed, or gender oriented. In this context, gender is not only a socially constructed category[2] but also a standpoint focusing on power dynamics, relations, and asymmetries among social groups. It can be defined

1 See Donna R Gabaccia (ed), *Seeking Ground: Multidisciplinary Studies of Immigrant Women in the United States* (Greenwood Press 1992); Arlie R. Hochschild, 'Global Care Chains and Emotional Surplus Value' in Will Hutton and Anthony Giddens (eds), *On the Edge: Living with Global Capitalism* (Jonathan Cape 2000) 130–146; Pierrette Hondagneu-Sotelo, *Gendered Transitions: Mexican Experiences of Immigration* (University of California Press 1994); Eleonore Kofman, 'Gendered Migrations, Social Reproduction and the Household in Europe' (2014) 38 (1) Dialectical Anthropology 79; Sarah J. Mahler and Patricia R. Pessar, 'Gendered Geographies of Power: Analyzing Gender Across Transnational Spaces' (2001) 7 (4) Identities: Global Studies in Culture and Power 441; Mirjana Morokvašić, 'Birds of Passage are also Women' (1984) 18 (4) International Migration Review 886; Rhacel S. Parreñas, *Servants of Globalization. Women, Migration and Domestic Work* (Stanford University Press 2001); Rachel Silvey, 'Power, Difference and Mobility: Feminist Advances in Migration Studies' (2004) 28 (4) Progress in Human Geography 490.

2 It is "a constitutive element of social relationships based on the perceived differences between the sexes" (see Joan W. Scott, 'Gender: A Useful Category of Historical Analysis' (1986) 91 (5) The American Historical Review 1067). These differences refer to "masculinity" and "femininity" – characteristics socially prescribed to individuals from birth.

DOI:10.1163/9789004467682_007

as “a social relation characterized by power inequalities that hierarchically produce, organize, and evaluate masculinities and femininities through the contested but controlling practices of individuals, organizations, and societies”.[3] An investigation of the existing gender gaps in migration scholarship requires an awareness of contemporary developments regarding the main object of analysis in the field – human spatial mobility.

Based on the latest data on migrations that cross national borders, the number of migrant men continues to exceed that of migrant women: 52 percent men versus 48 percent women out of 281 million migrants in 2020.[4] This gender imbalance raises the question of whether the numerical dominance of migrant men translates into comparatively more studies on them than on migrant women. What place do numerical minorities such as lesbian, gay, bisexual, transgender, queer (LGBTQ) migrants occupy in the migration scholarship?

The present chapter is based on the findings from qualitative and quantitative reviews of the literature on migration. The qualitative review examines the gender and migration scholarship and its temporal evolution in different regions of the world – the United States of America (USA), Europe, Asia, Africa, and Latin America. The quantitative review comprises a bibliometric analysis of the migration literature between 1980 and 2019 using two search engines that are widely used in research and academia (Web of Science and Google Scholar). Further input was obtained from the websites of two leading journals in the field (*Gender, Place & Culture* and *Journal of Ethnic and Migration Studies*). By adopting a mixed methodological approach, the present chapter aims to facilitate an in-depth understanding of the significant developments in migration studies and of the place of gender within this scholarship. It offers fresh insights as to which areas of the field should strive to become more gender sensitive.

The reviews presented here have certain limitations. First, they have a linguistic bias because they mainly examined publications written in English. Second, they focused on gender gaps, which leaves out issues related to other categories, such as ethnicity, age, and social class. Third, the quantitative review was limited to two widely used search engines, thus overlooking less popular and independent platforms at the national, regional, or international levels. However, despite these limitations, the qualitative and quantitative data analysis in the present chapter can contribute to migration scholars’ reflections

3 Myra Marx Ferree, ‘Filling the Glass: Gender Perspectives on Families’ (2010) 72 Journal of Marriage and the Family 424.

4 International Organization for Migration’s (IOM) Global Migration Portal, *Key Global Migration Figures, 2017 – 2021* (IOM 2021) <https://migrationdataportal.org/sites/default/files/2021-02/key-global-migration-figures.pdf> accessed on 29 November 2021.

on how transnational migration studies can be further developed, notably the gender and migration scholarship. Before presenting the quantitative review, the chapter examines the evolution of gender and migration studies in various social contexts. It concludes by identifying the gender gaps and issues still to be addressed in migration studies.

2 Gender and Migration Research: Evolution in Different Social Contexts

The development of the gender and migration scholarship is not entirely uniform across socio-geographic contexts, as "(c)oncepts of women's/gender and feminist ideas" that "travel across national, linguistic, cultural, and economic boundaries [...] are changed in the process".[5] The specific characteristics of each context as regards migration phenomena also vary, as does the situation of gender and migration research.

Prior to the birth of the gender and migration scholarship, the broader field of migration studies displayed several shortcomings related to gender. First, there was a male bias that viewed migration purely as a men's enterprise.[6] Second, most scholars adopted a "reductionist" perspective, that is, they considered women as mere followers and dependents of men.[7] Third, they approached migration in a gender-neutral way, and this gender blindness meant that they did not pay attention to the power dynamics and gender processes involved in migration. Fourth, as a result of these shortcomings, women migrants were mostly invisible in the study of migratory phenomena. And fifth, there was also a heterosexual bias linked to the heteronormative tendency in migration studies to analyse migration strictly as a heterosexual affair neglecting the idea that LGBTQ individuals are also capable of migrating. Now that gender perspectives have permeated migration studies, we can expect radical changes in the way scholars in the field conduct their investigations.

In the USA, Hondagneu-Sotelo describes the evolution of gender and migration research as having three stages.[8] The first stage is "women and migration"

5 Sondra Hale, 'Transnational Gender Studies and the Migrating Concept of Gender in the Middle East and North Africa' (2009) 21 (2) Cultural Dynamics 149.

6 Asuncion Fresnoza-Flot and Kyoko Shinozaki, 'Transnational Perspectives on Intersecting Experiences: Gender, Social Class and Generation among Southeast Asian Migrants and their Families' (2017) 43 (6) Journal of Ethnic and Migration Studies 867.

7 See Morokvašić (n 1).

8 Pierrette Hondagneu-Sotelo, 'Gender and Immigration: A Retrospective and Introduction' in Pierrette Hondagneu-Sotelo (ed), *Gender and U.S. Immigration: Contemporary Trends* (University of California Press 2003) 3–19.

(1970s to early 1980s) during which scholars wrote about women migrants. The second stage – "gender and migration" (late 1980s to early 1990s) – started when scholars turned their attention to gender processes in the realm of the family and households. The third and final stage, "gender as a constitutive element of immigration" began in the mid-1990s, when scholars started analysing larger social structures and institutions beyond the family, using a gender lens. The rise of queer migration studies is an important development in the USA. At present, as Hondagneu-Sotelo remarks,[9] sexuality is one of the main streams in gender and migration research,[10] thanks to the early initiatives of USA-based migration scholars.[11]

The evolution of gender and migration research in the USA, as described above, resembles the development of the same research field in Europe. In this region, the first stage of development of gender and migration research started in the late 1970s and ended in the 1980s. It is known as a "compensatory phase", that is, "focusing on women, showing them where they were not visible".[12] The visibilisation of women's active role as initiators and actors of migration characterised the 1980s.[13] The second stage occurred from the 1990s to the 2000s, during which the globalisation,[14] intersectionality,[15] and

9 Pierrette Hondagneu-Sotelo, 'Gender and Migration Scholarship: An Overview from a 21st Century Perspective' (2011) 6 (1) Migraciones Internacionales 219.

10 See the recent work on the subject: Shweta Majumdar Adur, 'In Pursuit of Love: 'Safe Passages', Migration and Queer South Asians in the US' (2018) 66 (2) Current Sociology 320; and Héctor Carrillo, *Pathways of Desire: The Sexual Migration of Mexican Gay Men* (University of Chicago Press 2017).

11 For example: Lionel Cantú Jr., *Border Crossings: Mexican Men and the Sexuality of Migration.* PhD dissertation (University of California 1999); Héctor Carrillo, 'Sexual Migration, Cross-Cultural Sexual Encounters, and Sexual Health' (2004) 1 (3) Sexuality Research and Social Policy 58; Eithne Luibhéid and Lionel Cantú Jr., *Queer Migrations: Sexuality, US Citizenship, and Border Crossings* (University of Minnesota Press 2005); and Martin Manalansan, IV, 'Queer Intersections. Sexuality and Gender in Migration Studies' (2006) 40 (1) International Migration Review 224.

12 Christine Catarino and Mirjana Morokvašić, 'Femmes, Genre, Migration et Mobilités' (2005) 21 Revue européenne des migrations internationales 1, 2.

13 See Laura Oso Casas, 'Femmes, Actrices des Mouvements Migratoires' (2005) 5 Cahiers Genre et développement 35.

14 See Parreñas 2001 and Saskia Sassen, 'Women's Burden: Counter-geographies of Globalization and the Feminization of Survival' (2000) 53 (2) Journal of International Affairs 503.

15 See Kimberlé Crenshaw, 'Demarginalizing the Intersection of Race and Sex: A Black Feminist Critique of Antidiscrimination Doctrine, Feminist Theory and Antiracist Politics' (1989) in *The University of Chicago Legal Forum: Feminism in the Law: Theory, Practice and Criticism*, 139–167; and Patricia Hill Collins, *Black Feminist Thought: Knowledge, Consciousness, and Politics of Empowerment* (Unwin Hyman 1990).

transnationalism[16] perspectives permeated European migration scholarship. It was during this period that studies on the international division of reproductive labour, domestic or care work, skilled migration, and transnational families burgeoned in Europe.[17] Consequently, women migrants, although they were already visible in migration studies before this period, attracted renewed scientific interest to the extent that scholars overlooked men while reinforcing their pre-existing heteronormative tendencies. During the third stage (from the 2010s to the present), migration scholars in Europe have been rectifying these shortcomings in the following ways: by examining men's experiences;[18] carrying out more gender informed, transnational, and/or intersectional research concentrating on power relations and inequalities;[19] and moving beyond care analysis to examine emerging phenomena in the region such as family and marriage,[20] refugee,[21] and LGBTQ[22] migrations.

16 Linda G. Basch, Nina Glick Schiller and Christina Szanton Blanc, *Nations Unbound. Transnational Projects, Postcolonial Predicaments, and Deterritorialized Nation-states* (Gordon and Breach 1995); and Nina Glick Schiller, Linda Basch and Christina Blanc-Szanton, 'Transnationalism: A New Analytic Framework for Understanding Migration' (1992) 645 (1) Annals of the New York Academy of Sciences 1.

17 For example: Deborah F. Bryceson and Ulla Vuorela (eds), *The Transnational Family: New European Frontiers and Global Networks* (Berg 2002); Asuncion Fresnoza-Flot, 'Migration Status and Transnational Mothering: The Case of Filipino Migrants in France' (2009) 9 (2) Global Networks 252; Helma Lutz, *The New Maids: Transnational Women and the Care Economy* (Zed Books Ltd. 2011); Janet Henshall Momsen (ed), *Gender, Migration, and Domestic Service* (Routledge 1999); and Parvati Raghuram, 'Gendering Skilled Migratory Streams: Implications for Conceptualizations of Migration' (2000) 9 (4) Asian and Pacific Migration Journal 429.

18 See Ester Gallo and Francesca Scrinzi, *Migration, Masculinities and Reproductive Labour. Men of the Home* (Palgrave 2016); Majella Kilkey, Diane Perrons and Ania Plomien, *Gender, Migration and Domestic Work: Masculinities, Male Labour and Fathering in the UK and USA* (Palgrave 2013).

19 Anna Amelina and Helma Lutz, *Gender and Migration: Transnational and Intersectional Prospects* (Routledge 2019); and Elisabetta Zontini, *Transnational Families, Migration and Gender: Moroccan and Filipino Women in Bologna and Barcelona* (Berghahn 2010).

20 Katharine Charsley (ed), *Transnational Marriage: New Perspectives from Europe and Beyond* (Routledge 2012); Joëlle Moret, Apostolos Andrikopoulos and Janine Dahinden, 'Contesting Categories: Cross-border Marriages from the Perspectives of the State, Spouses and Researchers' (2019) 47 (2) Journal of Ethnic and Migration Studies 325; and Saskia Bonjour and Betty de Hart, 'Intimate Citizenship: Introduction to the Special Issue on Citizenship, Membership and Belonging in Mixed-status Families' (2020) 28 (1) Identities 1.

21 For example: Betty De Hart, 'Sexuality, Race and Masculinity in Europe's Refugee Crisis' in Carolus Grütters, Sandra Mantu and Paul Minderhoud (eds), *Migration on the Move. Essays on the Dynamics of Migration* (Brill Nijhoff 2017) 27–53; and Jane Freedman, 'Engendering Security at the Borders of Europe: Women Migrants and the Mediterranean 'Crisis'' (2016) 29 (4) Journal of Refugee Studies 568.

22 See Jon Binnie, 'Critical Queer Regionality and LGBTQ Politics in Europe' (2016) 23 (11) Gender, Place & Culture 1631; and Sébastien Chauvin, Manuela Salcedo Robledo, Timo

In Eastern, South-Eastern, Southern, and Western Asia, migration studies began in the latter part of the 1920s with a gender-neutral tone. This was evident in the 1927 study by the South Manchuria Railway Company on migrant workers in Manchuria[23] and the early works of Japanese geographer Yoshiji Takemi on the Okinawans' overseas migration.[24] This tone persisted after the Second World War alongside the scholarly tendency to focus on male migration. In the 1970s, migration research continued in this direction, explicitly tackling refugee and labour migrations. Migrant women were almost absent from studies during this period, but as migratory movements within and from Asia to other continents increasingly feminised in the 1980s, scholarly works on women also started to increase.[25] Gender and migration research appears to have taken shape during this period, focusing on rural–urban and international migration of women.[26] As in Europe, gender and migration research in Asia during the period from the 1990s to the 2000s was characterised by the mushrooming of studies on women's migration,[27] notably examining their paid reproductive labour[28] and marriage- and family-related issues.[29] The influence of globalisation, intersectionality, and transnationalism perspectives

---

Koren and Joël Illidge, 'Class, Mobility and Inequality in the Lives of Same-sex Couples with Mixed Legal Statuses' (2019) 47 (2) Journal of Ethnic and Migration Studies 430.

23 Thomas R. Gottschang, 'Economic Change, Disasters, and Migration: The Historical Case of Manchuria' (1987) 35 (3) Economic Development and Cultural Change 461.

24 Yoshiji Takemi, 'Okinawa Jima Shutsuimin no Keizai Chirigakuteki Kousatsu' (1) (1928) 4 (2) Chirigaku Hyouron 1; and Yoshiji Takemi, 'Okinawa Jima Shutsuimin no Keizai Chirigakuteki Kousatsu' (1928) 4 (3) Chirigaku Hyouron 12.

25 See Maruja M. Asis and Nicola Piper, 'Researching International Labor Migration in Asia' (2008) 49 (3) The Sociological Quarterly 423.

26 See Nasra M. Shah and Peter C. Smith, 'Migrant Women at Work in Asia' in James T. Fawcett, Siew-Ean Khoo and Peter C. Smith (eds), *Women in the Cities of Asia: Migration and Urban Adaptation* (Routledge 1984) 297–322; and Lilian Trager, 'Family Strategies and the Migration of Women: Migrants to Dagupan City, Philippines' (1984) 18 (4) International Migration Review 1264.

27 Mary Beth Mills, *Thai Women in the Global Labor Force: Consuming Desires, Contested Selves* (Rutgers University Press 1999); and Nana Oishi, *Women in Motion: Globalization, State Policies, and Labor Migration in Asia* (Stanford University Press 2005).

28 Nicole Constable, *Maid to Order in Hong Kong: Stories of Filipina Workers* (Cornell University Press 1997); Pei-Chia Lan, *Global Cinderellas: Migrant Domestics and Newly Rich Employers in Taiwan* (Duke University Press 2006); and Rachel Silvey, 'Transnational Migration and the Gender Politics of Scale: Indonesian Domestic Workers in Saudi Arabia' (2004) 25 (2) Singapore Journal of Tropical Geography 141.

29 Rajni Palriwala and Patricia Uberoi (eds), *Marriage, Migration and Gender* (Sage 2008); Nicola Piper and Mina Roces (eds), *Wife or Worker?: Asian Women and Migration* (Rowman & Littlefield Publishers 2003); and Katie D. Willis and Brenda S. Yeoh, 'Gender and Transnational Household Strategies: Singaporean Migration to China' (2000) 34 (3) Regional Studies 253.

is clearly evident in the Asian literature on gender and migration. Nonetheless, in terms of theorisation, as Asis and Piper remark, "it appears still a challenge to advance from the descriptive to the more theoretical level of explanation".[30] Since 2011, gender and migration research in Asia has diversified in terms of analytical focus and orientation, with an increasing emphasis on marriage migration[31] and a holistic approach to Asian migrations.[32]

In the Latin American context, Herrera provides an overview of gender and international migration in the region.[33] She observes the "selective presence of gender in migration studies" there, which means that certain groups of migrant women are included in the studies "to the detriment of other subjects and other inequalities".[34] She highlights that it is necessary to examine internal migration in the Andean region in the 1970s and 1980s to understand international migration from Latin America. Through this approach, "migrations are analyzed as individual male trajectories articulated to family strategies in which women, gender relations and generational differences are taken as neutral variables".[35] Herrera also identifies the concepts most widely used in the study of internal migration in the 1980s – social networks and family survival strategies and reproduction. In the 1990s, these key concepts were also central to the analysis of Latin American international migration in the context of globalisation. She notes the scholarly interest in Latin American migrant women's paid domestic/care work and transnational families, particularly stay-behind family members such as wives and children.[36] Interestingly, many studies on Latin American migrants in Europe focus on women and often have a transnational dimension.[37] Herrera concludes that the issues that still need to be

30 See Asis and Piper (n 25) 432.

31 Sari K. Ishii (ed), *Marriage Migration in Asia: Emerging Minorities at the Frontiers of Nation-States* (NUS Press 2016); see also Asuncion Fresnoza-Flot and Gwénola Ricordeau (eds), *International Marriages and Marital Citizenship: Southeast Asian Women on the Move* (Routledge 2017).

32 See Gracia Liu-Farrer and Brenda S. Yeoh (eds), *Routledge Handbook of Asian Migrations* (Routledge 2018).

33 Gioconda Herrera, 'Género y Migración Internacional en la Experiencia Latinoamericana. De la Visibilización del Campo a una Presencia Selectiva' (2012) 49 (1) Política y Sociedad 35.

34 ibid 37.

35 ibid 40.

36 Jason Pribilsky, 'Nervios and 'Modern Childhood'. Migration and Shifting Contexts of Child Life in the Ecuadorian Andes' (2001) 8 (2) Childhood 251; and Johanna Dreby, *Divided by Borders: Mexican Migrants and their Children* (University of California Press 2010).

37 Paolo Boccagni, 'Practising Motherhood at a Distance: Retention and Loss in Ecuadorian Transnational Families' (2012) 38 (2) Journal of Ethnic and Migration Studies 261; Laura

explored in the context of Latin American migration include trafficking; the relationship between gender, state, and migration policies; and sexualities, notably migratory experiences of "transsexuals, transgender, gay and lesbian people".[38]

Like elsewhere in the world, migration studies in Africa started with a focus on men as leading actors of migration. Since the latter part of the 1970s, African migration research has embarked on the visibilisation of women.[39] For instance, Izzard remarks that studies in Southern Africa neglect migrant women "despite evidence" of their "increasing labour migration".[40] This gap can be attributed to the stereotypical view that men migrate and women stay behind, a cliché rooted in the historically male-dominated migration during colonial times. Such a stereotype also persists when it comes to rural–urban movement, which is generally viewed as male-predominated, although statistics demonstrate that it is dominated by women in many countries.[41] Because of this stereotyping, "the independent rural-urban migration of women has been grossly neglected in African studies to date".[42] Since the 2000s, gender perspectives have been progressively permeating migration studies in Africa. Nonetheless, Crush, Williams, and Peberdy pointed out that although "some attempts have been made to better understand the gender and dimensions of migration, the area remains unexplored", notably regarding "the impact of migration on gender" in the context of "changing roles for women, employment opportunities, household structure as well as [the] HIV/AIDS"[43] epidemic. During this time, studies have increasingly focused on women's internal migration, that is, rural–urban within a nation, circular movement within Africa,[44] and international migration to countries outside the African

Oso Casas, 'Money, Sex, Love and the Family: Economic and Affective Strategies of Latin American Sex Workers in Spain', 36 (1) Journal of Ethnic and Migration Studies 47.

38 See Herrera (n 33) 44.

39 Niara Sudarkasa, 'Women and Migration in Contemporary West Africa' (1977) 3 (1) Signs: Journal of Women in Culture and Society 178.

40 Wendy Izzard, 'Migrants and Mothers: Case Studies from Botswana' (1985) 1 (2) Journal of Southern African Studies 258.

41 Josef Gugler and Gudrun Ludwar-Ene, 'Gender and Migration in Africa South of the Sahara' in Jonathan Baker and Tade Akin Aina (eds), *The Migration Experience in Africa* (Nordiska Afrikainstitutet 1995).

42 ibid 261.

43 Jonathan Crush, Sally Peberdy and Vincent Williams, 'International Migration and Good Governance in the Southern African Region' (2006) Migration Policy Brief 17, 18.

44 Thomas Antwi Bosiakoh and Vera Williams Tetteh, 'Nigerian Immigrant Women's Entrepreneurial Embeddedness in Ghana, West Africa' (2019) 11 (1) International Journal of Gender and Entrepreneurship 38; and Stefania Gadia Meda, 'Single Mothers

continent.[45] The scholarly interest in studies on migrant men in and from the region through a gender lens has also surged,[46] notably those examining male refugees' experiences.[47]

Against this background of evolution of gender and migration research in different social contexts, we can conclude that advancements in the field have been taking place, moving through various phases, but in a non-uniform fashion. The USA and Europe appear to be at almost the same stage of progress in empirical and theoretical terms. Asia and Latin America have also advanced, but there is still a need for theorisations that go beyond Euro-American perspectives of migration. Africa underwent a long period of visibilisation of women in migration research compared to other regions in the world, which has culminated in the growth of separate areas of scholarship respectively focused on women and men. Making these areas converge will require more studies adopting gender perspectives in Africa. Finally, sexuality and queer perspectives have not yet received much attention in Asia, Latin America, and Africa, a gender gap that can be attributed to the challenging socio-legal situations of LGBTQ individuals in these regions. Analysing the debates around gender, migration, and globalisation over the past 40 years, Marchetti observes that a new era started in the late 2000s, during which two opposite tendencies became evident. Gender and migration became "a core element in a range of disciplines from the social sciences", while at the same time "several scholars are looking partially disappointed about what has been achieved, seen as a 'glass half-full'[48]".[49] Hence, the major challenge for gender and migration

---

of Nairobi: Rural-urban Migration and the Transformation of Gender Roles and Family Relations in Kenya' (2013) 15 (2) Lidé Města 279.

45 For example: Ameena Alrasheed, 'An Alternative Perspective: Islam, Identity, and Gender Migration of Sudanese Muslim Women in the UK' (2015) 9 (1) African Journal of Political Science and International Relations 1; and Marina De Regt, 'Ways to Come, Ways to Leave: Gender, Mobility, and Il/legality among Ethiopian Domestic Workers in Yemen' (2010) 24 (2) Gender & Society 237.

46 Dan Godshaw, 'A Masculinist Perspective on Gendered Relations of Power: Rwandan Migrant Men in the UK' (2014) Working Paper 72; and Netsai Sarah Matshaka, '"Marobot NeMawaya"–Traffic Lights and Wire: Crafting Zimbabwean Migrant Masculinities in Cape Town' (2010) 65 (13) Feminist Africa 65.

47 For example: Rosemary Jaji, 'Masculinity on Unstable Ground: Young Refugee Men in Nairobi, Kenya' (2009) 22 (2) Journal of Refugee Studies 177; and Samuel Muchoki, *Intimacies, Citizenship and Refugee Men* (Springer 2016).

48 Katharine M. Donato, Donna Gabaccia, Jennifer Holdaway, Martin Manalansan, IV and Patricia R. Pessar, 'A Glass Half Full? Gender in Migration Studies' (2006) 40 (1) International Migration Review 3.

49 Sabrina Marchetti, 'Gender, Migration and Globalization: An Overview of the Debates' in Anna Triandafyllidou (ed), *Handbook of Migration and Globalization* (Edward Elgar Publishing 2018) 449.

scholars in different socio-geographic contexts is how to finish filling that glass. In this respect, there is an immediate need to diversify gender and migration research by incorporating interdisciplinary perspectives. This will require dynamic collaborations among migration scholars from various disciplines and research fields. This represents another challenge due to the compartmentalised "nature of social science" in which, in the words of Hondagneu-Sotelo, "researchers [...] are mostly not in conversation with one another".[50]

3 State of Migration Studies in Quantitative Terms

A quantitative approach is needed to obtain a holistic view of the recent developments in migration studies and to find out whether gender gaps persist. The Web of Science and Google Scholar search engines, as well as websites of selected leading journals, provide interesting insights that are usually invisible in qualitative analyses of migration literature. These virtual research platforms enabled six major developments in the field to be identified, each of which is outlined below.

3.1 *Visibilised Women, Feminised Gender*

A search of Web of Science for the terms "gender, women, migration" and "gender, men, migration" in the title, abstract, and keywords of literature published from 1980 to 2019, identified 3,287 scholarly works for the former and 1,462 for the latter. Excluding self-citations, studies on "gender, women, migration" garnered more citations than those focusing on "gender, men, migration": 38,108 versus 20,939. The search with Google Scholar also identified more publications on the former than the latter: 430 versus 36 (see Figure 5.1).

Interestingly, the peak number of studies with the words "gender", "women", and "migration" in the title was reached during the period from 2000 to 2009. This coincided with the development of gender and migration research, particularly in the USA and Europe (see section 2 on the qualitative review of gender and migration scholarship). From 2010 to 2019, the number of studies on this theme dropped by 22 per cent, from 208 to 162. By contrast, the number of publications with "gender, men, migration" in the title showed a slow increase: from 0 (1980–1989), to 5 (1990–1999), 13 (2000–2009), and 18 (2010–2019). This suggests that the tendency to study women's migration through the prism of gender does not apply to men's migration. Although gender is

50 See Hondagneu-Sotelo (n 9) 227.

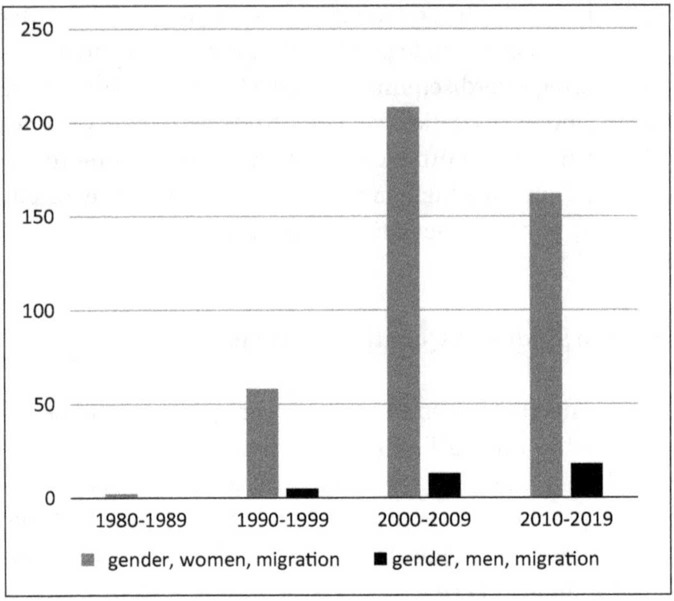

FIGURE 5.1 Google Scholar publications with gender, (wo)men, and migration in the title

relational and experiential,[51] gender often remains connoted with women and women with gender.

In terms of disciplines and research areas, Web of Science revealed that studies on "women, gender, migration" were mainly carried out in the fields of women's studies, demography, sociology, and geography. By contrast, studies on "men, gender, migration" were usually conducted in the fields of demography, sociology, geography, and public environmental and occupational health. The top five journals publishing studies on both topics were inscribed in one or more of the above disciplines and research areas. The following journals led in terms of numbers of publications on "women, gender, migration": *Gender, Place and Culture*; *Journal of Ethnic and Migration Studies*; *Women's Studies International Forum*; *International Migration*; and *International Migration Review*. Except *for Women's Studies International Forum*, all these journals also published work on "men, gender, migration". The list of leading journals publishing articles on "men, gender, migration" included the journal *Social Science Medicine*, which was not among the leading journals publishing articles on "women, gender, migration". *Gender, Place and Culture* and *Journal of Ethnic*

51 See Fresnoza-Flot and Shinozaki (n 6).

and Migration Studies ranked first and second, respectively, in both lists, confirming that women are no longer invisible in migration studies. From 1994 to 2019, *Gender, Place and Culture* published more articles with "women" and "migration" in the title than with "men" and "migration": 22 versus 5. This was also the case for the *Journal of Ethnic and Migration Studies* in which 74 articles with "women" and "migration" in the title were published from 1971 to 2019 versus 6 articles on men.

In addition, based on the address for reprints or the corresponding author of each publication, the regions that dominated research outputs on migration studies were North America – with the USA at the top of the list – and European countries such as England and Germany. Australia was also among the top ten countries with publications in Web of Science, whereas the People's Republic of China was the only Asian country that made it to the top ten. Latin American and African countries were not among the top ten countries. This suggests that it is not only social science that is compartmentalised, but also the geopolitical regions in which migration research takes place. Thus, the findings echo the results of the qualitative review earlier in this chapter showing that the USA and Europe are ahead of the developments in gender and migration research. It also illustrates the social inequalities migration scholars identify between the so-called "Global North" and the "Global South" as well as between "visible" women in the former and their "invisible" counterparts in the latter. Migration studies reflect these inequalities in knowledge production, which call for more collaborative research projects and exchanges among countries in these regions to fill this gap.

3.2 *Slowly Increasing Consideration of Sexuality and* LGBTQ

Through his doctoral dissertation on *Border crossings: Mexican men and the sexuality of migration*, Cantú introduced in 1999 sexuality in the study of migration. In 2004, Carrillo proposed conceptualising "sexual migration" in many ways, including by taking into account "sexual immigrants' transportation of practices across international borders, their lives in their places of origin", and "their exposure to local and foreign sexual ideologies before migrating",[52] among others. In 2005, Luibhéid and Cantú published their highly influential work on queer migrations, reinforcing the field of queer migration studies.[53] The following year, Manalansan called for sexuality and a queer perspective to be brought into migration studies.[54] This raises the question of whether

52 Carrillo (n 11) 58.
53 See Luibhéid and Cantú (n 11).
54 Manalansan (n 11).

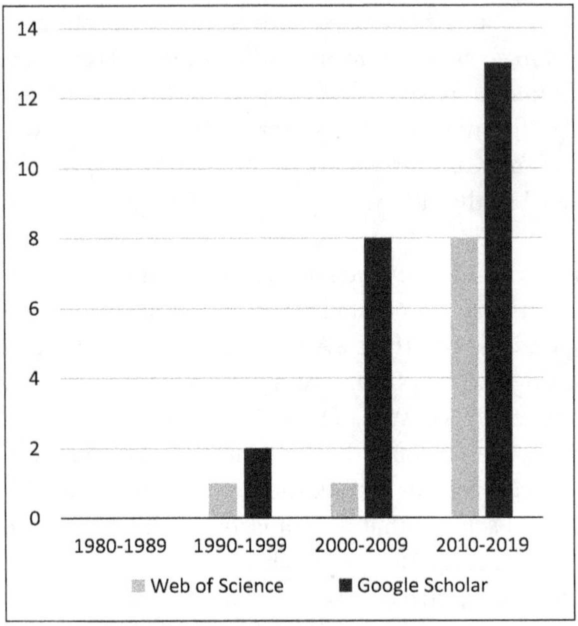

FIGURE 5.2 Publications with gender, sexuality, and migration in the title

scholars in the broader field of migration studies are following the path initiated by the above-mentioned pioneering scholars.

The search of Web of Science shows that studies with "gender, sexuality, migration" in the title remain at the margin of broader migration scholarship with only 10 publications from 1980 to 2019 (see Figure 5.2). Likewise, only 11 works with "men", "sexuality", and "migration" in the title were published during the same period. Google Scholar found 23 publications with "gender", "sexuality", and "migration" in the title (see Figure 5.2) and indicated that the first work with "men", "sexuality", and "migration" in the title appeared in 1999 – Cantú's doctoral dissertation. The period 2010 –2019 witnessed a sudden surge of publications on the topic, with 13 in total.

As scholars started to examine sexualities in migration, interest in LGBTQ migrants also increased, slowly at first, before intensifying from 2010 onwards. The search of Web of Science retrieved only 24 publications with "LGBT migrants" in the title, abstract, and keywords from the late 2000s to 2019. One of them appeared in 2007 following the publication of Manalansan's work,[55] and the others emerged during the 2010–2019 period. Surprisingly, the search

55 ibid.

engine found no study before 2007 with "LGBT migrants" in the title, abstract, and keywords. When the search term was changed to "LGBTQ migrants" and restricted to titles, Web of Science returned four results for the period 2010–2019. However, when the search for the keyword "LGBTQ migrants" was specified as a "topic" – a phrase appearing in the title, abstract, and keywords of a paper – instead of as a "title", Web of Science found 18 publications. Most of these studies were published between 2010 and 2019.

Similarly, the search of Google Scholar showed that publications with "LGBT migrants" in the title, abstract, and keywords came out during the same period, and so did the first set of publications (4) with "LGBTQ migrants" in the title. Before 2010, more studies included "LGBT, migration" in any part of their text than "LGBTQ, migration". In summary, since 2010, sexuality and LGBT(Q) migrants have been increasingly considered in the analysis of migration,[56] but generally remain marginal when compared to the bulk of publications on heterosexual migrants, as described in section 3.1. As previously observed, LGBTQ migrants "remain largely neglected in studies on transnational migrations".[57] Nonetheless, if the scholarly interest in sexuality and LGBTQ migrants continues, LGBTQ migration through the prism of sexuality and queer perspectives will occupy a central place in broader migration studies, similar to what has happened with studies on women's migratory movements.

3.3 *Continued Transnationalisation*

It is the pioneering work of Glick Schiller, Basch, and Blanc-Szanton that introduced the perspective of transnationalism in migration studies in the early 1990s.[58] This perspective highlights migrants' multi-faceted social relations, ties, and activities that connect the societies in which they are enmeshed. Before this perspective was adopted in migration studies, scholars mostly concentrated on international human mobility without necessarily examining the simultaneity and intensity of migrants' social being and practices "here" and "there", or, in other words, their embeddedness in social spaces traversing national borders.[59] The transnationalism perspective radically changed the

56 For example: see Chauvin et al. (n 22).

57 Asuncion Fresnoza-Flot, 'Negotiating Transnational Mobility and Gender Definitions in the Context of Migration' in *Oxford Research Encyclopedia of Education* (Oxford University Press 2021) 13.

58 See Glick Schiller, Basch and Blanc-Szanton (n 16), as well as Basch, Glick Schiller and Blanc-Szanton (n 16).

59 Thomas Faist, 'Transnational Social Spaces out of International Migration: Evolution, Significance and Future Prospects' (1998) 39 (2) Archives Européennes de Sociologie/European Journal of Sociology/Europäisches Archiv für Soziologie 213.

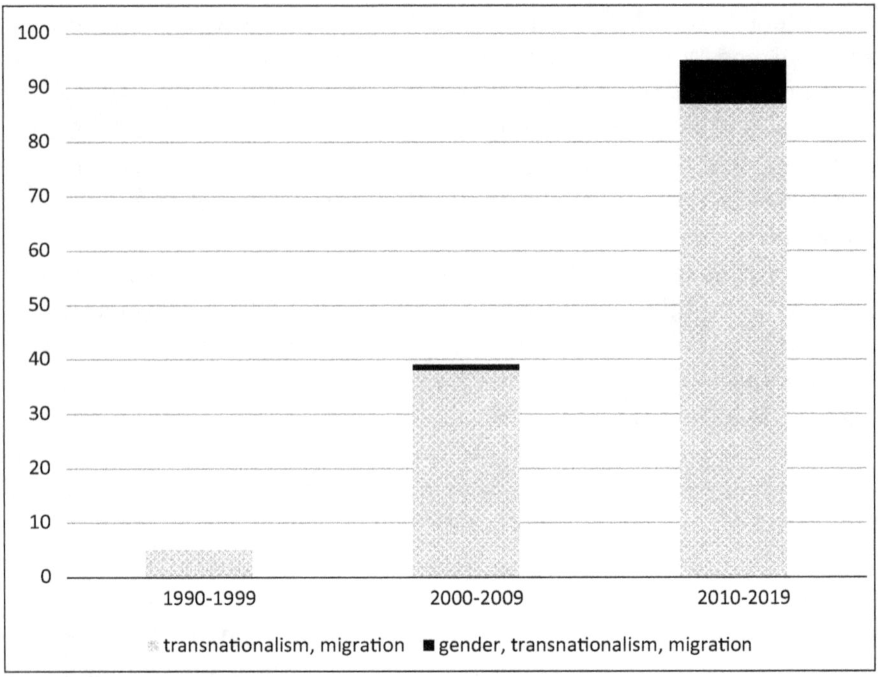

FIGURE 5.3 Web of Science publications on gender, transnationalism, and migration

way scholars viewed and examined migratory phenomena then and now. The search of Web of Science and Google Scholar provides quantitative proof of the continued transnationalisation of migration studies, that is, the process in which many migration scholars continue to adopt the lens of transnationalism in their studies.

Between 1990 and 2019, there were 130 publications listed in Web of Science with "transnationalism, migration" in their title (see Figure 5.3). When the search for the same words was extended to abstract and keywords, Web of Science identified 1,578 publications. These works garnered a total of 31,422 citations, reaching their peak in 2019 with 3,989 citations. When the search incorporated "gender" into the keywords "transnationalism, migration" and looked only at the title of publications, only nine publications were retrieved. However, Web of Science returned 224 results when the search covered the title, abstract, and keywords of publications (see Figure 5.3). Since 1990, the number of citations of these works has been steadily increasing.

In the search of Google Scholar, the number of publications including the keywords "transnationalism, migration" in the title was also found to be constantly increasing: for example, from 53 publications between 1990 and 2000 to 217 publications from 2011–2019. However, a search for the words "gender", "transnationalism" and "migration" in the titles of articles published during the 1990–2019 period gave only 17 results and none during the period 1980–1989. The comparison of data obtained from the two search engines confirms the lingering scholarly tendency to study migration using a transnational perspective. Interestingly, gender appears often out of the focus, which is surprising given the widely known studies on gender and migration (see section 2 about the evolution of this field), specifically about transnational families, care, and social reproduction.

3.4 *Rising Intersectionality, Prevailing Mobility Lens*

The intersectionality approach examines how the overlap of "categories of difference"[60] such as gender, social class, and "race" produces and reinforces marginality and oppression of social minorities, notably Black women. Although it was initially applied to the study of these minority women, it has become progressively more influential in migration studies in recent years. Likewise, the spatial turn in the social sciences led to the rise of the mobility perspective,[61] most notably in geography, sociology, and anthropology. In quantitative terms, this perspective has had a bigger influence on migration studies than the intersectionality approach and transnational perspective, as the data below from searches of the Web of Science and Google Scholar prove.

During the period 1980–2019, Web of Science registered eight publications with "intersectionality, migration" in the title, all of which emerged between 2011 and 2019. However, this search engine retrieved 325 studies with "intersectionality, migration" not only in their title but also in their abstracts and keywords. From 2008 onwards, there was an uninterrupted increase in the number of such works. Their highest peak of 84 publications was reached in 2019. A significant change took place in 2017 after two years with the same number of publications, which was probably due to the new tendency among scholars to combine analytical perspectives such as intersectionality and transnationalism: for example, the Special Issue on "Transnational perspectives on

60 See Crenshaw (n 15).

61 Peter Adey, David Bissel, Kevin Hannam, Peter Merriman and Mimi Sheller (eds), *The Routledge Handbook of Mobilities* (Routledge 2014); Weert Canzler, Vincent Kaufmann and Sven Kesselring, *Tracing Mobilities: Towards a Cosmopolitan Perspective* (Ashgate 2008); Noel B. Salazar, *Momentous Mobilities. Anthropological Musings on the Meanings of Travel* (Berghahn 2018); John Urry, *Mobilities* (Polity Press 2007); and Tanu Priya Uteng and Tim Cresswell (eds), *Gendered Mobilities* (Ashgate 2008).

intersecting experiences"[62] in *Journal of Ethnic and Migration Studies*. Out of 325 publications identified from Web of Science, 233 contained "gender" in their title, abstract, and keywords. Most of these publications appeared during the period 2011–2019, which is in line with the results of the Google Scholar search: 27 of 28 publications with "intersectionality, migration" in the title came out in the same period.

Concerning the mobility perspective, between 1980 and 2019, Web of Science registered 1,062 publications with "mobility, migration" in the title, and the largest number (714) appeared in the period 2011–2019. The number of these publications started with seven in 2000 and reached its highest point in 2019 with 121 studies. This increase coincided with an increased number of citations per year: from 41 in 2000 to 1,589 in 2019. When the search for "mobility, migration" included abstracts and keywords, Web of Science gave 18,720 results. However, the publications identified did not concern human migration alone but encompassed other types of movement from particles to ions and from cells to birds. The same observation also applied to the 1,220,000 works with "mobility, migration" elsewhere in the text retrieved by Google Scholar. Thus, it was more useful to search only for publications with "mobility, migration" in the title, giving 3,160 results of which 1,680 appeared between 2011 and 2019. As regards gender, in a search of Web of Science from 1980 to 2019, only 27 studies had "gender, mobility, migration" in their title, with the highest number – five publications – in 2009. When the search covered title, abstract, and keywords, it identified 1,044 publications. The largest increase in their number occurred in 2011 with 51 publications, up from 35 the preceding year. The highest peak was in 2019 with 159 publications. The influence of the mobility perspective in migration studies, as evident in the data presented above, rose following the launch of the journal *Mobilities* and Berghahn's *Worlds in Motion* series. Both have published several studies on mobility and migration often with a gender perspective.[63]

Figure 5.4 compares the number of publications with the words "mobility, migration", and "intersectionality, migration" in the title identified by a search in Google Scholar. It clearly shows that whereas the transnationalisation of

---

62 Fresnoza-Flot and Shinozaki (n 6).

63 Noelle K. Brigden, 'Gender Mobility: Survival Plays and Performing Central American Migration in Passage' (2018) 13 (1) Mobilities 111; Christian Groes and Nadine T. Fernandez (eds), *Intimate Mobilities. Sexual Economies, Marriage and Migration in a Disparate World* (Berghahn 2018); and Dawn Lyon, Erica Capussotti and Ioanna Laliotou (eds), *Women Migrants from East to West: Gender, Mobility and Belonging in Contemporary Europe* (Berghahn 2007).

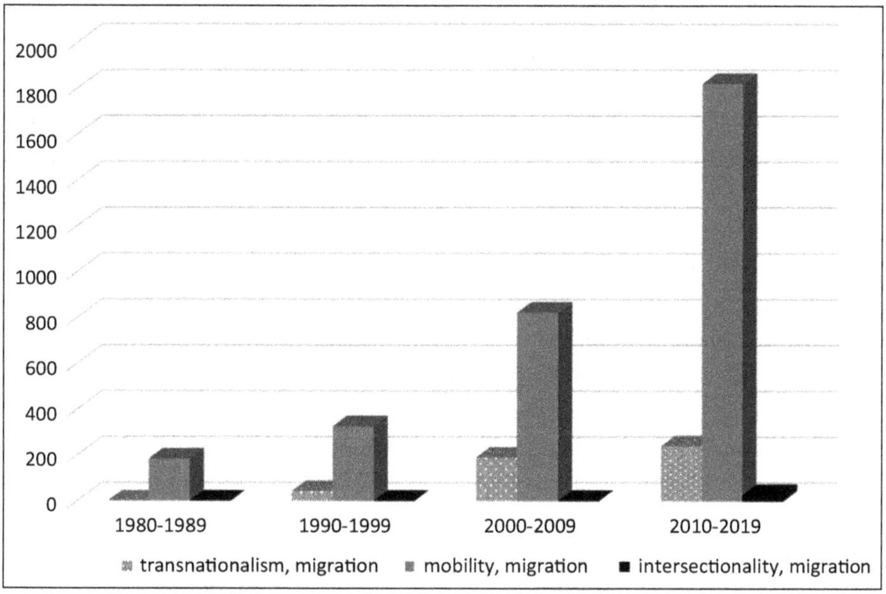

FIGURE 5.4 Google Scholar publications on transnationalism, mobility, and intersectionality

migration studies continues and the intersectionality approach is on the rise, the mobility perspective retains its dominant influence in the field. This dominance is probably due to the polyvalence of the "mobility" concept. Scholars in different research fields and disciplines are applying the concept in their inquiries, as well as combining it with other perspectives and approaches such as transnationalism and intersectionality (see for instance the Special Issue "Mobilities intersections"[64] in the journal *Mobilities*). Furthermore, it is noteworthy that the three analytical lenses above reinforce the value of the qualitative approach to migration studies. Web of Science, for instance, found more publications (523) with "gender, qualitative, migration" in their title, abstract, and keywords between 1980 and 2019 than with "gender, quantitative, migration" (236).

3.5 *Diversification of Research Focus*

In recent years, the research focus in the field of migration studies has diversified. Scholars are pursuing new lines of inquiry as migratory movements

64 Monika Büscher, Mimi Sheller and David Tyfield, 'Mobility Intersections: Social Research, Social Futures' (2016) 11 (4) Mobilities 485.

intensify. These include "super-diversity"[65] in global cities, migration of displaced people, and "family-related migration".[66]

"Super-diversity" is seen when various categories of difference such as religion, social class, ethnicity, and nationality intricately intersect at different facets of social life. The "decline of multiculturalism"[67] in Western countries has led to a rise in popularity of the "super-diversity" concept among migration scholars, most notably in Europe. Several publications using it as an analytical lens have revealed the heuristic value of this concept.[68] However, this burgeoning research field has been criticised for excluding from its analysis the "dimension of power" and for its "ethno-focal lens".[69] At the time of the bibliometric analysis presented here, 239 works in Google Scholar with "super-diversity" in the title were identified, but not one of them included "gender". Since a gender perspective considers power dynamics and processes, incorporating it in the analysis would be an effective solution to address the gaps above.

Another recent phenomenon that has been attracting scholarly attention, especially in Europe, involves asylum seekers and displaced people from war-torn and/or poverty-stricken countries in the Middle East and Africa. Since 2010, studies on migrant refugees have been increasing: Google Scholar showed 187 publications on this topic between 2000 and 2019, whereas Web of Science found 446. The latter search engine indicates that these works were mostly authored by scholars from major countries receiving displaced people: the USA, England, Australia, Germany, Canada, the Netherlands, Turkey, Italy, Sweden, and Switzerland. There are still only a few publications with "gender, refugees, migration" in their title: only five from 2000 to 2019. This suggests a need to engender the analysis of the movements of displaced people.

---

65 Steven Vertovec, 'Super-diversity and its Implications' (2007) 308 (6) Ethnic and Racial Studies 1024.

66 Eleonore Kofman, 'Family-related Migration: A Critical Review of European Studies' (2004) 30 (2) Journal of Ethnic and Migration Studies 243.

67 Amnon Rubinstein, 'The Decline, but not Demise, of Multiculturalism' (2007) 40 (3) Israel Law Review 763.

68 Mette Louise Berg, 'Super-diversity, Austerity, and the Production of Precarity: Latin Americans in London' (2019) 39 (2) Critical Social Policy 184; and Susanne Wessendorf, *Commonplace Diversity: Social Relations in a Super-diverse Context* (Palgrave 2014).

69 Nancy Foner, Jan Willem Duyvendak and Philip Kasinitz, 'Introduction: Super-diversity in Everyday Life' (2019) 42 Ethnic and Racial Studies 1, 3, 14.

Finally, the migratory wave that has intensified in recent years and has attracted the interest of scholars is related to families, notably migration by and/or for marriage leading to "mixed couples" with "different nationalities and/or ethnicities".[70] Web of Science retrieved 197 publications with "marriage, migration" in the title during the period 2000–2019. Aside from several articles and monographs, edited volumes[71], and Special Issues[72] on the subject mushroomed during the second decade of the 21st century. More and more publications have examined the migration by and/or for marriage through the prism of intimacy and mobility.[73] However, among the 197 publications identified in Web of Science, only 16 had "gender" in the title. None had "LGBTQ, marriage, migration" in the title. These two aspects represent a gap in this research field of marriage and migration.

3.6 *Expansion beyond the Core Disciplines*

Another significant development in migration studies is the unabated expansion beyond the borders of the core disciplines, namely geography, history, demography, sociology, anthropology, economics, and political science. This development can be mainly observed in theology and in biology. Web of Science and Google Scholar provide quantitative data showing the extent of this growth.

In theology, reflections on human migration can be traced back as far as the 1960s, during which the first initiatives took place: the organisation of "national and international theological conferences", and the publication of the "writings of some Scalabrinian missionaries" in Rome.[74] These missionaries

70 Betty de Hart, Wibo van Rossum and Iris Sportel, 'Law in the Everyday Lives of Transnational Families: An Introduction' (2013) 3 (6) Oñati Socio-Legal Series 995.

71 Nicole Constable (ed), *Cross-border Marriages: Gender and Mobility in Transnational Asia* (University of Pennsylvania Press 2010); see also Ishii (n 31) as well as Fresnoza-Flot and Ricordeau (n 31).

72 See Bonjour and de Hart (n 20); Beate Collet and Anne Unterrreiner, 'Introduction. Mixités conjugales et Familiales' (2017) 14 (1) Recherches familiales 49; Hélène Le Bail, Marylène Lieber and Gwénola Ricordeau, 'Migrations par le Mariage et Intimités transnationales' (2018) 64 (1) Cahiers du Genre 5 ; Maïté Maskens, 'L'amour et ses frontières: Régulations étatiques et migrations de mariage (Belgique, France, Suisse et Italie)' (2013) 150 (6) Migrations société 41; Moret et al. (n 20); and Laura Odasso, 'Introduction. Special Issue "Migration, amour et état: Un ménage à trois"' (2015) 85 Revue de l'Institut de Sociologie 11.

73 See Groes and Fernandez (n 63).

74 Gioacchino Campese, 'The Irruption of Migrants: Theology of Migration in the 21st Century' (2012) 73 (1) Theological Studies 7.

founded Centres for Migration Studies in seven cities around the world to gain "a deeper understanding of migration in all its aspects": "New York, Paris, Rome, Cape Town, São Paulo, Buenos Aires, and Manila".[75] It was in the late 1970s in the USA that "the first attempts to craft a theology of migration" were made.[76] During the first decade of the 21st century, several theological gatherings took place and publications appeared. In 2008, Groody and Campese proposed a theology of immigration in their book *A promised land. A perilous journey.*[77] The following years witnessed the publication of several books[78] and articles, notably in the journal *Theological Studies*. Since it first began, theology of migration has promoted interdisciplinarity, drawing from different disciplines of migration. It is not surprising that the Centres for Migration Studies that the Scalabrinian missionaries founded are the home of some of the leading journals in the broader field of migration studies, such as *International Migration Review* and the *Asian and Pacific Migration Journal*.

Quantitatively speaking, of the four decades from 1980–2019, Web of Science and Google Scholar identified the second decade of the 21st century as the period with the highest number of publications with "theology, migration" in the title: 37 and 83 respectively. Hence, the second decade of the 21st century marks the sharp take-off of the theology of migration. This development coincided with the surge of scholarly interest in religion in the broader field of migration studies. As Google Scholar reveals, this increase started in the period from 1990 to 1999 when 69 publications had "religion, migration" in the title. This number more than doubled between 2000 and 2009, but the peak was reached in the period 2010–2019 with 389 publications (see Figure 5.5), as confirmed by Web of Science. During the same period, six publications appeared with "gender, religion, migration" in the title. However, there are so far no publications with "gender, theology, migration" in the title in Web of Science, which indicates a critical gap to address in the theological study of migration.

75 Scalabriniani, *Networks of Study Centers* (2015) <https://www.scalabriniani.org/en/federazione-dei-centri-di-studio-sulle-migrazioni/> accessed 28 November 2020.

76 ibid.

77 Daniel G. Groody and Gioacchino Campese (eds), *A Promised Land, a Perilous Journey. Theological Perspectives on Migration* (University of Notre Dame Press 2008).

78 Gemma T. Cruz, *An Intercultural Theology of Migration. Pilgrims in the Wilderness* (Brill 2010); Judith Gruber and Sigrid Rettenbacher (eds), *Migration as a Sign of the Times. Towards a Theology of Migration* (Brill 2015); and Kristin E. Heyer, *Kinship across Borders: A Christian Ethic of Immigration* (Georgetown University Press 2012).

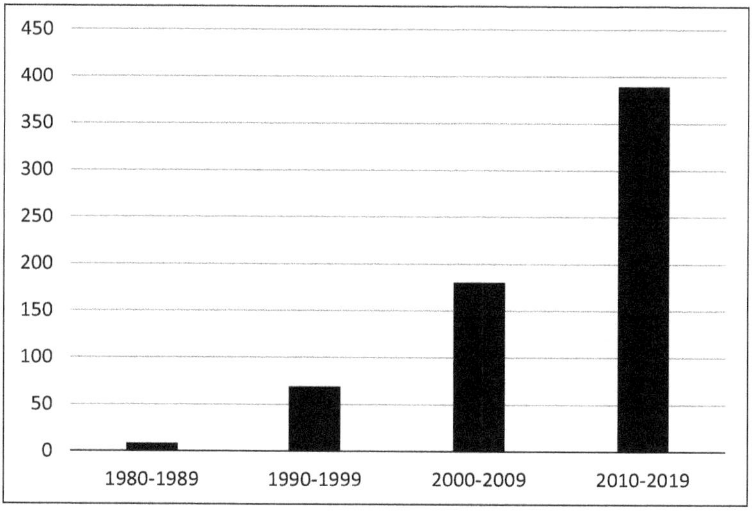

FIGURE 5.5 Google Scholar publications with religion and migration in the title

Since the 2000s, the biological research field of genetics has been contributing new findings regarding migration by analysing human DNA (deoxyribonucleic acid). This process involves examining the Y chromosome that fathers pass on to their male children and/or the mitochondrial DNA (mtDNA) that mothers transfer to both their male and female offspring. Studies employing these methods provide fresh knowledge on human mobility across time and geographical spaces. For example, mtDNA analysis has shown that the early waves of human migration occurred first within Africa, specifically from the region called "Makgadikgadi"[79] in Southern Africa, before proceeding to different continents.[80] Like the theology of migration, the genetic study of human mobility promotes interdisciplinarity. Scholars in this field integrate and draw from various disciplines such as anthropology, archaeology, paleoclimatology, and linguistics to obtain evidence corroborating their DNA

79 See the latest findings regarding the "cradle of humanity" by Eva K. F. Chan, Axel Timmermann, Benedetta F. Baldi, Andy E. Moore, Ruth J. Lyons, Sun-Seon Lee, Anton M. F. Kalsbeek, Desiree C. Petersen, Hannes Rautenbach, Hagen E. A. Förtsch, M. S. Riana Bornman and Vanessa M. Hayes, 'Human Origins in a Southern African Palaeo-wetland and First Migrations' (2019) 575 (7781) Nature 185.

80 See also mtDNA "haplogroup migration pattern" in Michelangelo Mancuso, Massimiliano Filosto, Daniele Orsucci and Gabriele Siciliano, 'Mitochondrial DNA Sequence Variation and Neurodegeneration' (2008) 3 (1) Human genomics 71.

analysis. Recently, Reich has demonstrated the value of analyses of ancient human DNA in the study of human mobility.[81] Studies using this method contribute to refuting or calling into question racialising stereotypes and discourses regarding majority and minority populations in society. They also help us understand power inequalities in the past that left genetic imprints on the present-day human population. For example, Reich discusses[82] how the analysis of the Y chromosome can identify "star clusters" in which a population of men sharing a common male ancestor is spread across many countries and generations.

Despite its novel findings, genetic research on migration appears to be gaining ground more slowly than the theology of migration in quantitative terms. Google Scholar and Web of Science identified only 12 and 8 publications, respectively, with "genetics, human migration" in the title between 2000 and 2019. Likewise, these search engines found only 41 and 29 works, respectively, with "DNA, human migration" in the title, and not all of these studies focused on human migration. Moreover, no publications with "gender, DNA, human migration" and "gender, genetics, human migration" in the title were retrieved by Web of Science. As with theology of migration, there is a need in this new field of migration research to adopt a gender frame in the analysis, a lens that focuses on relational aspects and moves beyond the mere description of differences between sex categories of "male" and "female".

4 Discussion and Conclusion

The present chapter provides new insights regarding the state of gender and migration scholarship and on the broader migration studies. It unveils lacunas that should be addressed to attain gender equality in migration studies and to deepen the reflection about the gender–power nexus in this research field.

Based on the quantitative data and, to a lesser extent, on the qualitative data analyses, the gender gaps in migration studies identified in this chapter can be summarised as follows. First, the visibility of women, or for other scholars the "over-visibility of women" in migration studies, unintentionally leads to feminised gender in the field, which overlooks other socially constructed categories of difference and the dynamics of power among them. Hence, the

81 David Reich, *Who We are and How We Got Here: Ancient DNA and the New Science of the Human Past* (Oxford University Press 2018).

82 ibid.

numerical dominance of migrant men that we observe in present-day migration statistics does not automatically translate into many more publications about them compared to research focusing on migrant women. Second, heteronormativity still prevails in migration studies, which slows down the inclusion of sexuality and queer perspectives. This explains why the voices and experiences of LGBTQ migrants, notably beyond Europe and the USA, remain marginal in migration scholarship compared to their heterosexual counterparts. And third, although gender and migration scholarship has brought to the fore the analytical effectiveness of a gender approach to migration, its influence has not yet permeated the broader migration studies: for example, the theology of migration and genetic studies of human mobility. The reflex of "bringing gender in"[83], therefore, does not appear to be well developed in this field as yet.

There are at least three factors that can explain the gaps described above, which are not necessarily related to one another. First, since the evolution of gender and migration scholarship across countries and regions is not uniform, neither are the broader migration studies; there are many socio-geographic contexts in the world where gender and migration research is still in its first or second phase of development. Second, the compartmentalised "nature of social science"[84] engenders compartmentalised migration studies in which scholars continue to working within the constraints of their disciplines or research areas, with little or no contact or dialogue with scholars outside their fields. And third, there is also a compartmentalised geography of migration studies reflecting the "Global South–Global North" relations of inequalities. Widely held theoretical perspectives on migration still originate mostly from the "Global North" and scholars from this region still dominate in terms of the number of publications and research outputs on human mobility.

To address the non-uniform development and compartmentalised characteristics of transnational migration studies, the present chapter calls for more analytical rigour in migration research. This can be achieved in three ways: adopting an intersectional approach, considering its "*contextuality*", and paying attention to "the issue of simultaneity in analysing transnational experiences and practices".[85] The lens of transnationalism appears effective

83 Patricia R. Pessar and Sarah J. Mahler, 'Transnational Migration: Bringing Gender In' (2003) 37 (3) International Migration Review 812.

84 Hondagneu-Sotelo (n 9) 227.

85 Fresnoza-Flot and Shinozaki (n 6) 875.

to pursue inclusiveness in migration studies as it compels scholars to expand their analytical horizons to the societies of origin of migrants, their historical ties (colonial or post-colonial) with migrant-receiving countries, the social and legal norms that prevail, and their influence on migrants' lives, positionality and sense-making. Combining the lens of transnationalism with other analytical approaches, such as intersectionality, makes it powerful tool to unveil the nuances and subtleties of migrants' experiences.

Furthermore, there is a need for immediate transnational collaborative actions to bring migration studies to the next level by making the field more diversified, interdisciplinary, and gender sensitive. These actions will entail cooperation among scholars with diverse socio-demographic backgrounds, working in distinct research fields and disciplines, from economically developing and developed countries, as well as at different stages in their research and/or academic careers. Such cooperation can take various forms, such as collaborative research projects, sharing data, co-authoring scholarly publications, co-organising scientific events such as seminars and conferences, or making these events accessible to researchers with little or no funding, particularly in the times of a global pandemic that exacerbates the social inequalities around the world. It is through these collaborations that scholars can avoid "methodological nationalism",[86] remedy the "unequal internationalization"[87]of the field, and, by doing so, reduce inequalities in knowledge production. Transnational collaborations are urgently needed to understand human migration in terms of the gender–power nexus.

Acknowledgements

Previous versions of this chapter were presented at two events in Switzerland: the *Know the GAP Lecture Series* focusing on "Talking gender, equality and diversity" at the World Trade Institute (WTI) at the University of Bern on 19 February 2020; and as a keynote lecture on 2 July 2021 during the 4th Neuchâtel Graduate Conference of Migration and Mobility Studies organised by the NCCR – On the Move of the Swiss National Science Foundation. I thank

86 Andreas Wimmer and Nina Glick Schiller, 'Methodological Nationalism and Beyond: Nation-state Building, Migration and the Social Sciences' (2002) 2 (4) Global Networks 301.

87 Eleonore Kofman, 'Unequal Internationalisation and the Emergence of a New Epistemic Community: Gender and Migration' (2020) 8 (36) Comparative Migration Studies 2.

Elisa Fornalé of the WTI, Robin Stünzi of the NCCR – On the Move, and Janine Dahinden of University of Neuchâtel for giving me the opportunity to share my analysis and reflections regarding gender gaps in migration studies.

References

Adey P, Bissel D, Hannam K, Merriman P and Sheller M (eds), *The Routledge Handbook of Mobilities* (Routledge 2014).

Amelina A and Lutz H, *Gender and Migration: Transnational and Intersectional Prospects* (Routledge 2019).

Basch LG, Glick Schiller N and Szanton Blanc C, *Nations Unbound. Transnational Projects, Postcolonial Predicaments, and Deterritorialized Nation-states* (Gordon and Breach 1995).

Bryceson DF and Vuorela U (eds), *The Transnational Family: New European Frontiers and Global Networks* (Berg 2002).

Canzler W, Kaufmann V and Kesselring S, *Tracing Mobilities: Towards a Cosmopolitan Perspective* (Ashgate 2008).

Cantú Jr. L, *Border Crossings: Mexican Men and the Sexuality of Migration*. PhD dissertation (University of California 1999).

Carrillo H, *Pathways of Desire: The Sexual Migration of Mexican Gay Men* (University of Chicago Press 2017).

Charsley K (ed), *Transnational Marriage: New Perspectives from Europe and Beyond* (Routledge 2012).

Fresnoza-Flot A and Ricordeau G (eds), *International Marriages and Marital Citizenship: Southeast Asian Women on the Move* (Routledge 2017).

Constable N, *Maid to Order in Hong Kong: Stories of Filipina Workers* (Cornell University Press 1997).

Constable N (ed), *Cross-border Marriages: Gender and Mobility in Transnational Asia* (University of Pennsylvania Press 2010).

Cruz G T, *An Intercultural Theology of Migration. Pilgrims in the Wilderness* (Brill 2010).

Dreby J, *Divided by Borders: Mexican Migrants and their Children* (University of California Press 2010).

Gabaccia DR (ed), *Seeking Ground: Multidisciplinary Studies of Immigrant Women in the United States* (Greenwood Press 1992).

Gallo E and Scrinzi F, *Migration, Masculinities and Reproductive Labour. Men of the Home* (Palgrave 2016).

Groes C and Fernandez NT (eds), *Intimate Mobilities. Sexual Economies, Marriage and Migration in a Disparate World* (Berghahn 2018).

Groody D G and Campese G (eds), *A Promised Land, a Perilous Journey. Theological Perspectives on Migration* (University of Notre Dame Press 2008).

Gruber J and Rettenbacher S (eds), *Migration as a Sign of the Times. Towards a Theology of Migration* (Brill 2015).

Hill Collins P, *Black Feminist Thought: Knowledge, Consciousness, and Politics of Empowerment* (Unwin Hyman 1990).

Hondagneu-Sotelo P, *Gendered Transitions: Mexican Experiences of Immigration* (University of California Press 1994).

Henshall Momsen J (ed), *Gender, Migration, and Domestic Service* (Routledge 1999).

Heyer K E, *Kinship across Borders: A Christian Ethic of Immigrat*ion (Georgetown University Press 2012).

Ishii S K (ed), *Marriage Migration in Asia: Emerging Minorities at the Frontiers of Nation-States* (NUS Press 2016).

Kilkey M, Perrons D and Plomien A, *Gender, Migration and Domestic Work: Masculinities, Male Labour and Fathering in the UK and USA* (Palgrave 2013).

Lan PC, *Global Cinderellas: Migrant Domestics and Newly Rich Employers in Taiwan* (Duke University Press 2006).

Luibhéid E and Cantú L Jr., *Queer Migrations: Sexuality, US Citizenship, and Border Crossings* (University of Minnesota Press 2005).

Lutz H, *The New Maids: Transnational Women and the Care Economy* (Zed Books Ltd. 2011).

Mills MB, *Thai Women in the Global Labor Force: Consuming Desires, Contested Selves* (Rutgers University Press 1999).

Lyon D, Capussotti E and Laliotou I (eds), *Women Migrants from East to West: Gender, Mobility and Belonging in Contemporary Europe* (Berghahn 2007).

Muchoki S, *Intimacies, Citizenship and Refugee Men* (Springer 2016).

Oishi N, *Women in Motion: Globalization, State Policies, and Labor Migration in Asia* (Stanford University Press 2005).

Palriwala R and Uberoi P (eds), *Marriage, Migration and Gender* (Sage 2008).

Parreñas RS, *Servants of Globalization. Women, Migration and Domestic Work* (Stanford University Press 2001).

Piper N and Roces M (eds), *Wife or Worker?: Asian Women and Migration* (Rowman & Littlefield Publishers 2003).

Reich D, *Who We are and How We Got Here: Ancient DNA and the New Science of the Human Past* (Oxford University Press 2018).

Salazar NB, *Momentous Mobilities. Anthropological Musings on the Meanings of Travel* (Berghahn 2018).

Uteng T P and Cresswell T (eds), *Gendered Mobilities* (Ashgate 2008).

Urry J, *Mobilities* (Polity Press 2007).

Zontini E, *Transnational Families, Migration and Gender: Moroccan and Filipino Women in Bologna and Barcelona* (Berghahn 2010).

Wessendorf S, *Commonplace Diversity: Social Relations in a Super-diverse Context* (Palgrave 2014).

CHAPTER 6

Unpaid Work during the COVID-19 Pandemic

Amount, Allocation and the Aftermath: A European Perspective

Zsuzsa Blaskó

1 Introduction

The division of unpaid work between men and women has long been a central theme of scholarly work on gender inequalities and with very good reasons.[1] Household duties and caring for family members were considered female territories in the past and the underlying gender norms as well as the actual practice have changed surprisingly little considering the massive changes in other spheres of life. Despite their active participation in the labour market, women still shoulder most of the domestic labour and their home responsibilities continue to be a major factor behind their labour market disadvantages.[2]

One of the most immediate and profound social consequences of the COVID-19 crisis hit exactly this area of persistent gender inequalities: the sphere of domestic work. With social distancing measures forcing a large part of the population – children included – to carry out their daily activities in their homes, the amount of domestic work was bound to expand and family life to be reorganised. It was expected that the change would be most marked in households with (younger) children, where institutional care and education needed to be replaced by parental effort. Consideration of these disruptions led to two parallel predictions concerning the crisis' longer-term impact on gender equality. The stronger, pessimistic argument warned about the possible implications of women continuing to do the major part of the excessive household duties during lockdowns, while the second, optimistic suggestion

1 The views expressed are purely those of the author and may not in any circumstance be regarded as stating an official position of the European Commission. The author would like to thank to Beatrice D'Hombres for her support and helpful comments on an earlier version of this chapter. This manuscript was closed in May 2021.

2 E.g. Man Yee Kan et al., 'Gender Convergence in Domestic Work: Discerning the Effects of Interactional and Institutional Barriers from Large-Scale Data' (2011) 45 (2) Sociology 234.

 | DOI:10.1163/9789004467682_008

considered men's potentially increasing contributions to these duties and some of the benefits that might arise.[3]

From the beginning it was expected that women would continue to undertake the major share of the potentially excessive workload, both childcare and chores. This assumption was to a large extent based on pre-COVID research evidence on how households organise their duties in normal times and on how prevailing gender norms and the labour market status of men and women reinforce the gendered allocation of work in the household. From this scenario a major risk follows: the massive household burden might jeopardise women's employment prospects, both in the short and in the long run, thus further widening the gender gap in employment.

At the same time, however, a carefully phrased positive scenario also appeared. Once again based on pre-COVID knowledge, scholars expected that also men would substantially increase the time they spent on household duties – even if they remained the secondary care providers in the vast majority of households. If such a behavioural change were to take place, it could then generate a shift towards a somewhat more equal division of tasks as well as more egalitarian gender norms that could persist in the longer term.

While "predictions" and "speculations" at the time, one year later we are already in a (somewhat) better position to re-examine these early scenario in the light of new evidence collected during the first year of the pandemic. This chapter brings together pre-COVID research evidence and early-COVID predictions and compares them with empirical research findings on the gendered division of unpaid labour from the first pandemic lockdown period in Europe. Our review of the available evidence shows that COVID-19 studies tend to support, albeit not (yet) fully confirm the early hypotheses. The lockdown situation did indeed force women, particularly mothers, into balancing a heavy workload – both paid and unpaid. But, at the same time, many men increased their involvement in household duties to unprecedented levels. After describing these main tendencies, we move on to the two more complex questions and discuss the possible consequences of these substantial changes. First, we look at the possible labour market effects of women's increased household burden, considering both the short- and the long-term consequences. We then discuss the possibility of a shift towards more egalitarian gender norms; that

3 United Nations, 'The Impact of COVID-19 on Women' (2020) Policy Brief; Titan Alon et al., 'The Impact of COVID-19 on Gender Equality' (2020) NBER Working Paper No. 26947; Zsuzsa Blaskó et al., 'How Will the COVID-19 Crisis Affect Existing Gender Divides in Europe?' (2020) Publications Office of the European Union.

is, towards more support for a gender-equal distribution of labour in Europe. Undoubtedly, this prediction is the most difficult one to assess at this stage.

Our discussion is limited to Europe[4], a – relatively – homogenous set of countries. Unfortunately, data is still too limited to allow an in-depth and full exploration, let alone to enable us to understand cross-country differences within Europe. The existence of such differences, however, is more than likely given the variations in the cultural- and institutional conditions. Nevertheless, keeping such a focus also helps to call attention to the need to avoid automatically applying findings from other contexts to Europe – using them instead to cross-fertilise European investigations. Finally, notwithstanding the heterogeneity across countries, most European societies are still among the highest achievers in gender equality globally. Due to path-dependence,[5] it is very likely that whatever negative impact the crisis has on gender equality in Europe, it is still relatively moderate when compared to the global situation.

The aim of this chapter is to provide a first assessment, and not a complete review with definitive answers to the questions raised. This is due both to the long-term nature of these questions and to the limitations of data availability. First, more than a year since the pandemic started, the situation is still evolving and measures, including those that are important from a gender perspective, are still in effect in most European countries. Second, data and research evidence is also limited even many months on from the start of the pandemic. In some areas, available evidence remains scattered and certain details of the underlying mechanisms might never be measured. This is because research and data collection are time-consuming and costly processes and (understandably) the research sector could not keep pace with the speed of the changes and collect evidence on all the relevant aspects.

Importantly, we do not have internationally comparable real-time data on how household members spent their time in lockdown, and most probably never will.[6] Still we are very fortunate to have such data from several European

---

4 In this chapter by Europe, we mean the 27 Members States of the EU plus the United Kingdom.

5 World Economic Forum, 'Global Gender Gap Report 2020' <weforum.org> accessed 23 June 2021.

6 Eurofound's Living, working and COVID-19 online survey, although a rich and important resource in many regards, is unfortunately not very useful here. As it collected time use information in the second and not in the first wave of the survey, it only provides such data for the summer period when school closures were no longer key factors in shaping parental time use.

countries that also represent various welfare regimes in Europe.[7] In particular, we will discuss research findings from the UK (liberal regime), the Netherlands and Germany (conservative); Italy and Spain (Mediterranean) and Hungary (post-socialist).[8] The small number of studies and the variations in the research methodologies preclude linking the heterogeneities in the findings to the characteristics of the regimes. However, any similarities found across these countries are important, as they are likely to represent general tendencies that persist in Europe despite the variations in structural and cultural circumstances and national COVID-19 responses.

2 Amount: a Heavily Increased Workload in the Households

The change that COVID-19 wrought on homes and families all over the world is massive and unprecedented. From a place that primarily served as a site for recreation and private life, households were transformed into an environment with multiple functions where adults and children alike spent the greater part of their days for several weeks or even months in 2020 and early 2021. The changes were driven by some widely applied confinement measures: mainly the physical closure of schools and childcare institutions but also by teleworking and social distancing measures that reduced the mobility of people between households.

By far the most significant change in the amount of unpaid work occurred in households with children and in periods when schools and childcare institutions were closed. During these times, younger children required full-time care to be provided at home while school-age children needed support with distance learning. Without school-meals provided, regular meal-preparation was needed and also additional household chores could appear. At the same time, stay-at-home requirements also limited access to external help. Grandparental help – a major childcare and sometimes housework support

---

7 Gosta Esping-Andersen, *The Three Worlds of Welfare Capitalism* (Polity Press 1989); Gosta Esping-Andersen, *Social Foundations of Postindustrial Economies* (OUP 1999); Makiko Fuwa, 'Macro-Level Gender Inequality and the Division of Household Labor in 22 Countries' (2004) 69 American Sociological Review 751; Makiko Fuwa and Philip N Cohen, 'Housework and Social Policy' (2007) 36 Social Science Research 512; Tanja van der Lippe et al., 'Persistent Inequalities in Time Use between Men and Women: a Detailed Look at the Influence of Economic Circumstances, Policies, and Culture' (2011) 27 (2) European Sociological Review 164.

8 Unfortunately no comparable study from any Scandinavian regimes was found.

for many families – became unavailable[9] and access to paid domestic help was restricted.

A rapid shift to teleworking for many could also have had some impact on the workload in the household by increasing the demand for food consumed at home and possibly also for cleaning and small maintenance tasks. However, working from home was also key to meeting the increased demand for care provision when children had to stay at home. The Eurofound's Living, working and COVID-19 online survey survey suggests that in April 2020, 39% and in June up to 48% of European employees were working from home[10] – a massive and rapid increase from 2019 when only 5.4% of EU-27 employees "usually" worked from their homes.[11]

Consequently, parents have been facing a constantly and often unpredictably changing demand for care, home schooling and household work. The extent of this increase is likely to vary significantly by household type, demographic and other individual circumstances, as well as by country. Unfortunately, to the best of our knowledge, no cross-country research was carried out to document what was happening in the households across the European countries. At the same time a set of national studies are available from the first lockdown period to explore these issues. These provide important, albeit not fully comparable, insights into the extent of this increase and its consequences.[12] Several of these

---

9 Across ten European countries, the percentage of parents that regularly used grandparental support to look after their children varied between 4% (Denmark and Sweden) and 25% (Greece). Data from the SHARE study, 2004/05. Participating countries were Denmark, Sweden, the Netherlands, Germany, France, Austria, Belgium, Spain, Italy and Greece. Giorgio Di Gessa et al., 'What Drives National Differences in Intensive Grandparental Childcare in Europe?' (2016) 71 The Journals of Gerontology: Series B 141.

10 Eurofound, 'Living, Working and COVID-19 – First Findings – April 2020' (2020) Publications Office of the European Union; Eurofound, 'COVID-19: Implications for Employment and Working Life' (2021) Publications Office of the European Union.

11 Eurostat, 'Database' <europa.eu> accessed 29 November 2021.

12 This chapter mainly relies on findings from real-time national lockdown surveys in the UK (Alison Andrew et al., 'How Are Mothers and Fathers Balancing Work and Family Under Lockdown?' (2020) IFS Briefing Note BN290; Almudena Sevilla and Sarah Smith, 'Baby Steps: The Gender Division of Childcare during the COVID-19 Pandemic' (2020) 36 (S1) Oxford Review of Economic Policy S169); Spain (Lidia Farré et al., 'How The COVID-19 Lockdown Affected the Gender Equality in Paid and Unpaid Work in Spain' (2020) IZA DP No. 13434); Hungary (Éva Fodor et al., 'The Impact of COVID-19 on the Gender Division of Childcare Work in Hungary' (2020) 23 (S1) European Societies S95); Germany (Michaela Kreyenfeld et al., 'Coronavirus and Care: How the Coronavirus Crisis Affected Father's Involvement in Germany' (2021) 44 Demographic Research 99; Gundula Zoch et al., 'Who Cares When Care Closes? Care-Arrangements and Parental Working Conditions during the COVID-19 Pandemic in Germany' (2021) 23 (S1) European Societies S576; Lena Hipp and Mareike Bünnig, 'Parenthood as a Driver of Increased Gender Inequality during

studies (from the UK,[13] Spain,[14] Hungary,[15] and Germany[16]) asked the respondents to give an estimate of the number of hours spent on various activities. While the actual numbers of hours are difficult to compare across the studies, it is very indicative that the percentage increase compared to pre-COVID times in the overall time spent on childcare ranges from 25 to 70%.[17] One of the UK studies[18] even found that families with children below the age of 12 years reported an average of 40 additional hours spent on childcare, which is more than twice as much as they spent on such activities before the crisis.

The various studies used different approaches to differentiate by children's age, but there is little doubt that the biggest additional burden had to be shouldered in households with children of primary school age and younger. In Italy, for example, parents with a primary school-age child were twice as likely to report an increase in the time devoted to childcare than parents of lower secondary age children.[19] Distinguishing further among the youngest children, a German study found the increase in time spent on childcare to be the greatest among parents with children aged 3–5 years[20] and a Spanish survey[21] identified parents with children aged under 5 years as those who had to increase the time spent on childcare most significantly.

COVID-19? Exploratory Evidence from Germany' (2021) 23 (S1) European Societies S658); and the Netherlands (Mara Yerkes et al., "Intelligent' Lockdown, Intelligent Effects? Results from a Survey on Gender (in)Equality in Paid Work, the Division of Childcare and Household Work, and Quality of Life among Parents in the Netherlands during the Covid-19 Lockdown' (2020) 15 (11) PLoS One e0242249). Each of these real-time surveys were carried out in April–May 2020, during the first period of lockdown and school closure measures. They all used representative samples, either directly targeting the adult population with children in the household, or selecting such groups for some of the analyses. As the specification of the population studied as well as the modes of measurement varied, their findings are not directly comparable, but systematically put together, they nevertheless provide an insight into the main tendencies in the field.

13 Andrew et al. (n 12); Sevilla and Smith (n 12); Claudia Hupkau and Barbara Petrolongo, 'Work, Care and Gender During the Covid-19 Crisis' (2020) CEP Discussion Paper.

14 Farré et al. (n 12).

15 Fodor et al. (n 12).

16 Kreyenfeld et al. (n 12); Zoch et al. (n 12).

17 To calculate overall time used by the parents we aggregated mean number of hours reported by males and mean number of hours reported by females in the sample. This can be considered as a fair approximation of what was happening in the households as most of the studies only looked at two-parent households.

18 Sevilla and Smith (n 12).

19 Daniela Del Boca et al., 'Women's Work, Housework and Childcare, before and during COVID-19' (2020) IZA Discussion Papers.

20 Kreyenfeld et al. (n 12).

21 Farré et al. (n 12).

Data to quantify the change in time spent on housework is somewhat more limited, but, there again, research confirms that an increase was certainly taking place. In the Italian survey, around two-thirds of working women (mothers and childless) reported having devoted more time to such duties, while 40% said that their partner had (also) increased his involvement.[22] Estimates of weekly time spent on chores were only collected in the Spanish study. These show that men and women who live with children below the age of 16 years spent on average 23% more time on household work (childcare excluded) than before the pandemic.[23]

Thus, available evidence makes it clear that the crisis-enforced increase of unpaid work – especially childcare and home schooling – was significant and affected many families in Europe. Furthermore, in most countries it did so for prolonged periods during the first year of the pandemic. According to data from the United Nations Educational, Scientific and Cultural Organization, the number of weeks during which schools were closed across the entire country due to the pandemic up to 28 February 2021 added up to only 3 weeks in Denmark but reached 16–19 weeks in Bulgaria, Poland and the Czech Republic.[24] In most countries, there was more than one period of closure, responding to the various waves of the virus. Beyond the full, national school closures, additional regional or local measures for distance teaching were introduced, while individual institutions or classes were sometimes also quarantined to stop the spread of the virus. Moreover, confinement measures also curtailed children's extra-curricular activities. This meant that services that would usually help parents to keep children active after school and during school breaks became unavailable. All these conditions made the excessive workload measured during the first lockdowns a reality for a large part of the first pandemic year for millions of families across Europe.

3 Allocation: Women Doing the Lion's Share – but also a Real Shock for Men

Long before any new data appeared, there was little doubt that women would continue to bear most of the increased unpaid workload.[25] This was a logical

22 Del Boca et al. (n 19).

23 Farré et al. (n 12).

24 UNESCO, 'Education: From Disruption to Recovery' <unesco.org> accessed 29 November 2021. Author's calculations: Sweden was the only country in Europe whose schools never fully closed.

25 Alon et al. (n 3).

expectation, following from the strongly gendered pre-COVID task allocations as well as the related gender norms in Europe. First, research has consistently shown that despite some convergence, domestic work has remained rather unequally distributed within couples, with women spending significantly more time on, and taking the main responsibility for, these activities.[26] Second, prevailing gender norms in Europe are still often centred around the idea of female home-making and intensive motherhood,[27] both of which raise expectations that women will respond more than men to newly emerging household tasks.

The lockdown surveys reviewed here uniformly confirm that women on average were doing substantially more care and housework during the crisis than men did, so the allocation of work remained highly unbalanced even in this period of extreme unpaid workloads. While men also increased their contributions, the size of the *absolute* gap between males and females grew larger when compared to pre-COVID times. Based on the surveys measuring hours spent on different activities we can calculate that, during an average lockdown week, women were engaged in childcare for 12 to 19 hours longer than men,[28] or even more.[29] These estimated time gaps are either comparable to – or notably bigger than they were in pre-COVID times, depending on the study we look at.

Moreover, studies also agree that, at most, a small proportion of this gap can be explained by the employment situation of the partners. Overall, women's childcare (and household) involvement was less dependent on their employment situation than men's.[30] Consequently, mothers who continued doing paid work during the lockdowns had to bear particularly heavy loads. In Germany, for example, even the incidence of exclusive maternal care remained unchanged also when mothers did more hours of paid work than before the pandemic.[31]

It is less clear how mothers in the various working situations differed in their responses to the crisis. In the UK, working mothers reported very similar numbers of additional childcare hours, irrespective of their place of employment, but they took on less extra childcare responsibilities than did

26 E.g. Jennifer L Hook, 'Gender Inequality in the Welfare State: Sex Segregation in Housework' 1965–2003 (2010) 115 (5) American Journal of Sociology 1480; Kan et al. (n 2).

27 Daniela Grunow et al., 'Gender Ideologies in Europe: a Multidimensional Framework' (2018) 80 (1) Journal of Marriage and Family 42.

28 Andrew et al. (n 12); Fodor et al. (n 12); Sevilla and Smith (n 12); Hupkau and Petrolongo (n 13).

29 Kreyenfeld et al. (n 12).

30 Sevilla and Smith (n 12); Del Boca et al. (n 19); Farré et al. (n 12); Fodor et al. (n 12).

31 Zoch et al. (n 12).

non-working mothers.[32] In Hungary, on the other hand, teleworking mothers spent on average 6 hours per week more on childcare than women working from their workplaces did.[33] No difference in the probability of increasing the time spent on childcare was found between teleworking and non-working women in Italy, while women working from their workplaces were less likely to make changes.[34]

Together with the worryingly large increase in women's burden, a substantial growth in paternal involvement as measured in actual hours was also reported. In fact, the results from several studies suggest that the average *relative* gender gap (e.g. calculated as men's share of the overall parenting time) remained largely unchanged during the lockdown, implying a massive increase in fathers' involvement too.[35] The only study that also looked closely at housework even found an increase in the share of men's contribution to that.[36] In absolute terms, the surveys show that fathers on average increased their weekly contribution to childcare by at least 5–7 hours,[37] but potentially up to around 18 hours or more[38] depending on the country as well as on how exactly the contribution was measured.

Unlike mothers, fathers were most likely to react to the lockdown with an increased involvement in childcare if they found themselves without paid work. In the UK, both furloughed and non-working fathers did several hours more childcare per week than either teleworking or workplace-based men[39] and similar patterns were found in Hungary.[40] To a lesser extent, men also adjusted to their partners' employment situation. Italian men were more likely to increase their involvement in childcare if their partner was working either from home or at the workplace.[41] Men in Spain were also more likely to adapt to their partners' status than women did.[42]

There is little doubt that many details of households' adjustment to the crisis remain hidden and, although likely, cross-country variations have not been studied. However, the case studies already provide strong evidence on some

32 Sevilla and Smith (n 12).
33 Fodor et al. (n 12).
34 Del Boca et al. (n 19).
35 Fodor et al. (n 12); Farré et al. (n 12); Sevilla and Smith (n 12); Kreyenfeld et al. (n 12).
36 Farré et al. (n 12).
37 Farré et al. (n 12); Fodor et al. (n 12).
38 Kreyenfeld et al. (n 12); Sevilla and Smith (n 12); Andrew et al. (n 12).
39 Fodor et al. (n 12).
40 ibid.
41 Del Boca et al. (n 19).
42 Farré et al. (n 12).

major trends. Women with young children were extremely overloaded during the lockdown, especially if they continued working. This remains true even though many fathers made massive contributions and shared part of the burden. We now consider two possible major consequences of the increase – and the reallocation – of household tasks during the pandemic. We start with the pessimistic proposal, which claims that sooner or later, women would have to face negative labour market consequences due to their increased family responsibilities during the pandemic. Then we move on to evaluating the more optimistic scenario proposing that the increased paternal involvement could generate a shift towards more equal gender roles in Europe.

4 The Aftermath

4.1 *Could Women's Employment be Affected?*

The massive unpaid workload mothers had to shoulder during the pandemic is in itself a cause for concern, as it is most likely to have had adverse effects on their wellbeing.[43] But it is also feared that it will negatively affect their employment prospects both in the short and the longer run and thus widen the gender gap in the labour market. It has been widely suggested that this de-equalising effect would come on top of another main trend that put women in a particularly vulnerable labour market position in this crisis, which is the typically female occupations' and economic sectors' greater susceptibility to furloughs and dismissals.[44] While the consequences of pre-existing gender segregation in the labour market constitute an important gender aspect of the crisis, we continue to focus here on unpaid work and on trying to understand whether women's employment prospects can indeed be further affected by their increased workload in the household.

To answer this question, we look first at some related discussions and research findings from the USA, where the concerns about some very direct gender impacts of the crisis were first raised. In particular, Alon and his colleagues[45] suggested very early on that women might respond to their increased

43 E.g. Hipp and Bünning (n 12); Katja Möhring et al., 'The COVID-19 Pandemic and Subjective Well-Being: Longitudinal Evidence on Satisfaction with Work and Family' (2021) 23 (S1) European Societies S601.

44 Alon et al. (n 3); ILO, 'ILO Monitor: COVID-19 and the World of Work. Fifth Edition' (2020); Eleni Papadimitriou and Zsuzsa Blaskó, 'Economic Sectors at Risk Due to COVID-19 Disruptions: Will Men and Women in the EU be Affected Similarly?' (2020) JRC Science for Policy Report.

45 Alon et al. (n 3).

care responsibilities by temporarily dropping out of the labour market altogether. At the time, this suggestion appeared somewhat too extreme from a European perspective,[46] given the better availability of leave options and flexible work arrangements at least in some of the European countries, as well as the short-time work schemes put in place shortly after the outbreak of the virus.

Immediately quitting the labour market, however, is not the only way in which employment of women can be affected by their caring responsibilities. To accommodate the family's needs, women can also reduce their work hours while remaining in employment. This is possible either by taking various forms of paid and unpaid leave or by reducing the number of working hours in other ways. Cumulatively, such disruptions might result in skill losses leading to reduced wages and more limited career prospects in the longer run, creating a loss similar to the motherhood penalty – a well-known consequence of taking maternal leave or reducing working hours to care for young children even in "normal" times.[47] Thus, COVID-19-induced work-time reduction could take its toll later on, contributing to long-term increases in gender inequality by increasing both the employment gap and the gender pay gap.

US data confirms predictions that the present crisis is very different from earlier ones in having a more negative impact on women's than on men's employment.[48] Moreover, a growing body of US evidence suggests that the reduction in women's presence in the labour market is at least partially attributable to their growing care responsibilities. Researchers calculate that opening schools earlier rather than later and thus relieving women of the additional burden of home education and making it possible for them to re-enter the labour market, could help to avoid a large part of their recession-induced relative skill losses. This could also substantially mitigate the expected COVID-induced increase in the gender wage-gap.[49] In a US study from May to June 2020, 13% of the working parents surveyed reported having lost their job or having reduced their working hours due to lack of childcare. Among those who lost their jobs, a quarter of the women, but only an eighth of the men, cited lack of childcare

46 Papadimitriou and Blasko (n 44).

47 Ewa Cukrowska-Torzewska and Anna Matysiak, 'The Motherhood Wage Penalty: a Meta-Analysis' (2020) 88–89 Social Science Research 1.

48 Titan Alon et al., 'This Time It's Different: The Role of Women's Employment in a Pandemic Recession' (2020) NBER Working Paper No. 27660.

49 Alon et al. (n 48).

as the reason for this.[50] Finally, a study that used temporal and geographical variations in the US pandemic-related school closures to identify their impacts found that parents with children aged 6–12 years decreased their working hours when schools were closed, and this reduction was significantly bigger for women than for men.[51]

In Europe, the overall gender balance of the crisis in the labour market is not yet fully clear. Not only are the consequences still unfolding, the tendencies also vary across countries as changes appear at a very different pace, depending both on the spread of the virus and the particular national policies applied to mitigate the effects. Overall, the initial shock seemed to have hit women harder. Across the 27 EU Member States, the overall number of working hours as well as the level of employment declined more sharply for women than for men in the first half of 2020 according to Eurostat.[52] Looking at the first three-quarters of 2020, the European Institute for Gender Equality (EIGE) also finds that the recovery is slower for women and suggests that this might indicate longer-lasting impacts for women than for men.[53] Data from the last months of 2020, however, do not justify this concern. Instead, they show that, compared to one year earlier, men's employment reduced more significantly both in relative and in absolute terms, with only a small number of countries displaying opposite tendencies.[54]

Even if the fear of an overall bigger employment loss for women remains unjustified, the question is valid: can we link any aspect of European women's employment losses to their childcare responsibilities? Research on this topic so far is limited and inconclusive. Some evidence comes from detailed analyses of the UK lockdown surveys. In their analysis, Andrew and her colleagues[55] control for occupation as well as the percentage of tasks that can be done at home. They test whether gender differences in these could explain women's

50 Alicia Sasser Modestino et al., 'The Importance of Childcare in Reopening the Economy' Econofact (29 July 2020) <https://econofact.org/the-importance-of-childcare-in-reopening-the-economy> accessed 29 November 2021.

51 Catalina Amuedo-Dorantes et al., 'COVID-19 School Closures and Parental Labor Supply in the United States' (2020) IZA DP No. 13827.

52 Eurostat data, author's calculations. https://ec.europa.eu/eurostat/databrowser/view/LFSI_EMP_Q__custom_850298/default/table?lang=en.

53 EIGE, 'Gender Equality and the Socio-Economic Impact of the COVID-19 Pandemic' (2021) Publications Office of the European Union.

54 Eurostat, 'Male Employment More Affected by the COVID-19 Crisis than Female Employment' (30 April 2021) <https://ec.europa.eu/eurostat/web/products-eurostat-news/-/ddn-20210430-1> accessed 29 November 2021.

55 Andrew et al. (n 12).

increased risk of losing their jobs in the early phase of the crisis. As a significant gender gap in job losses persists, they speculate that women's childcare and home schooling responsibilities could be a contributing factor. Similarly, Sevilla and her colleagues[56] find that the 4-percentage points gender gap in the likelihood of being furloughed and the 2-percentage points difference in being out of work due to the crisis reduces little when men and women with similar occupational characteristics are compared. These patterns, however, are not significantly different between mothers and childless women. Consequently, we cannot be sure that the additional care work that resulted from the school closures made women more likely to accept being furloughed or even to give up employment. Since no other studies testing for such an effect in Europe were identified, it is not yet possible to conclude whether or not the increased amount of unpaid work directly influenced women's labour market situation during the first year of the pandemic.

It is, however, not only a loss in the *quantity* but also in the *quality* of working hours that can induce long-term deterioration in women's labour market prospects, and lead to reduced productivity and relative skills losses. Andrew et al.[57] provide a measure of uninterrupted working hours – that is the number of working hours when parents are not engaged in childcare while also working. They not only find that, compared to pre-COVID times, the proportion of such working time reduced significantly for all parents, but also that mothers' working hours were affected more than fathers'. Fathers spent 70% of their working time focusing solely on their paid work, while mothers spent only 53%.

More fragmented work patterns can lead to reduced productivity and thus to reduced wages.[58] In fact, a gender gap in productivity related to the lockdowns has already been shown to exist for a particular group of workers: academics. In this labour market segment, productivity can be relatively accurately measured through the number of papers submitted to academic journals. A detailed study of manuscripts submitted to Elsevier between February and May 2020 shows that compared to males, female researchers – especially younger ones that are most likely to have childcare responsibilities – produced significantly fewer academic outputs in all the science areas. However, results for Europe are not distinguishable.[59]

56 Sevilla and Smith (n 12).

57 Andrew et al. (n 12).

58 Abi Adams-Prassl et al., 'The Gender Wage Gap in an Online Labour Market: The Cost of Interruptions' (2020) CEPR Discussion Paper No. DP14294.

59 Flaminio Squazzoni et al., 'Only Second-Class Tickets for Women in the COVID-19 Race. A Study on Manuscript Submissions and Reviews in 2329 Elsevier Journals'.

To sum up, so far there is only limited evidence from European countries linking women's increased domestic responsibilities during the pandemic to their employment prospects either in the short or in the long run. National real-time lockdown surveys could potentially be further exploited to test for associations between short-term consequences for employment and women's increased burden of care work, especially women with young children. Longer-term consequences on the other hand are still unfolding, and we would argue that existing evidence on the amount of housework mothers were doing and the reduced quality of the time they had for paid work during the pandemic make a strong case for closely monitoring how the employment prospects of mothers will evolve.

4.2 *A Shift towards More Egalitarian Gender Norms?*

Discussions about gender equality after COVID-19 are dominated by well-underpinned concerns, as discussed above. Still, there seems to be one ray of hope. This again is associated with the reallocation of unpaid work during these unusual times and suggests that the shock that led to men's participation in household duties might provoke a persistent positive shift in gender norms, and make a more equal division of tasks more widely accepted and followed. This possibility too was raised before any new evidence became available[60] and has been repeatedly discussed since.[61] This section presents some of the underlying arguments and looks at the (limited) empirical evidence available so far.

In normal circumstances, gender norms and the actual division of unpaid work constitute the slowest changing dimensions of gender inequality.[62] Gender attitudes and allocation of housework are, however, strongly interrelated and it is reasonable to expect that an external shock influencing one will generate a shift in the other. Research carried out before the COVID-19 pandemic provides abundant evidence that men and women that have more egalitarian attitudes to gender roles are more likely to share domestic work more evenly. The association appears both directly, and indirectly, through the influence of their employment characteristics (number of work hours, earnings, etc.).[63] Most studies, however, have assumed – but not systematically tested – that attitudes to gender roles precede, and thus shape, participation in unpaid

60 Alon et al. (n 48).

61 E.g. Hupkau and Petrolongo (n 13); Andrew et al. (n 12).

62 Scott Coltrane, 'Research on Household Labor: Modeling and Measuring the Social Embeddedness of Routine Family Work' (2020) 62 (4) Journal of Marriage and Family 1208.

63 Fuwa (n 7).

labour. A study based on the National Survey of Families and Households in the US however shows that the association is most likely to be reciprocal, and attitudes towards gender roles and allocation of household duties in couples are mutually adjusted.[64] The findings suggest that the way couples divide housework also affects their beliefs about the right way of allocating tasks – especially among males.

Additional relevant evidence comes from studies looking at the longer-term impact of non-transferable paternal leave schemes. Some (but not all) research on the effects of such measures show that a temporary, enforced move towards equalisation of childcare tasks can shape how couples share their duties even several years later. Across several countries, fathers that took up paternal leave were more likely to continue shouldering not only more of the childcare but also more housework responsibilities.[65] The periods of paternal caregiving due to these leave schemes were two weeks to two months long. With the school closures due to COVID-19 and thus the lockdown-enforced reorganisations of the work in households being a minimum of three weeks long across the European countries, it is reasonable to expect qualitatively similar outcomes in the long term.

Which types of households are the most likely to be affected? Looking at the various work-situation combinations of couples during the pandemic, we certainly see unusually large scope for moving towards a paternal caretaking model in several arrangements. Among couples with young children in Germany as many as 30% of the fathers had more flexible working arrangements than the mothers did.[66] In the UK,[67] 15% of women with dependent children worked in a critical job and had a partner who stayed at home either teleworking or without a job. Of course, such situations do not directly lead to a more equal allocation of tasks let alone to reversed gender roles. Some studies, however, provide some – albeit subjective – indications as to the

64 Daniel L Carlson and Jamie L Lynch, 'Housework: Cause and Consequence of Gender Ideology?' (2013) 42 (6) Social Science Research 1505.

65 Anna-Lena Almqvist and Ann-Zofie Duvander, 'Changes in Gender Equality? Swedish Fathers' Parental Leave, Division of Childcare and Housework' (2014) 20 (1) Journal of Family Studies 19; Lídia Farré and Libertad González, 'Does Paternity Leave Reduce Fertility?' (2019) 172 Journal of Public Economics 52; Ankita Patnaik, 'Reserving Time for Daddy: The Short and Long-Run Consequences of Fathers' Quotas' (2014) SSRN Electronic Journal; Marcus Tamm, "Fathers' Parental Leave-Taking, Childcare Involvement and Labor Market Participation' (2019) 59 Labour Economics 184.

66 Melanie Arntz et al., 'Working from Home and COVID-19: the Chances and Risks for Gender Gaps' (2020) 55 (6) Intereconomics 381.

67 Hupkau and Petrolongo (n 13).

occurrence of such reversals. In the Netherlands, 10% of the fathers reported doing much more caregiving than their partners during the lockdown, and the proportion of those taking most of the responsibility for housework was similar.[68] As many as one-fifth of fathers acted as the main provider of childcare in the UK[69] while, in Germany, childcare was provided exclusively by the father in 4–6% of two-parent families during the first weeks of the pandemic.[70]

Data clearly links the largest increase in fathers' involvement in childcare to loss of their jobs[71] – a pattern not unknown from pre-COVID times.[72] Even if women continued to take on a large part of the unpaid duties in these families too, and thus it would often be an exaggeration to speak of "reversed gender roles",[73] we can expect the most significant attitude changes to take place under these circumstances. Indeed, to the best of our knowledge, the only study that has so far tested the prediction that a non-traditional reallocation of tasks provoked more egalitarian gender norms during the lockdowns, found supportive evidence in the group of fathers that lost their jobs.[74] The study covered Germany, the USA and Singapore between May and June 2020, and found that men who lived in a relationship became unemployed during the crisis reported significantly more egalitarian gender attitudes than other men did. Even though the research design does not allow for strong causality claims, it offers convincing evidence that losing paid activity during the lockdown could make men more open to the idea of equally shared responsibilities between men and women. Due to the reciprocal association between gender attitudes and involvement in domestic labour, this might well be a sign of longer-term changes in paternal behaviour.[75]

The aforementioned study found no comparable attitude shift among teleworking fathers. Still, there are good reasons to believe that not only the men who stopped working might have reconsidered their attitudes towards housework. Teleworking fathers in particular found themselves in a position (possibly for the first time in their lives) to closely observe the household and

68 Yerkes et al. (n 12).
69 Hupkau and Petrolongo (n 13).
70 Zoch et al. (n 12).
71 Fodor et al. (n 12); Del Boca et al. (n 19); Andrew et al. (n 12); Sevilla and Smith (n 12).
72 Tanja van der Lippe et al., 'Unemployment and the Division of Housework in Europe' (2018) 32 (4) Work, Employment and Society 650.
73 Andrew et al. (n 12).
74 Malte Reichelt et al., 'The Impact of COVID-19 on Gender Inequality in the Labor Market and Gender-Role Attitudes' (2021) 23 European Societies 228.
75 Carlson and Lynch (n 64).

childcare demands that are usually met by women.[76] Compared to fathers working from their workplace, they also became more involved not only in childcare but also in household work according to some studies[77] (but not others[78]). More research is needed to test if and how the behaviour and the attitudes of these groups were affected.

In an optimistic scenario, fathers in their redefined roles can also become role models spreading the attitude shift still further, beyond their own families. While most of the household and care work takes place behind closed doors, some of the duties newly taken over by men are still visible and might initiate a shift in gender norms in the broader society. Examples include time men spent with their children in public places, but also doing the grocery shopping, which became a predominantly male activity in Spain during the lockdowns.[79] Finally, we should not forget, that among teleworking men, who now have first-hand experience of both the ups and the downs of childcare and household work, there are also employers and managers well positioned to introduce changes in working cultures that have so far not offered much support for a good work–life balance.

5 Conclusion: Room for Research, Room for Intervention

This chapter brought together pre-COVID research with new evidence from Europe to reflect upon some key aspects of the changes this crisis has induced in households. Estimates from national real-time surveys, albeit not fully comparable, indicate that parents spent a minimum of 25%, but possibly even 100% more hours on childcare and home schooling during the lockdowns than before, while also faced with an increased amount of housework. As school closures were recurring and often long-lasting episodes during the first year of the pandemic, the possible consequences for parents cannot be underestimated. Looking at the distribution of this heavy workload, research clearly confirms that the heaviest burden was taken up by mothers, particularly those with young children. Not only were they more likely to adjust to the situation by massively increasing the time spent on unpaid duties, but their involvement was to a large extent independent of their working situation. However, at the same time, fathers also became more involved, many of them taking up several

---

76 Alon et al. (n 48).
77 Zoch et al. (n 12).
78 Fodor et al. (n 12).
79 Farré et al. (n 12).

hours of duties at home – even if it only led (close) to an equal distribution of the workload in a small share of cases.

While these are important changes in themselves, the most interesting questions relate to the possible longer-term consequences of the lockdown-induced disruptions. Will mothers' labour market prospects be damaged as a result of their heavy COVID-19 burden? Will a more equal division of household tasks prevail and reshape gender norms at least in some parts of society? So far only limited research has been done to answer these questions for Europe, although some data is already available to illustrate what is happening and to help better formulate our questions for future research.

Not enough research was available to enable us to understand if women's employment losses so far can, to some extent, be attributable to their increased family responsibilities. Therefore, we conclude that, in contrast to the USA, it is not (yet) possible to evaluate this assumption for Europe. There are, however, several indications that women's and especially mothers' number of uninterrupted working hours and productivity could have been badly affected – the possible labour market consequences of these will require continuous monitoring in the future. Regarding a potential shift in gender norms, we conclude that paternal involvement, especially in childcare activities, in some cases (particularly where the father had stopped working but also to some extent when they teleworked) became intense enough to raise hopes of a positive and persistent shift in the division of household labour as well as the related gender norms. Again, more studies will be needed to see if this is really happening.

How the situation eventually evolves and how gender relations will (or will not) be reshaped in Europe will also depend upon the institutional responses. National governments and employers have a great responsibility to help people to fit both paid and unpaid work into their lives and maintain an acceptable work–family balance during and beyond the pandemic. Flexible working arrangements and teleworking will most likely be an integrated part of the "new normal".[80] It is crucial, however, that they do not become a solution for female employees only: such arrangements need to be equally available but also acceptable for men. The positive shift away from the unequal distribution of labour that this crisis might have created will need to be reinforced by both public communication and other supportive measures.

80 Katherine Guyot and Isabel V Sawhill, 'Telecommuting Will Likely Continue Long after the Pandemic' Brookings (6 April 2020) <www.brookings.edu> accessed 29 November 2021; Sandrine Ceurstemont, 'Teleworking is Here to Stay – Here's What it Means for the Future of Work' Horizon (01 September 2020) <www.horizon-magazine.eu> accessed 29 November 2021.

This chapter mainly looked at women's relative disadvantages and discussed how they could be mitigated through the increased involvement of their male partners. While considering the undoubtedly crucial issue of gender gaps in the context of the pandemic, it would, however, be a big mistake to overlook another gap that the crisis is likely to create: the gap between parents and non-parents. This chapter compared women to men and mothers to fathers. While the comparisons showed that fathers also had an increased workload during lockdowns, they did not ask how this might affect fathers' labour market prospects, when compared to childless male employees. Future research will have to consider this question, and policy-makers should pay attention to the parental – and not solely the maternal – responsibilities.

References

Almqvist AL and Duvander AZ, 'Changes in Gender Equality? Swedish Fathers' Parental Leave, Division of Childcare and Housework' (2014) 20 Journal of Family Studies 19.

Alon T et al., 'The Impact of COVID-19 on Gender Equality' (2020) NBER Working Paper 26947.

Alon T et al., 'This Time it's Different: the Role of Women's Employment in a Pandemic Recession' (2020) NBER Working Paper 27660.

Andrew A et al., 'How Are Mothers and Fathers Balancing Work and Family under Lockdown?' IFS Briefing Note BN 290.

Arntz M et al., 'Working from Home and COVID-19: the Chances and Risks for Gender Gaps' (2020) 55 (6) Intereconomics 381.

Blaskó Z et al., 'How Will the COVID-19 Crisis Affect Existing Gender Divides in Europe?' (2020) Publications Office of the European Union.

Boca D et al., 'Women's Work, Housework and Childcare, before and during COVID-19' (2020) 18 Review of Economics of the Household 1001.

Carlson DL and Lynch JL, 'Housework: Cause and Consequence of Gender Ideology?' (2013) 42 (6) Social Science Research 1505.

Coltrane S, 'Research on Household Labor: Modeling and Measuring the Social Embeddedness of Routine Family Work' (2020) 62 (4) Journal of Marriage and Family 1208.

Cukrowska-Torzewska E and Matysiak A, 'The Motherhood Wage Penalty: a Meta-Analysis' (2020) 88–89 Social Science Research 1.

EIGE, 'Gender Equality and the Socio-Economic Impact of the COVID-19 Pandemic' (2021) Publications Office of the European Union.

Esping-Andersen G, *The Three Worlds of Welfare Capitalism* (Polity Press 1989).

Esping-Andersen G, *Social Foundations of Postindustrial Economies* (OUP 1999).

Eurofound, 'COVID-19: Implications for Employment and Working Life' (2021) Publications Office of the European Union.

Farré L and González L, 'Does Paternity Leave Reduce Fertility?' (2019) 172 Journal of Public Economics 52.

Fodor É et al., 'The Impact of COVID-19 on the Gender Division of Childcare Work in Hungary' (2021) 23 (S1) European Societies S95.

Fuwa M, 'Macro-Level Gender Inequality and the Division of Household Labor in 22 Countries' (2004) 69 American Sociological Review 751.

Fuwa M and Cohen PN, 'Housework and Social Policy' (2007) 36 Social Science Research 512.

Di Gessa G et al., 'What Drives National Differences in Intensive Grandparental Childcare in Europe?' (2016) 71 The Journals of Gerontology: Series B 141.

Grunow D et al., 'Gender Ideologies in Europe: a Multidimensional Framework' (2018) 80 Journal of Marriage and Family 42.

Hipp L and Bünning M, 'Parenthood as a Driver of Increased Gender Inequality during COVID-19? Exploratory Evidence from Germany' (2021) 23 (S1) European Societies S658.

Hook JL, 'Gender Inequality in the Welfare State: Sex Segregation in Housework, 1965–2003' (2010) 115 (5) American Journal of Sociology 1480.

Kan MY et al., 'Gender Convergence in Domestic Work: Discerning the Effects of Interactional and Institutional Barriers from Large-Scale Data' (2011) 45 (2) Sociology 234.

Kreyenfeld M et al., 'Coronavirus and Care: How the Coronavirus Crisis Affected Father's Involvement in Germany' (2021) 44 Demographic Research 99.

Möhring K et al., 'The COVID-19 Pandemic and Subjective Well-Being: Longitudinal Evidence on Satisfaction with Work and Family' (2021) 23 (S1) European Societies S601.

Papadimitriou E and Blaskó Z, 'Economic Sectors at Risk due to COVID-19 Disruptions: Will Men and Women in the EU be Affected Similarly?' (2020) JRC Science for Policy Report.

Patnaik A, 'Reserving Time for Daddy: the Short and Long-Run Consequences of Fathers' Quotas' (2019) 37 (4) Journal of Labor Economics 1009.

Reichelt M et al., 'The Impact of COVID-19 on Gender Inequality in the Labor Market and Gender-Role Attitudes' (2021) 23 (S1) European Societies S228.

Sevilla A and Smith S, 'Baby Steps: the Gender Division of Childcare during the COVID-19 Pandemic' (2020) 36 (S1) Oxford Review of Economic Policy S169.

Squazzoni F et al., 'Only Second-Class Tickets for Women in the COVID-19 Race. A Study on Manuscript Submissions and Reviews in 2329 Elsevier Journals' (2020) 16 (10) PLoS ONE e0257919. October 10, 2021 https://doi.org/10.1371/journal.pone.0257919, Available at SSRN: https://ssrn.com/abstract=3712813 or http://dx.doi.org/10.2139/ssrn.3712813.

Tamm M, "Fathers' Parental Leave-Taking, Childcare Involvement and Labor Market Participation' (2019) 59 Labour Economics 184.

Van der Lippe T et al., 'Persistent Inequalities in Time Use between Men and Women: a Detailed Look at the Influence of Economic Circumstances, Policies, and Culture' (2011) 27 (2) European Sociological Review 164.

Van der Lippe T et al., 'Unemployment and the Division of Housework in Europe' (2018) 32 (4) Work, Employment and Society 650.

Yerkes MA et al., "Intelligent' Lockdown, Intelligent Effects? Results from a Survey on Gender (in)Equality in Paid Work, the Division of Childcare and Household Work, and Quality of Life among Parents in the Netherlands during the COVID-19 Lockdown' (2020) 15 (11) PLos One.

Zoch G et al., 'Who Cares When Care Closes? Care-Arrangements and Parental Working Conditions during the COVID-19 Pandemic in Germany' (2021) 23 (S1) European Societies S576.

CHAPTER 7

The Unequal Ivory Tower

The Effects of COVID-19 on Academic Mothers

Sara Martucci, Alessandra Minello, and Lidia Katia C. Manzo

1 Introduction

Millions of professionals around the world switched to remote working in spring 2020 when nearly every country had imposed some form of lockdown as a result of the COVID-19 pandemic. For academics, this meant that campuses were abandoned, research labs were closed, teaching was moved online, and writing had to be done at home. Almost immediately, popular media outlets began publishing stories about the obstacles women encountered as a result of this abrupt shift.[1] While essential workers continued to work outside the home and faced their own challenges around childcare, "non-essential" working parents had to cope with a sudden spatial and temporal collision of their work with their domestic responsibilities.[2] For academic mothers, this meant redeveloping courses and teaching them online, continuing to perform administrative tasks and service work within their departments, and struggling to find the time to pursue their research agendas and to concentrate on writing academic texts. Since teaching and departmental commitments cannot be postponed, it was the research and writing that had to be put on hold when childcare and household duties became a priority during the workday.[3] Several articles in the popular press focused specifically on academic mothers who

1 Nancy Jo Sales, 'Dispatches from the Gender Gap: Work-From-Home Moms in the Time of Coronavirus' *Vanity Fair* (3 April 2020). Patricia Cohen and Tiffany Hsu, 'Pandemic Could Scar a Generation of Working Mothers' *The New York Times* (3 June 2020). Nora Ellmann et al., 'What Women Need in Response to the Coronavirus Pandemic' *Center for American Progress* (8 June 2020).

2 Lidia KC Manzo and Alessandra Minello, 'Mothers, Childcare Duties, and Remote Working under COVID-19 Lockdown in Italy: Cultivating Communities of Care' (2020) 10(2) Dialogues in Human Geography.

3 Kyle R Myers et al., 'Unequal Effects of the COVID-19 Pandemic on Scientists' (2020) 4 Nature Human Behavior 880. Sara Martucci, 'He's Working from Home and I'm at Home Trying to Work: Experiences of Childcare and the Work-Family Balance Among Mothers During Covid' *Journal of Family Issues* (2021).

struggled to fit the time for research and writing into their schedule of teaching, childcare, cooking, and other domestic chores.[4] These reports exposed a fact that was later confirmed by scientific research, namely that fewer article manuscripts were submitted by women than men during the lockdown across a broad range of disciplines, and that numbers of submissions from women were lower in 2020 than in 2019.[5] The consequences of this are material. Within academia, publications are needed for job appointments, promotion, and tenure. Beyond these external requirements, research and publication are important aspects of professional identity: both are needed for academics to be recognised within their intellectual communities, and are even necessary for their recognition of themselves as scholars. With these concerns in mind, we asked: how did the lack of time available for research and writing affect the careers of academic mothers during lockdown?

This chapter focuses on the daily experiences of academic mothers in the United States of America (USA) and Italy during the lockdown imposed in spring 2020 to curtail the pandemic of COVID-19. It is part of a 'larger research project, the Smart-Mama study, where the social effects of the COVID-19 crisis are explored through the lens of domestic rearrangements of parenting duties as a result of the increase in remote working during the lockdown in the USA and Italy'.[6] At the beginning of this project, in late March 2020, Italy was the

4 Colleen Flaherty, 'Early Journal Submission Data Suggest COVID-19 Is Tanking Women's Research Productivity' *Inside Higher Ed* (21 April 2020). Trisalyn Nelson and Jessica Early, 'Covid-19 and the Academic Parent' *The Chronicle of Higher Ed* (27 April 2020). Megan Frederickson, 'Women Are Getting Less Research Done than Men during This Coronavirus Pandemic' *The Conversation* (18 May 2020).

5 National Academies of Sciences, Engineering, and Medicine, 'Impact of COVID-19 on the Careers of Women in Academic Sciences, Engineering, and Medicine' <https://www.nap.edu/catalog/26061/impact-of-covid-19-on-the-careers-of-women-in-academic-sciences-engineering-and-medicine> accessed 29 November 2021. Rebecca A Krukowski et al., 'Academic Productivity Differences by Gender and Child Age in Science, Technology, Engineering, Mathematics, and Medicine Faculty during the Covid-19 Pandemic' (2021) 30 (3) Journal of Women's Health 341.

6 The Smart-Mama study was initially designed as a non-funded research project with the aim of getting an immediate, firsthand account of the lived experiences of working mothers during the Spring 2020 COVID-19 lockdown in Italy, the second country facing the spread of the COVID-19 after China. The US followed quite immediately in March 2020. Consequently, the Italian research team decided to include the US as a comparative country to explore how both Italian and American working mothers were dealing with the limitations in their job activities and the management of childcare at home. This project had approval from the Institutional Review Board at Mercy College. There were a total of 45 American and 23 Italian participants between April 2020–August 2020. Alessandra Minello, Sara Martucci, Lidia KC Manzo 'The Pandemic and the Academic Mothers: Present Hardships and Future Perspectives' (2020) 23 (1) European Societies 1.

worst affected country in the Western hemisphere. At this time, Americans were looking to Italy as the prime example of how the virus might unfold in the USA. Italian schools and universities were closed on the fourth of March while in the USA, states, counties, and individual schools made decisions to close at different times, with most closing in mid- to late March. Interviews with women from both countries allowed us to find out about their experiences during different moments in the lockdown timeline – beginning, middle, and in the Italian case, nearly to the end of the Phase 1 lockdown.

Women's experiences during the lockdown were directly affected by the amount of childcare and domestic labour they were responsible for in the home. We wanted to understand the effects of the gendered division of unpaid labour on academic mothers. For this reason, we focused on women who are currently in domestic partnerships with men. According to the Organisation for Economic Co-operation and Development, American women spent 241 minutes per day doing unpaid labour in 2019, compared with 145 minutes for men. In Italy, these numbers were 306 minutes and 130 minutes per day, respectively.[7] When we take paid and unpaid labour into account, women in the USA worked 22 minutes more per day than men; in Italy women worked 90 minutes more per day. Research demonstrates that during the lockdown the gender gap in care was not closed; overall, women spent more time on necessities – e.g., household chores and caring responsibilities – than men.[8] Among academics, mothers spent more time on childcare and housework than fathers.[9]

The preliminary reports about mothers' reduced output during the lockdown, and the quantitative data demonstrating that mothers spent more time providing care, raised several new research questions for understanding the everyday realities during this unprecedented situation. The following is an exploratory account of academic mothers' experiences specifically at the time of the COVID-19 spring 2020 lockdown. We focus on the following questions: First, how did academic mothers feel about their simultaneous work and home duties during the COVID-19 lockdown in spring 2020? Second, how did the reduction of productivity due to care duties impact their perception of

7 Organisation for Economic Cooperation and Development, 'Employment: Time Spent in Paid and Unpaid Work, by Sex' <https://stats.oecd.org/index.aspx?queryid=54757> accessed 29 November 2021.

8 Laura M Giurge et al., 'Why Time Poverty Matters for Individuals, Organisations and Nations' (2021) 118 (12) Proceedings of the National Academy of Sciences of the United States of America.

9 Katie Langin, 'Pandemic Hit Academic Mothers Especially Hard, New Data Confirm' (2021) Science 660.

their career trajectories in the long term? Third, what are some of the strategies women adopted to keep up with their research agenda and produce scholarship?

2 Gendered Division of Labour in the Home and at Work

Ample research has exposed the hardships that women face when balancing an academic career and a family.[10] Ward & Wolf-Wendel refer to both academia and parenting as intensive, even "greedy", contexts that require an individual's full dedication.[11] Prestigious or research-oriented academic jobs have garnered a reputation for being incompatible with family life, especially for women. According to a 2006 survey of more than 1,000 doctoral students in the University of California system, 46% of women (compared with 21% of men) cited "issues related to children" as a very important factor in their decision not to pursue a research-oriented academic career.[12] It is not news that a good work–family balance – between being a full-time academic and a mother – is hard to achieve. In the home, mothers dedicate more time to childcare, thus reducing their availability for academic tasks.[13] Compared with academic fathers and academics who are not parenting, academic mothers experience a "motherhood penalty" because of time lost due to maternity leave and childcare responsibilities.[14] In academia, women are also more likely to take on certain roles at work – mentoring students, administrative responsibilities to the school – and to prioritise teaching over writing.[15] The COVID-19

10 Rachel H Bassett, *Parenting and Professing: Balancing Family Work with an Academic Career* (Vanderbilt University Press 2005). Maureen Baker, 'Choices or Constraints? Family Responsibilities, Gender and Academic Career' (2010) 41 (1) Journal of Comparative Family Studies 1. Kelly Ward, 'Having it All: Women, Work, Family, and the Academic Career' (2014) 73 Labour / Le Travail 255.

11 Kelly Ward and Lisa Wolf-Wendel, 'Mothering and Professing: Critical Choices and the Academic Career' (2017) 10 (3) NASPA Journal About Women in Higher Education 229.

12 Mary Ann Mason et al., 'Why Graduate Students Reject the Fast Track' (2009) 95 (1) Academe 11.

13 Arlie Hochschild and Anne Machung, *The Second Shift: Working Families and the Revolution at Home* (Viking 1989).

14 J Scott Long, 'The Origins of Sex Differences in Science' (1990) 68 (4) Social Forces 1297. Nicholas H Wolfinger et al., 'Problems in the Pipeline: Gender, Marriage, and Fertility in the Ivory Tower' (2008) 79 (4) The Journal of Higher Education 388. Mary Ann Mason et al., *Do Babies Matter?: Gender and Family in the Ivory Tower* (Rutgers University Press 2013).

15 Johana Kantola, 'Why Do All the Women Disappear? Gendering Processes in a Political Science Department' (2008) 15 (2) Gender, Work & Organization 202.

lockdown of spring 2020 further amplified the gender inequalities present in parenthood and academia.[16]

Women perform more childcare and domestic labour than men, even when they are working full-time outside the home.[17] This domestic workload imbalance has been decreasing since the 1970s, although women still do more of the work and often feel like they are the managers of the household.[18] For academic women, the gendered division of labour at work also plays a role. Some degree of "service", like advising students, working on accreditation, or committee work within a department or campus, is necessary for sustained employment and promotion. However, too much service work can get in the way of publications, professional development, and even promotion, and women are more likely to take on service responsibilities beyond those that are required.[19]

Several studies on the effect of parenting on academic productivity for both men and women have been published. A study of academics in Germany found that having children had a more negative impact on publishing rates for mothers than for fathers, especially if mothers were publishing infrequently before having children.[20] Even academics who were not yet (or never planning on) parenting emphasised the potential impact of having children. A 2017 study of early-career Italian academics found that women were more preoccupied than men with the negative effects of potential work-life interferences that would

---

16 Alessandra Minello et al., 'The Pandemic and the Academic Mothers: Present Hardships and Future Perspectives' (2021) 23 (1) European Societies S82.

17 Man Yee Kan et al., 'Gender Convergence in Domestic Work: Discerning the Effects of Interactional and Institutional Barriers from Large-scale Data' (2011) 45 (2) Sociology 234. Suzanne M Bianchi et al., 'Housework: Who Did, Does or Will Do it, and How Much Does it Matter?' (2012) 91 (1) Social Forces 55.

18 Shira Offer, 'The Costs of Thinking About Work and Family: Mental Labor, Work–family Spillover, and Gender Inequality Among Parents in Dual-earner Families' (2014) 29 (4) Sociological Forum 916. Tomi Oinas, 'The Division of Labour Within Households: Men's Increased Participation?' in Mia Tammelin (ed.), *Family, Work and Well-Being: Emergence of New Issues, Springer Briefs in Well-Being and Quality of Life Research* (Springer International Publishing 2018). Lindsey G Robertson et al., 'Mothers and Mental Labor: A Phenomenological Focus Group Study of Family-related Thinking Work' (2019) 43 (2) Psychology of Women Quarterly 184.

19 Lisa Wolf-Wendel and Kelly Ward, 'Academic Mothers: Exploring Disciplinary Perspectives' (2015) 40 (1) Innovative Higher Education 19.

20 Mark Lutter and Martin Schröder, 'Is There a Motherhood Penalty in Academia? The Gendered Effect of Children on Academic Publications' (2020) 36 (3) European Sociological Review 442.

result from having children.[21] Examining professional and familial outcomes in the USA, Mason & Goulden confirmed that gender inequality permeates both the work and home environments of academic women.[22] They found that, compared with academic fathers, mothers reported having less time or mental space for writing and were more likely to miss professional development opportunities because of childcare commitments. This double bind of gender inequity at work and at home means that academic mothers gain tenure or promotion less frequently than fathers. In a sample of 30,000 American academics with young children at the beginning of tenure-track jobs, only 53% of women achieved tenure, compared with 77% of men.[23] The authors interpreted this to mean that some women were being denied tenure, but that others had moved to different positions within academia that made fewer demands.

During the global pandemic of COVID-19, all non-essential work was suddenly being done in the home. For academics this meant that childcare, housework, teaching, service work, and research responsibilities were in constant conflict. Because gender equity is already lacking in the home and the workplace, these deficits interacted to the detriment of many women's careers, specifically limiting their capacity for the research and writing that are required for tenure and promotion.

The requirements for tenure vary across disciplines, positions, and between universities. Wolf-Wendel & Ward exemplified how the specific norms of academic disciplines and the requirements of individual departments affected an academic's perceptions of her own productivity, but they found overall that experiences were more similar than they were different across contexts.[24] The present study does not distinguish between disciplines or prestige of the university, although the individual's position within the university is included in the data below.

Professors who are already tenured may have been less concerned with their productivity during the lockdown. In the USA, non-tenure track faculty may not have felt pressured to publish, but may have been more concerned about the precariousness of their positions. In Italy, publications are nearly always

---

21 Rosella Bozzo et al., 'Work–life Interferences in the Early Stages of Academic Careers: The Case of Precarious Researchers in Italy' (2017) 16 (2–3) European Educational Research Journal 332.

22 Mary Ann Mason and Marc Goulden, 'Marriage and the Baby Blues: Redefining Gender Equity in the Academy' (2004) 596 (1) Annals of the American Academy of Political and Social Science 86.

23 Mary Ann Mason and Marc Goulden, 'Do Babies Matter? The Effects of Family Formation on the Lifelong Careers of Academic Men and Women' (2002) 88 (6) Academe 21.

24 Wolf-Wendel and Ward (n 19).

necessary to obtain promotion, secure long-term employment, and continue professorship. The role of publications became extremely important after 2010, when the Gelmini Law introduced the National Scientific Qualification. This is a complex system of evaluation of an academic's productivity, mainly based on published articles and books, which is necessary to obtain the title of associate or full professor.[25]

Although the variations among departments, institutions, and disciplines are likely to have influenced pressures around productivity during the COVID-19 lockdown, the focus here is on the division of labour in the home that helped or hindered mothers' productivity. In our analysis, we will first examine the new balance between childcare and academic work, and the reorganisation of family life in spring 2020. Then, we will discuss our hypothesis that the reduction in productivity would be perceived by the women as detrimental to their careers. Finally, we explore a new direction: what, if any, childcare strategies did women put in place to ameliorate their workload and assuage fears of long-term career damage?

3 Sample and Methodology

This research is based on 25 in-depth interviews with academic mothers from the USA and 13 from Italy. Because we were interested in the gendered division of domestic labour and its effect on academic mothers, we focused on self-identifying women who were coupled with men and who had children aged 0–5 years. The literature demonstrates that mothers of children aged 0–5 years were the ones who suffered the most from reduced worktime during the early stages of the pandemic.[26] [27] [28] Women of colour have historically

25 The recent university reform introduced the National Scientific Qualification by disciplinary field, based on a series of standardized criteria defined by the MIUR, the Ministry of Education, University and Research. Obtaining the National Scientific Qualification has become a precondition for appointment to the position of associate or full professor. The same reform introduced two categories of fixed-term researchers (type A and type B), one with a three-year contract renewable for a maximum of two further years, the other with a three-year contract that guarantees appointment as an associate professor following a positive evaluation.

26 Myers et al. (n 3).

27 Meghan C Halley et al., 'The Intersection of Work and Home Challenges Faced by Physician Mothers during the Coronavirus Disease 2019 Pandemic: A Mixed-methods Analysis' (2021) 30 (4) Journal of Women's Health 514.

28 Caterina Balenzano et al., 'Families in the Pandemic between Challenges and Opportunities: An Empirical Study of Parents with Preschool and School-age Children' (2020) 10 Italian Sociological Review 777.

TABLE 7.1 Ethnic/Racial background of American respondents versus American female academics overall, from the National Center for Education Statistics (NCES), 2017

	White	Black/African American	Asian	Hispanic	Middle Eastern
Sample, n (percentage)	16 (64%)	3 (12%)	3 (12%)	1 (4%)	2 (8%)
Academics overall	76%	6%	11%	6%	*

*NCES data does not include numbers for Middle Eastern academics: they are often classified as white or Asian; however, two participants in this study identified their ethnic/racial background as Middle Eastern.

been undersampled in research on academic parents. Therefore, we purposely oversampled non-white women among American participants (see Table 7.1). In Italy less than 8% of the population is non-white: all respondents in that sample identified as Italian.

Participants were recruited from various ranks of academia, provided their academic position was a full-time job. This included tenure-track, tenured, and non-tenure track faculty, lecturers, and graduate students. Part-time or adjunct professors were not included in this research. The participants came from teaching – as well as from research-focused institutions in the USA; this distinction is not as prevalent in Italian universities. Most of the women in the sample were considered "early-career" although some were newly tenured.

This study aimed to obtain an immediate, first-hand response to the pandemic conditions. As a result, convenience and snowball sampling methods were used. Three methods of recruitment were used: identifying women who posted content on Twitter about being an academic mother; advertising the study in academic mothers' groups on social media; and contacting personal networks of academics. We acknowledge that mothers particularly affected by the worktime constraints may have been more likely to express interest in the study. However, it is also important to note that the mothers experiencing the worst constraints may not have had time to participate in an interview. Because of these selective recruitment methods, we do not claim to have obtained a representative sample of academic mothers in the USA or in Italy.

All interviews with academics took place during the coronavirus lockdown in the USA and Italy between the 13th of April and 10th of June 2020. The interviews were conducted by the three authors of this paper over tele-conferencing applications. We each used the same interview script and the interviews lasted from 30 minutes to 1 hour, on average. We asked participants questions about their daily work and childcare schedules both before COVID-19 and during the lockdown. Participants were also asked about their sources of emotional support, as well as positive and negative experiences of the lockdown. An information sheet and a consent form were given to participants prior to conducting the interview, and anonymity was guaranteed.

4 Childcare Organization and Feelings of Despair

Neither the USA nor Italy had put a national plan in place relating to work and childcare during the lockdown. Most mothers in our sample noted that their universities and departments failed to make any arrangements to help parents. The only institutional support given during this time was technical help for getting classes online; any accommodations to ease time constraints were at the discretion of individual research teams or department chairs. Our participants reported considerable variation in the level of sympathy and support offered to them by their institutions, and rarely felt that they had enough time to adequately perform as both an academic and a parent.

The sudden lockdown during the COVID-19 pandemic meant an immediate reorganisation of daily life for everyone, especially parents. Predictably, the bulk of the childcare duties fell to the women: almost half (48%) of the American and 38% of the Italian academics in our sample define themselves as the main caretaker (See Table 7.2). Twenty three percent of the Italian academic mothers interviewed outsourced the care duties to family members or babysitters, compared with 28% of the Americans. It was more common for Italian women to report that they split childcare with their husbands (30%), while American women were more likely to have a husband who took over the bulk of the care (12% compared with 7.7% of Italians). Even when men were more involved with childcare, mothers noted that their children would still come to them for certain needs, for example, emotional comfort. We will explore below how the reorganisation of work and family load affected mothers' perceptions of current and future productivity and which strategies mothers adopted for alleviating the feelings of despair.

Academic mothers prioritised childcare and crucial tasks like teaching or departmental meetings. All other aspects of their academic identity, including research, submitting grant proposals, and writing, were put on hold indefinitely. This sudden loss of part of their academic identity, as well as the uncertainty about when things would return to normal, created a profound sense

TABLE 7.2 Household childcare arrangements for families in our study

	Babysitter/ nanny	Family help	Self-employed/ underemployed partner	Arranged to split care with partner	Mother is the main caretaker	Total
American Sample, n (percentage)	3 (12%)	4 (16%)	3 (12%)	3 (12%)	12 (48%)	25
Italian Sample, n (percentage)	1 (7.7%)	2 (15%)	1 (7.7%)	4 (30%)	5 (38%)	13
Total	4 (10.5%)	6 (15.8%)	4 (10.5%)	7 (18.4%)	17 (44.7%)	38

of despair about their current and future work, for mothers in both the USA and Italy.

Our participants consistently reported a lack of ability to concentrate as a result of being home with their children around the clock. One dual-professor couple who were both at home with their children even conducted a brief experiment during the lockdown, published in *The Washington Post.*[29] They took turns at being the "on duty" parent for three-hour stretches. The on-duty parent, while still working, was the children's go-to person for snacks, questions, help, and other needs. The couple found that the average length of uninterrupted time for the on-duty parent was only 3 minutes and 24 seconds. In their article, the couple explained that: "Our personal responsibilities interrupt our professional ones, which interrupt our personal ones – and we feel we are failing at *all* our jobs". Most of the women in our sample were acting as the on-duty parent for most of the day, meaning that they had very short time windows to complete academic work during their children's waking hours.

Charlotte, an American tenured professor mentioned a *"daily moment of panic"* when she thought about everything that needed to get done. She noted how it was difficult to do any kind of work that requires the time to think: *"It happens so often that I'm like, when am I going to do that .... .it's just kind of a constant sense of dread that blankets my day".* Natalie, a tenure-track professor in the USA, was worried that she was only able to work about three hours per day,

29 Suzanne M Edwards and Larry Snyder, 'Perspective: Yes, Balancing Work and Parenting Is Impossible. Here's the Data' *The Washington Post* (10 July 2020).

compared with ten before the lockdown. She said that she felt *"a real cognitive deficit"* from being home with her children all day. Monia, an Italian doctoral student, acknowledged that her husband does help around the house, but only when it fits into his schedule. She complained that this made her work feel very fragmented. Even when her husband helped, it was hard to get intellectual work done at home.

Camilla and Vanda both spoke of the inability to work on academic publications, citing a lack of concentration:

> *I've put aside the whole part of the research … that was, unfortunately, the first to go. In the sense that I didn't have the time, the concentration, the possibility right now.*
>
> CAMILLA, Professor, Italy

> *But in terms of research and concentration, I have to be honest, it was impossible to go on. I recovered a little in the evening but I was also tired.*
>
> VANDA, Professor, Italy

Academic mothers were not just worried about the spring 2020 semester, but also about what the disruption would mean for their future careers, especially if day-care providers and schools remained closed in the summer and even the autumn. Some women felt that they had already "fallen behind" in their careers during maternity leave. Now, with this return to full-time parenting, many women were reminded of their child's infancy in terms of the isolation and the constant demands of motherhood, giving them the impression that they were once again falling behind.

As a mother of four children, it was impossible for Abigail, an American doctoral student studying health, to work during the lockdown. She felt frustrated at night when she read the news, thinking about what she could contribute if she had not had small children: *"I would have more brain space to run with these ideas and take this moment for what it is and what we need to contribute as social scientists … and then it's like 'oh God what are we going to have for dinner' … I feel like I'm going to be even more behind because I'm not doing this cutting edge research that I would want to be doing and I know I have the skills, I just don't have the time, or space, or brainpower".*

This sense of long-term adverse effects on their academic careers was reflected among the Italian and American mothers.

> *I haven't even opened the file … teaching has its urgency … but research is like oh well, I can do this later … and also you need concentration when*

> *you're doing research and I'm too distracted by this kid. So my plan is postponed probably for another year, which is already nothing new for me. One night I felt this complete sadness of my whole career ... sometimes I doubt myself.*
>
> OLIVIA, Tenured Professor, USA

> *This thing will certainly have an impact: I'll publish less. That's a fact. I feel at a disadvantage compared to the others ... I don't know if it will affect my career in the long term, but it will certainly have a negative effect on scientific production.*
>
> CLAUDIA, Professor, Italy

> *I'm worried, the longer this lockdown will last, the lower the probability of having a good CV.*
>
> FRIDA, Post-doc, Italy

> *I do appreciate the time I get with my children, but I have to block out the career aspirations and not think about that. I'm really curious about the PTSD* [*post-traumatic stress disorder*] *that comes out of this, the retention of female professors with children.*
>
> CINDY, Tenure-track Professor, USA

The constant interruptions prevented the accomplishment of all but the most modest professional tasks by academic mothers. Our respondents reported feeling overwhelmed with the amount of work they needed to do, coupled with the lack of time and space for concentration. Many mothers felt that being home with their children all day affected their ability to do intellectual work and were fearful about how this would affect their future careers.

5 Alternative Strategies for Combining Care and Work

Academic work was already perceived as very flexible before the global pandemic. Except for departmental meetings and teaching obligations, professors and graduate students can complete much of their work on their own schedule. When teaching moved online during the lockdown, this work appeared even more flexible as many professors opted for an asynchronous format, meaning that lectures and other teaching responsibilities could be performed at any time of the day. Most of the participants in our study claimed that they took on the bulk of the childcare because their partners' jobs were less flexible than their own. It was more common in Italy than in the USA for parents to split the workday. In terms of sharing childcare with their partners, the US women with underemployed partners had the most success with getting their work done.

Brittany's husband is an adjunct professor at the same university where Brittany is on the tenure track. During the lockdown they took turns at childcare, with her husband waking up around 5 am and taking care of the baby until noon. Brittany spent this time writing and on self-care before taking over the childcare in the afternoons. Marlene's husband was self-employed and arranged his schedule so that they could split care during the day. Cora's husband was also self-employed and took care of the children while she taught her classes online or attended meetings. Although none of these women felt that they were doing the same amount of work as before the lockdown, these were some of the cases where academic mothers in the USA were able to continue to be productive.

The women who reported having the most success with maintaining their workload during the lockdown had full-time assistance with childcare which was provided either by members of the extended family or hired help. These arrangements had their own drawbacks: families being separated temporarily, flouting quarantine regulations, or spending a significant portion of their income on hired care.

Ali is a tenure-track professor in the USA with two children. At the beginning of the lockdown, her in-laws made the decision to move in with her. The children were primarily cared for by their grandmother throughout the day. Ali would take breaks with them for meals and to do one planned activity during the day. Unlike most of the women in the sample, Ali was not worried that her work was affected by the lockdown: *"I've been writing grants, doing some research, mostly I've been managing projects and editing. I've been showing up to meetings and disseminating information".* She acknowledged that it was only manageable because she had her in-laws helping out and a staff of mostly childless graduate students who were still able to work. If her in-laws had not taken over the childcare, she said it would have been *"a complete mess".*

Beth's husband worked in IT for a hospital, and at the beginning of lockdown his job was extremely demanding as he spearheaded efforts to set up a telehealth infrastructure. Because of this, Beth, a tenured professor, decided to move in with her parents, several states away. During the lockdown Beth exercised in the mornings and then took care of her children until 10am when her parents took over. Beth was mostly able to get her work done under this arrangement. She did not foresee any long-term negative impacts on her career, and had even been able to support others who did not have assistance with childcare: *"because of my parents' help, I've been able to do a few additional things to help other people in similar boats that I'm in".*

In Italy, Claudia struggled to complete her research and writing, as described above, but made use of family support to finish her teaching duties. She admitted to having disregarded the Italian lockdown rules in an effort to complete her work: *"Despite the strict limits, my parents live in the same town, in fact, they live very close by … I know very well that we did not respect the rules … but unfortunately, I could not manage both with my little daughter at home … there's never an hour of tranquillity … And so, since the grandparents lived nearby, and they had locked themselves in the house like us, in the end we decided to do as we did".*

Before the lockdown Farah, a doctoral student in the USA, would write for four to five hours per day. During the lockdown her productivity diminished to one to three hours, on a good day. As a result, she had to postpone her grant application and her oral exams: *"It became overwhelming to not have an infrastructure in place".* She said that she did not do well in her qualifying exams because her daughter was going stir crazy. Because of this, and the impending delivery of her second child, Farah ended up sending her daughter to a relative's house so that she could focus on her exams.

When mothers had full-time assistance with childcare, they were able to more or less continue with their career paths. Of course, there were still more interruptions during the day compared to pre-lockdown when mothers were at work and children were cared for outside the home. Even with sitters or grandparents doing the bulk of the childcare, mothers would take breaks to breastfeed babies, soothe toddlers, put children down for naps, and mediate sibling conflict.

6 Discussion

In every country tracked by the Organisation for Economic Co-operation and Development, women spend more time per day on domestic, unpaid labour than men. Since women were already performing more of the domestic labour before the lockdown, it felt "normal" for women to take on the bulk of the childcare during lockdown, especially during the workday. For academics, the increase in domestic duties conflicted with extremely demanding careers.

Most women expressed feelings of panic when trying to balance meeting the day-to-day needs of their families with their job commitments. It was rare that mothers in this sample were able to keep up with their research and writing agendas during the initial phases of the lockdown, and many were overwhelmed with the uncertainty about when schools would reopen and day-care provisions would resume. This led to fears about how the interruption would affect their career trajectories in the long-term.

All of the women in our sample were able to complete their teaching duties for the semester, but they complained that impaired concentration and the increased cognitive load of full-time childcare impacted their ability to conduct research and write. Before the lockdown, nearly all of these women had some form of full-time care for their children. The shift to caring for their children full-time while still being expected to work full-time, created a sense that none of these tasks could be done properly. The only women who consistently felt successful as academics and mothers during the lockdown had access to full-time assistance from family members, babysitters, or nannies – the ones for whom a more "sustainable" version of life persisted. The lockdown served to expose the concessions women must make when trying to balance an academic career with family life.[30]

7 Future Research and Recommendations

This research focused on academic work and motherhood in only two countries during a nearly worldwide lockdown. We acknowledge that academia is a specific career field, and that focusing on academics, rather than professionals in general, limits the generalizability of our research findings. Since ours was an exploratory study of women's initial lockdown experiences, generalizability was not among our aims – the academic profession has been a subject of robust research in the past, especially with respect to concerns around gender and childcare.[31] This critical and unique moment demanded the timely exploration of the experiences of mothers in academia during the COVID-19 pandemic.

Data from additional countries would enrich our understanding of motherhood in academia during the COVID-19 pandemic. As is often the case, our findings raise more questions: What about single mothers working from home during the lockdown? Did academic fathers experience the lockdown differently than mothers? If we interviewed both members of a couple, how would their responses differ? What were the experiences of mothers who were

---

30 Candice Harris et al., 'Academic Careers and Parenting: Identity, Performance and Surveillance' (2019) 44 (4) Studies in Higher Education 708.

31 Venitha Pillay, 'Academic Mothers Finding Rhyme and Reason'(2009) 21 (5) Gender and Education 501. Maureen Baker, 'Choices or Constraints? Family Responsibilities, Gender and Academic Career' (2010) 41 (1) Journal of Comparative Family Studies. 16. Ward (n 10).

essential workers? Follow-up research on the long-term effects of the lockdown on women's academic careers will also be necessary.

In the short term, universities need to come up with a plan for assisting parents, and especially mothers, who will struggle to catch up after the COVID-19 lockdown. Some universities have suspended the tenure clock for a year, but many research projects will be delayed for much longer. If academic mothers are facing a two- or three-year delay in their publication pipeline, what sort of protections can be put in place if their tenure is postponed? The publication requirements for tenure and promotion in academia have been steadily increasing: is it time for departments, schools, or entire fields to rethink the 'publish or perish' culture?

The interviews illustrated the various strategies used to reconcile academic work and family care work during the COVID-19 lockdown in both the USA and Italy. As long as unequal division and gendered assumptions of care work prevail, full "citizenship" for the majority of women in academia will remain out of reach.[32] More than two years into the pandemic, it is time to pause and assess the impact that it has had on academic parents – especially on mothers, 'who face disproportionately more caregiving work at home' and corresponding curbs on their productivity.[33]

In the USA, the reliance on adjunct labour means that the shrinking full-time faculty need to take on increasing amounts of the administrative and service work.[34] This is problematic in itself, as adjunct labour is chronically underpaid, precarious, and without benefits. If universities relied less on part-time labour and hired more full-time faculty, there would be a larger "safety net" of faculty members available to pick up the slack when life interrupts work for some of them. In the short-term, departments can consider supporting academic parents by organising a temporary redistribution of tasks, potentially giving work requiring only short periods of concentration to caretakers,

32 Lidia KC Manzo and Sara Martucci, 'Academic Mothers Being Left Behind during Covid-19: Challenges and Opportunities Toward a New Culture of Care and Citizenship' (2021) Working Paper presented at the second international conference of the journal Scuola Democratica <https://www.scuolademocratica-conference.net> accessed 29 November 2021.

33 <https://www.insidehighered.com/news/2021/03/10/covid-19-moment-women-stem> accessed 29 November 2021.

34 Adjuncts are faculty members who teach one or more courses per semester but are not employed full-time by the university. The work is typically low-paid and often without benefits like health care. In the USA, more than half of all faculty appointments are part-time, adjunct labor. While some courses are staffed by specialists who have full-time work in other industries like law firms, non-profits, or corporations, most are taught by graduate students and individuals who have PhDs but have not secured full-time positions.

for the time being. Perhaps faculty who are less burdened by care could take on heavier workloads, in exchange for "credits" that they can take advantage of at a later point in their careers.

Finally, we know from our research that women who had access to full-time childcare support were the most successful during the spring 2020 lockdown. Previous research on the topic has shown the need to consider the lockdown period as a time of leave, as a way of compensating for the loss in productivity.[35] Others have advocated for the increased weighting of teaching in the evaluation of academic careers.[36] Here we ask: what would potential future lockdowns or other interruptions look like if governments funded programmes to pay unemployed or underemployed family members or neighbours to provide childcare during the mother's workday? This perhaps would not alleviate the motherhood penalty, but it would prevent it increasing in the way that we witnessed during the current pandemic.

The pandemic has laid bare many inequalities in our societies concerning race, class, and gender. The plight of a relatively privileged group – highly educated women with professional careers – in the so-called ivory tower of academia may seem trivial, but it reflects wider issues around motherhood and work in modern Western societies. Academia is an especially demanding career and motherhood is a taxing job, especially when the children are young. The COVID-19 lockdown brought to the forefront the gender inequality that exists in the home and at work. It is not enough to acknowledge that the COVID-19 crisis has exposed underlying issues, now is the time for creative alternatives to a system that never worked to begin with.

References

Balenzano C et al., 'Families in the Pandemic between Challenges and Opportunities: An Empirical Study of Parents with Preschool and School-age Children' (2020) 10 Italian Sociological Review 777.

Baker M, 'Choices or Constraints? Family Responsibilities, gender and academic career' (2010) 41 (1) Journal of Comparative Family Studies 1.

Bassett RH, *Parenting and Professing: Balancing Family Work with an Academic Career* (Vanderbilt University Press 2005).

---

35 Alessandra Minello, 'The Pandemic and the Female Academic' (2020) Nature.

36 Candace Miller and Josipa Roksa, 'Balancing Research and Service in Academia: Gender, Race, and Laboratory Tasks' (2020) 34 (1) Gender & Society 131.

Bianchi SM et al., 'Housework: Who Did, Does or Will Do it, and How Much Does it Matter?' (2012) 91 (1) Social Forces 55.
Bozzon RAM et al., 'Work–life Interferences in the Early Stages of Academic Careers: The Case of Precarious Researchers in Italy' (2017) 16 (2–3) European Educational Research Journal 332.
Giurge LM et al., 'Why Time Poverty Matters for Individuals, Organisations and Nations' (2021) 118 (12) Nature Human Behavior 993–1003.
Halley MC et al., 'The Intersection of Work and Home Challenges Faced by Physician Mothers during the Coronavirus Disease 2019 Pandemic: A Mixed-methods Analysis' (2021) 30 (4) Journal of Women's Health 514.
Harris CB et al., 'Academic Careers and Parenting: Identity, Performance and Surveillance' (2019) 44 (4) Studies in Higher Education 708.
Hochschild A and Machung A, *The Second Shift: Working Families and the Revolution at Home* (Viking 1989).
Kan MY et al., 'Gender Convergence in Domestic Work: Discerning the Effects of Interactional and Institutional Barriers from Large-scale Data' (2011) 45 (2) Sociology 234.
Kantola J, 'Why Do All the Women Disappear?' Gendering Processes in a Political Science Department' (2008) 15 (2) Gender, Work & Organization 202.
Krukowski RA et al., 'Academic Productivity Differences by Gender and Child Age in Science, Technology, Engineering, Mathematics, and Medicine Faculty during the COVID-19 Pandemic' (2021) 30 (3) Journal of Women's Health 341–347.
Langin K, 'Pandemic Hit Academic Mothers Especially Hard, New Data Confirm' (2021) Science 660.
Long JS, 'The Origins of Sex Differences in Science' (1990) 68 (4) Social Forces 1297.
Lutter M and Schröder M, 'Is there a Motherhood Penalty in Academia? The Gendered Effect of Children on Academic Publications' (2020) 36 (3) European Sociological Review 442.
Manzo LKC and Minello A, 'Mothers, Childcare Duties, and Remote Working under COVID-19 Lockdown in Italy: Cultivating Communities of Care' (2020) 10 (2) Dialogues in Human Geography 120.
Martucci S, 'He's Working from Home and I'm at Home Trying to Work: Experiences of Childcare and the Work-Family Balance Among Mothers During Covid' (2021) Journal of Family Issues.
Mason MA and Goulden M, 'Do Babies Matter? The Effects of Family Formation on the Lifelong Careers of Academic Men and Women' (2002) 88 (6) Academe 21.
Mason MA and Goulden M, 'Marriage and the Baby Blues: Redefining Gender Equity in the Academy' (2004) 596 (1) Annals of the American Academy of Political and Social Science 86.

Mason MA et al., 'Why Graduate Students Reject the Fast Track' (2009) 95 (1) Academe 11.

Mason MA et al., *Do Babies Matter?: Gender and Family in the Ivory Tower* (Rutgers University Press 2013).

Miller C and Roksa J, 'Balancing Research and Service in Academia: Gender, Race, and Laboratory Tasks' (2020) 34 (1) Gender & Society 131.

Minello A et al., 'The Pandemic and the Academic Mothers: Present Hardships and Future Perspectives' (2020) 23 (1) European Societies S82–S94.

Minello A, 'The Pandemic and the Female Academic' (2020) Nature.

Myers KR et al., 'Unequal Effects of the COVID-19 Pandemic on Scientists' (2020) 4 Nature Human Behavior 880.

Offer S, 'The Costs of Thinking about Work and Family: Mental Labor, Work–family Spillover, and Gender Inequality among Parents in Dual-earner Families' (2014) 29 (4) Sociological Forum 916.

Oinas T, 'The Division of Labour within Households: Men's Increased Participation?' in Tammelin M (ed.), *Family, Work and Well-Being: Emergence of New Issues, Springer Briefs in Well-Being and Quality of Life Research* (Springer International Publishing 2018).

Picardi I, *Labirinti di Cristallo. Strutture di Genere nella Ricerca e nell'Accademia* (Franco Angeli 2020).

Pillay V, 'Academic Mothers Finding Rhyme and Reason' (2009) 21 (5) Gender and Education 501.

Robertson LG et al., 'Mothers and Mental Labor: A Phenomenological Focus Group Study of Family-related Thinking Work' (2019) 43 (2) Psychology of Women Quarterly 184.

Ward K, 'Having it all: Women, Work, Family, and the Academic Career' (2014) 73 Labour / Le Travail 255.

Ward K and Wolf-Wendel L, 'Mothering and Professing: Critical Choices and the Academic Career' (2017) 10 (3) NASPA Journal About Women in Higher Education 229.

Wolf-Wendel L and Ward K, 'Academic Mothers: Exploring Disciplinary Perspectives' (2015) 40 (1) Innovative Higher Education 19.

Wolfinger NH et al., 'Problems in the Pipeline: Gender, Marriage, and Fertility in the Ivory Tower' (2008) 79 (4) The Journal of Higher Education 388.

CHAPTER 8

Women and Financial Equality

Rewriting the Rules

Mara Catherine Harvey and Federica Cristani

1 Financial Equality: A Preliminary Theoretical and Legal Background

Since the commitment to gender equality made in 1995 at the United Nations (UN) Fourth World Conference on Women,[1] "gender mainstreaming" has become an important international strategy to advance women's equality (see also Chapter 3 of this volume). According to the UN Economic and Social Council (ECOSOC), "[m]ainstreaming a gender perspective is the process of assessing the implications for women and men of *any* planned action, including legislation, policies or programmes, in all areas and at all levels" [emphasis added].[2]

As highlighted by several international instruments,[3] equality of women is a goal for *all* policies and sectors, including the economic and financial ones. Among others, the Convention on the Elimination of All Forms of Discrimination against Women (CEDAW)[4] requires parties to take appropriate measures "in particular in the political, social, economic and cultural fields [...] to ensure the full development and advancement of women".[5] Moreover, several (non-governmental) declarations and documents have stressed the need to empower women's economic rights. For example, the Montreal Principles

1 Fourth World Conference on Women, Declaration, UN Doc. A/CONF/177/20, 15 September 1995, para 24 <https://www.un.org/en/development/desa/population/migration/generalassembly/docs/globalcompact/A_CONF.177_20.pdf> accessed 29 November 2021.

2 UN General Assembly, Resolution A/52/3, Report of the Economic and Social Council for 1997, 18 September 1997 <https://undocs.org/A/52/3> accessed 29 November 2021.

3 For a general review of the relevant international legal framework, see Christine Chinkin, 'Women, Rights of, International Protection' (2010) Max Planck Encyclopedia of Public International Law <https://opil.ouplaw.com/view/10.1093/law:epil/9780199231690/law-9780199231690-e1745> accessed 29 November 2021.

4 Convention on the Elimination of All Forms of Discrimination against Women (CEDAW), UNTS 1249, adopted on 8 December 1979 and entered into force on 3 September 1981, 13.

5 CEDAW, article 3.

DOI:10.1163/9789004467682_010

on Women's Economic, Social and Cultural Rights, adopted at a meeting of experts in Montréal from 7 to 10 December 2002,[6] and the 2012 Declaration of the G20 Leaders, recognised "[…] the need for women and youth to gain access to financial services and financial education […]".[7]

Women's economic empowerment was listed as a global priority in the 2015 G7 Leader's Joint Declaration, where they "[…] reaffirm [their] commitment to continue our work to promote gender equality as well as full participation and empowerment for all women and girls [… and] to overcome discrimination […] and other cultural, social, economic and legal barriers to women's economic participation".[8] Two years later, in 2017, the priority theme for the 61st session of the UN Commission on the Status of Women (CSW)[9] was "Women's economic empowerment in the changing world of work".[10] The background document for the preparatory meeting in the Asia-Pacific region made it very clear that "[t]here is an urgent need to analyse […] the role of fiscal policy in upholding the right to life for girls and women".[11] Overall, we find several references and commitments to advancing the economic empowerment of women and to adopting the "gender mainstreaming" approach in the economic and fiscal discourse.[12]

But what do we mean by economic empowerment of women? A report prepared for the International Center for Research on Women has developed

6 'Montréal Principles on Women's Economic, Social and Cultural Rights' (2004) 26 (3) Human Rights Quarterly 760.

7 G20 Leaders Declaration, Los Cabos, Mexico, 19 June 2012, para 53 <http://www.g20.utoronto.ca/2012/2012-0619-loscabos.html> accessed 29 November 2021.

8 G7 Leaders' Declaration at the G7 Summit of 7–8 June 2015 <https://www.unwomen.org/en/news/stories/2015/6/g7-leaders-highlight-women-empowerment-as-a-top-priority> accessed 29 November 2021.

9 The Commission on the Status of Women (CSW) is the principal UN intergovernmental body exclusively dedicated to the promotion of gender equality and the empowerment of women. It was established by ECOSOC resolution 11(II) of 21 June 1946. See the official website at <https://www.unwomen.org/en/csw> accessed 29 November 2021.

10 The 61st session of the Commission on the Status of Women took place from 13 to 24 March 2017. See the dedicated website at <https://www.unwomen.org/en/csw/previous-sessions/csw61-2017> accessed 29 November 2021.

11 UN Economic and Social Commission for Asia and the Pacific (ESCAP), UN Women, Regional preparatory meeting in the Asia-Pacific region for CSW61, Background document (2016) 14 <https://www.unwomen.org/-/media/headquarters/attachments/sections/csw/61/the%20future%20of%20work%20in%20a%20changing%20world%2020170220.pdf?la=en&vs=3414> accessed 29 November 2021.

12 Christine Chinkin, 'Gender and Economic, Social, and Cultural Rights', in Eibe Riedel et al (eds), *Economic, Social, and Cultural Rights in International Law: Contemporary Issues and Challenges* (Oxford University Press 2014) 136.

the following definition, which effectively draws together the elements of economic empowerment: "[a] woman is economically empowered when she has both the *ability* to succeed and advance economically and the *power* to make and act on economic decisions [...] women need the skills and resources to compete in markets, as well as [...] the ability to make and act on decisions and control resources and profits" [emphasis added].[13]

In the financial sector, in particular, economic empowerment can be achieved by promoting financial inclusion, meaning the possibility to access, and actively and effectively use, all the relevant financial services, such as bank accounts, loans, and insurance.[14] One tool that has been used to promote economic empowerment of women in the fiscal policy framework is the so-called "gender budgeting",[15] which allows fiscal authorities "to ensure that tax and spending policies and/or public financial management instruments address gender inequality and the advancement of women in areas such as education, health, and economic empowerment".[16] As underlined in one of the expert papers prepared for the 61st session of CSW, "[g]ender budgeting is ideally a fiscal innovation that translates gender commitments into fiscal commitments"[17]; however, "[a] tremendous amount of confusion exists on the concept of gender budgeting [...]".[18]

Indeed, particular stress has been laid on the need to enhance the capacity building of national governments so that they can adequately address the question of fiscal equality. In this regard, UN agencies and other international

---

13 Anne Marie Golla et al, *Understanding and Measuring Women's Economic Empowerment* (International Center for Research on Women 2011) 4 <https://www.empowerwomen.org/en/resources/documents/2013/8/understanding-and-measuring--womens-economic-empowerment?lang=en> accessed 29 November 2021.

14 Leora Klapper and Jake Hess, *Financial Inclusion and Women's Economic Empowerment* (UNHLP 2016) 2 <https://www.empowerwomen.org/en/resources/documents/2016/11/financial-inclusion-and-womens-economic-empowerment?lang=en> accessed 29 November 2021.

15 Janet G. Stotsky, *Using Fiscal Policy and Public Financial Management to Promote Gender Equality. International Perspectives* (Routledge 2020) 30.

16 Lisa Kolovich, 'Gender Budgeting: How Fiscal Policy Can Promote Gender Equality', in Lisa Kolovich (ed), *Fiscal Policies and Gender Equality* (International Monetary Fund 2018) 2.

17 Lekha Chakraborty, Expert paper for the UN Women Expert Group Meeting 'Women's economic empowerment in the changing world of work' Geneva, Switzerland, 26–28 September 2016; EGM/CWW/EP, 'Fiscal Policy Practices for Women's Economic Empowerment' (8 September 2016) 3 <https://www.unwomen.org/en/csw/previous-sessions/csw61-2017/preparations/expert-group-meeting> accessed 29 November 2021.

18 ibid 13.

organisations have been providing technical assistance and training to countries over the years.[19] For example, the International Monetary Fund has supported countries to use fiscal policy to promote gender equality.[20]

Nevertheless, women's financial inclusion still faces several barriers.[21] Increasing women's financial inclusion is not just a matter of providing the relevant financial instruments, it is also a matter of improving women's skills and capabilities to use them effectively.[22] In this respect, financial literacy, which provides individuals with the "knowledge, aptitude, and skill base necessary to become questioning and informed consumers of financial services"[23] is an effective instrument to achieve financial equality and, consequently, strengthen women's economic empowerment.[24]

In this chapter, we want to stress the overall need for a new narrative when it comes to financial equality. The following section illustrates what we mean by "new narrative" together with an overview of the most significant obstacles that women are still facing in the financial sector.

2 Financial Equality: the Need for a New Narrative

It is a fact that wealth is increasingly growing in the hands of women around the world. According to the statistics, women worldwide already hold more than 30% of global wealth,[25] and will hold even more in the next couple of decades as a result of the wealth transfer down the generations.

19 Kolovich (n 16) 7.

20 ibid 1–2.

21 Klapper and Hess (n 14) 2.

22 Mark Napier et al, *Promoting Women's Financial Inclusion: A Toolkit* (DFID UK 2013), 17 <https://www.empowerwomen.org/en/resources/documents/2014/5/promoting-womens-financial-inclusion-a-toolkit?lang=en> accessed 29 November 2021.

23 Carolynne Mason and Richard M S Wilson, 'Conceptualising Financial Literacy' (2000) 7 Loughborough University Occasional Paper 5.

24 Jodi Jarecke et al, 'Financial Literacy Education for Women' (2014) 2014 (141) New Directions for Adult and Continuing Education. Special Issue: Financial Literacy and Adult Education 38.

25 This will rise at a compound annual growth rate of 5.7% to US$ 97 trillion by 2024, according to Boston Consulting Group (BCG). See Anna Zakrzewski et al, 'Managing the Next Decade of Women's Wealth' (*BCG Publications*, 9 April 2020) <https://www.bcg.com/publications/2020/managing-next-decade-women-wealth> accessed 22 May 2021 and UBS, *Women's Wealth 2030 Report* (8 March 2021) <https://www.ubs.com/global/en/wealth-management/women/2021/women-wealth-parity-power-purpose.html> accessed 29 November 2021.

This means that there is a huge opportunity for the finance industry to focus more on women. Even though women hold a significant part of the global wealth, they still suffer from inequalities: recent research published by UBS shows a dramatic picture of how a pay gap can influence women's wealth accumulation over her lifetime. The research simulates the earnings, savings and wealth accumulation of a professional woman and the impact of a potential pay gap compared to a man's earnings in a similar professional position. A pay gap of 10% can lead to the woman accumulating 38% less wealth over the course of her life. Furthermore, the woman's wealth gap can increase dramatically if other life circumstances are taken into consideration, as we will explore below.[26]

Women face several barriers to financial participation and access to capital. And in many countries, financial equality is still very new: let us take for example Switzerland, where it has been barely 35 years since married women were first allowed to open bank accounts without the consent of their husbands.[27] Accordingly, the financial empowerment of women in the country is also still in its infancy. And, according to the 2019 "UBS Investor Watch. Own your worth" report, although 80% of daily household financial decisions are taken by women, only 23% take the lead on long-term financial decisions. Moreover, 8 in 10 women still believe their male partners know more about money than they do.[28]

Although it is true that companies are increasingly implementing policies aimed to foster equal opportunities,[29] significant gaps in pay and funding remain.[30] In this respect, it is worth noting the report "Women's Empowerment

---

26 See GenderSmart, 'Unlocking Women's Wealth: An Interview with Mara Harvey' (*GenderSmart Blog*, 19 November 2020) <https://www.gendersmartinvesting.com/gendersmart-blog/2020/11/19/unlocking-womens-wealth-an-interview-with-mara-harvey> accessed 29 November 2021.

27 In 1985, the new Swiss Marriage Law, introducing legal equality between women and men within marriage, was ratified by referendum. See Claudia Kaufmann, 'Marriage Law Revision. Occasion for Hope?' (1986) 9 (1) Women's Studies International Forum 35.

28 See UBS, 'UBS Investor Watch. Own your Worth' Global insights: What's on Investors' Minds. Volume 1 (2019) 7, <https://www.ubs.com/global/en/wealth-management/our-approach/investor-watch/2019/own-your-worth.html> accessed 29 November y 2021.

29 Equileap's report on implementation of gender policies by companies, for example, shows that there was an overall improvement in performance among companies ranked in Equileap's Global Top 200 in 2018 compared to 2017. See Equileap, *Gender Equality. Global Report & Ranking* (Equileap 2018) <https://equileap.com/wp-content/uploads/2020/08/Equileap-Gender-Equality-Global-Report-and-Ranking-2018.pdf> accessed 29 November 2021.

30 UBS (n 28).

and Business: 2020 Trends and Opportunities" prepared by the UN Global Compact initiative in partnership with the nonprofit organisation Business for Social Responsibility. This report effectively highlights that, while 68% of the companies surveyed have made a leadership commitment or offer 'support for gender equality and women's empowerment, only 28% of them have time-bound, measurable goals and targets' in terms of gender policies.[31]

Overall, there is a need for a new narrative when it comes to advancing financial inclusion and equality: it is not enough to address the issue with businesses solutions of "pink marketing" (marketing targeting female clients), "pink products" (offerings targeting female clients) or "pink teams" (female teams focusing on female clients). Instead, there is an immediate need to reconsider the entire value chain of the business, to make it more appealing (and functional) for women: both outside-in (making it attractive for female clients to engage with businesses) and inside-out (making it more attractive for women to join, grow and remain within organisations).[32]

Promoting and improving gender equality policies in the financial and business sectors is not only a social and moral issue, but can also have a significant positive impact on boosting gross domestic product (GDP) growth. According to the 2020 European Investment Bank's report "Funding Women Entrepreneurs", promoting gender diversity 'could lead to a potential increase of 26% of the annual global GDP and US$ 160 trillion of human capital wealth' as well as improving business performance by 15%.[33]

When creating a new narrative on financial equality, three main questions arise: what would the financial industry look like if it focused on women? What is the true cost of pay gaps and funding gaps? Isn't it time for fewer words and more action?

Thus, gender equality represents one of the biggest challenges and opportunities for every country. The following sections highlight the barriers women are currently facing and the steps that can be taken to boost financial literacy and, consequently, financial equality.

---

31 United Nations Global Compact, Business for Social Responsibility, *Women's Empowerment and Business: 2020 Trends and Opportunities* (2020) <https://www.bsr.org/reports/WEP-AnnualReport2020.pdf> accessed 22 May 2021. See also UBS (n 28) 5.

32 GenderSmart (n 26).

33 See Surya Fackelmann and Alessandro De Concini, *Funding Women Entrepreneurs. How to Empower Growth* (European Investment Bank June 2020) 7 <https://www.eib.org/en/publications/why-are-women-entrepreneurs-missing-out-on-funding-report> accessed 22 May 2021. See also UBS, *Women's Wealth 2030 Report* (8 March 2021) 4 <https://www.ubs.com/global/en/wealth-management/women/2021/women-wealth-parity-power-purpose.html> accessed 29 November 2021.

3 Barriers to Gender Equality in the Financial World: What Are We Talking About?

What are the main barriers to gender equality? The five most common are: (1) pay gaps – the long-term impact of lower earnings on wealth gaps and pension gaps; (2) career discontinuity – when women take time off to care for family members; (3) flexible work – particularly in Switzerland, where the percentage of women working part-time is higher than in other European countries;[34] (4) longevity – if women live 5 to 7 years longer than men, statistically, their (more modest) wealth has to last longer, impacting their quality of life; and (5) and risk appetite – aggregate statistics show that women tend to sit on more cash and fixed income investments than men do, which means they compound their wealth over decades at a low interest rate.[35]

A simulation of a lifetime wealth curve was carried out in the 2017 study "UBS Wealth management research: Taking action". The study showed how the cumulative impact of the above-mentioned factors can prevent women from being able to accumulate the wealth needed to sustain their longevity.[36]

The overall picture is not very encouraging: according to the "Global Gender Gap Report 2020" of the World Economic Forum, 'it would take 257 years for women and men to reach pay parity'.[37] This should be coupled with the findings of the UBS research, which shows that a 10% gender pay gap alone can lead to a 38% gender wealth gap, while a 20% pay gap can lead to an 85% wealth gap.[38] For example, in Switzerland, the pay gap between male and female full-time employees stands at 19%, according to the Federal Statistical Office.[39]

In light of this analysis, we need to reflect on the broader meaning of risk when we talk about women and financial participation. Conventional notions of risk relate to stock market risk or volatility; and a lack of financial confidence

---

34 See Switzerland, Federal Statistical Office, *Swiss Labour Force Survey: Labour Market Participation 2010–2018* (23 April 2019) <https://www.bfs.admin.ch/bfs/en/home/news/whats-new.gnpdetail.2019-0464.html> accessed 29 November 2021.

35 See UBS, 'Taking Action. How Women Can Best Protect and Grow Their Wealth' *Women and Investing UBS Wealth Management* (October 2017) 4 <https://www.ubs.com/global/en/wealth-management> accessed 29 November 2021.

36 ibid.

37 See World Economic Forum, *Global Gender Gap Report 2020* (World Economic Forum 2019) <https://www.weforum.org/reports/gender-gap-2020-report-100-years-pay-equality> accessed 29 November 2021.

38 UBS (n 28) 5.

39 Switzerland, Federal Statistical Office, *Wage Gap 2018* (2019) <https://www.bfs.admin.ch/bfs/en/home/statistics/work-income/wages-income-employment-labour-costs/wage-levels-switzerland/wage-gap.html> accessed 29 November 2021.

can lead women to shy away from investing. However, the real risk that women need to assess is whether they will be able to afford to maintain their quality of life after retirement, especially if they do not capture the compound, long-term benefits of investing.

The above-mentioned UBS report shows that a woman's life 'circumstances, financial confidence, and attitude to investing can actually make it harder for her to achieve her financial goals'.[40] And indeed, one factor that has been consistently underestimated is the role that gender can play in the investment decision-making process.[41] Women and men build up and invest their wealth differently; accordingly, finding the right investment approach can make a big difference by improving women's financial well-being as well as their quality of life.[42] For example, women tend to make investments in businesses that have a meaning and purpose for them.[43]

There are several steps than can be taken to reduce the impact of the gender pay gap on women's wealth: focusing more on the financial goals of women, and defining and recommending portfolios accordingly; and, above all, helping women feel more confident about investing.[44]

This leads to the issues of financial literacy and financial equality, which are discussed in the following section.

4 Financial Literacy and Financial Equality: Where Do We Stand?

Financial literacy, namely the "ability to use one's knowledge and skills to effectively manage financial resources",[45] is important for everyone, not only for those working in the financial sectors, but also for the consumers of financial products to help them know how best to save and invest their money.[46]

---

40 See UBS, 'Taking Action. How Women Can Best Protect and Grow Their Wealth' *Women and Investing UBS Wealth Management* (October 2017) 4 <https://www.ubs.com/global/en/wealth-management> accessed 29 November 2021.

41 ibid.

42 ibid.

43 ibid.

44 ibid 16.

45 See Andras Horvai and Andrey A. Bokarev, 'Financial Literacy – Helping Citizens Make Smart Financial Choices' (*World Bank – Opinion*, 21 June 2018) <https://www.worldbank.org/en/news/opinion/2018/06/21/financial-literacy-helping-citizens-make-smart-financial-choices> accessed 29 November 2021.

46 See Leora Klapper et al, *Financial Literacy Around the World. Insights from the Standard & Poor's Ratings Services Global Financial Literacy Survey* (2015) 4 <https://gflec.org/initiatives/sp-global-finlit-survey> accessed 29 November 2021.

Research has demonstrated that financial literacy can actually help people plan their investments and savings better.[47] However, financial literacy is still a goal that has yet to be achieved for a large proportion of the population, A good overview is provided by the 2015 *Standard & Poor's Ratings Services Global Financial Literacy Survey*, which builds on previous similar initiatives undertaken by the International Network on Financial Education of the Organisation for Economic Co-operation and Development (OECD)[48] and the World Bank,[49] as well as on several national survey initiatives.[50] The *Standard & Poor's Ratings Services Global Financial Literacy Survey* represents the "first and most comprehensive global gauge of financial literacy to date", based on interviews with more than 150,000 people in more than 140 countries. According to the findings of the survey, on average, only one in three adults worldwide are financially literate.[51] In Switzerland, for example, financial literacy is 57% (meaning that roughly one in every two adults does not fully understand the impact of inflation, of diversification and of compound interest on their wealth accumulation over a lifetime), versus >70% in top scoring countries.[52] And the numbers get worse when factors such as gender, educational

---

47 See Jere R. Behrman et al, 'The Effects of Financial Education and Financial Literacy: How Financial Literacy Affects Household Wealth Accumulation' (2012) 102 American Economic Review 3, 300 and Annamaria Lusardi, and Olivia S. Mitchell, 'The Economic Importance of Financial Literacy: Theory and Evidence' (2014) 52 (1) Journal of Economic Literature 5.

48 OECD Member States established the International Network on Financial Education in 2008, with the aim of collecting relevant data and sharing experiences and good practices on financial literacy worldwide. For more information see the official website <https://www.oecd.org/financial/education/oecd-international-network-on-financial-education.htm> accessed 29 November 2021.

49 See the Financial Literacy survey prepared as part of the World Bank Financial Governance Consumer Protection in Financial Services Program, Alpha Research, *Financial Literacy Survey* (World Bank 2010) <https://openknowledge.worldbank.org/handle/10986/12876> accessed 29 November 2021.

50 See, for example, the financial literacy survey prepared by the National Bank of Italy (Giovanni D'Alessio et al, 'Financial literacy in Italy: the results of the Bank of Italy's 2020 survey' (*Banca d'Italia – Questioni di Economia e Finanza. Occasional Paper No. 588*, December 2020) <https://www.bancaditalia.it/pubblicazioni/qef/2020-0588/index.html?com.dotmarketing.htmlpage.language=1> accessed 29 November 2021) and the financial literacy survey prepared by the US National Foundation for Credit Counseling, *2020 Annual Financial Literacy Survey* (2021) <https://www.nfcc.org/resources/client-impact-and-research/2020-consumer-financial-literacy-survey> accessed 29 November 2021.

51 Leora Klapper et al, *Financial Literacy Around the World. Insights from the Standard & Poor's Ratings Services Global Financial Literacy Survey* (2015), 4, <https://gflec.org/initiatives/sp-global-finlit-survey> accessed 22 May 2021.

52 See the relevant data from Klapper et al (n 51) 8.

level, income, and age are taken into account. In particular, according to the survey, '35% of men worldwide are financially literate compared with 30% of women', and this average gender gap of 5% can be found equally in both advanced economies and emerging ones.[53]

Together with the low rate of financial literacy, we should also consider the semantics around money and financial matters. Indeed, the language normally used by 'investors, finance professionals and the media' is still biased against women.[54] For example, a study conducted at the London Business School highlighted that women wishing to start an investment plan are usually asked mainly "about the potential for losses", while men are asked "about the potential for gains".[55]

Also, the media is biased against women in its publications on financial matters.[56] In a linguistic study of 300 articles, Starling Bank highlighted huge discrepancies 'in the way men and women are spoken to about money'. Around 65% of financial articles in women's magazines define 'women as excessive spenders'; on the other hand, in articles aimed at men, 70% emphasise the concept that making money is a masculine ideal.[57] Thus, there is a need for a new narrative to overcome the biased semantics around financial matters, which affect women's access to capital and women's involvement in managing money and investment.[58]

Turning to the question of how engaged women are in financial matters, it is worth recalling that, according to the 2019 UBS "Own Your Worth" report, most married women worldwide tend to leave financial decisions to their male spouses. This is mainly because of "historical and social precedents to

53 ibid 12.

54 UBS (n 40).

55 Dana Kanze et al, 'Male and Female Entrepreneurs Get Asked Different Questions by VCs – and it Affects How Much Funding They Get' (2017) *Harvard Business Review* <https://www8.gsb.columbia.edu/cbs-directory/sites/cbs-directory/files/publications/H03QHY-PDF-ENG.PDF> accessed 29 November 2021. See also UBS, *Women's Wealth 2030 Report* (8 March 2021) 15 <https://www.ubs.com/global/en/wealth-management/women/2021/women-wealth-parity-power-purpose.html> accessed 29 November 2021.

56 ibid.

57 Starling Bank, *#Makemoneyequal. Linguistic Analysis 2018* (February 2018) <https://www.starlingbank.com/docs/reports-research/MakeMoneyEqual-Research.pdf> accessed 22 May 2021. See also Anne Boden, 'Why we need to #Makemoneyequal' (*Starling Bank Blog*, 13 March 2018) <https://www.starlingbank.com/blog/make-money-equal/> accessed 29 November 2021.

58 Mara C. Harvey, *Women and Risk: Rewriting the Rules* (Nicolai Publishing & Intelligence 2019).

family, gender roles and confidence levels".[59] The 2019 UBS report detailed the findings of a survey of about '3,700 married women, widows and divorcees in Brazil, Germany, Hong Kong, Italy, Mexico, Singapore, Switzerland, the United Kingdom and the United States', on the question of 'how women around the world engage with their finances'.[60]

The findings highlight that women tend to focus more on short-term financial responsibilities and tasks, such as the daily household expenses. Only 23% of women are reported to have a say on long-term 'financial planning decisions like investing and insurance' (and this seems most common in Hong Kong and Switzerland). There are many reasons for this, including women's belief that their male spouses know more about finance (82%), or are generally the ones earning more in the family (78%) or because women have never been encouraged (58%) or even discouraged (56%) from being involved in long-term financial planning and investing.[61]

Women often only grasp the risks of not getting involved in long-term financial management decisions when they divorce or are widowed: statistics show that 76% of widows and divorcees wish they had been more involved in long-term financial planning, while 77% urge others to become so.[62] Indeed, when women are actively engaged in making long-term financial decisions with their male spouses, they feel more positive about their future financial security.[63]

Another noteworthy finding is that the involvement of women in long-term financial decision-taking is less today than for the previous generation.[64] According to the 2019 UBS report, nearly 60% of women under 50 years old defer long-term financial decisions to their male spouses, compared to 55% of women over 50 years old.[65]

Accordingly, finance needs a profound transformation; in particular, the narrative around financial participation should be focused on life goals, purpose

59 See UBS, 'UBS Investor Watch. Own your worth' *Global insights: What's on investors' minds. Volume 1* (2019) 3 <https://www.ubs.com/global/en/wealth-management/our-approach/investor-watch/2019/own-your-worth.html> accessed 29 November 2021 and UBS, *Women's Wealth 2030 Report* (8 March 2021) 11 <https://www.ubs.com/global/en/wealth-management/women/2021/women-wealth-parity-power-purpose.html> accessed 29 November 2021.

60 See UBS, 'UBS Investor Watch. Own your worth' *Global Insights: What's on Investors' Minds. Volume 1* (2019) 4 <https://www.ubs.com/global/en/wealth-management/our-approach/investor-watch/2019/own-your-worth.html> accessed 29 November 2021.

61 ibid 7.

62 ibid 12.

63 ibid 11.

64 ibid.

65 ibid 13.

and impact, instead of just evaluating clients' risk profiles. A new narrative should also emphasise that every investment decision is actually a reflection of values, such as in the case of "impact investing", which is "an investment strategy that aims to generate specific beneficial social or environmental effects in addition to financial gains".[66] And, indeed, according to a recent report of the Boston Consulting Group (BCG), 64% of women tend to take into account 'environmental, social, and governance concerns' when making investment decisions.[67]

Financial literacy should be on school curriculum for all age groups, from primary through university. This will enable a new narrative to be built up around finance – and reaching financial equality – starting from the younger generations, as discussed further in section 5.

5 Building up a New Narrative around Money for the Younger Generations

Financial education needs to begin at a young age, especially for girls, to build up financial confidence as early as possible.[68] In 2015, a study from the University of Washington revealed that by the age of 5 years, 'children have a sense of self-esteem comparable to that of adults',[69] and money habits are largely shaped by the age of 7 years. This is why it is important to start a conversation about finance with children quite early.[70] Research shows that pay gaps start with pocket money: by the age of 10 years, many girls are already facing pocket money pay gaps that range between 10% and 30%.[71] And this is

66 James Chen, 'Impact Investing' (*Investopedia*, 2 March 2021) <https://www.investopedia.com/terms/i/impact-investing.asp> accessed 29 November 2021.

67 Anna Zakrzewski et al, 'Managing the Next Decade of Women's Wealth' (*BCG Publications*, 9 April 2020) <https://www.bcg.com/publications/2020/managing-next-decade-women-wealth> accessed 29 November 2021. See also UBS, *Women's Wealth 2030 Report* (8 March 2021) 25 <https://www.ubs.com/global/en/wealth-management/women/2021/women-wealth-parity-power-purpose.html> accessed 29 November 2021.

68 ibid 23.

69 Molly McElroy, 'Children's Self-esteem Already Established by Age 5, New Study Finds' (*Washington University News*, 2 November 2015) <https://www.washington.edu/news/2015/11/02/childrens-self-esteem-already-established-by-age-5-new-study-finds> accessed 29 November 2021.

70 UBS, *Women's Wealth 2030 Report* (8 March 2021) 23 <https://www.ubs.com/global/en/wealth-management/women/2021/women-wealth-parity-power-purpose.html> accessed 29 November 2021.

71 See, among others, Mara C. Harvey, *Women and Risk: Rewriting the Rules* (Nicolai Publishing & Intelligence 2019), 55; Hilary Osborne, 'Boys Get More Pocket Money Than

happening partly because of the above-mentioned biased semantics around financial matters, that permeate not only our business lives but our family lives, too. This needs to change if we want to empower the next generation of girls to enter the labour force, access capital and manage wealth on equal terms with men. This underpins the need for a new narrative around money and finances that would encourage girls and women to deal positively with earning and investing, boosting financial literacy and financial equality.

Financial literacy can and should start at home, by teaching children the value of money, the ways in which they can start earning and, importantly for girls, training them to negotiate their pay for a given job. Financial training should also include teaching children that every financial decision has an impact on our world. In this way, they will soon learn that every spending decision or investment decision they make has a social and environmental impact.[72] It is essential to bear in mind that "when spending your pennies, you want to know where your money ends up, and which companies care: do they care about forests and oceans and seas? Do they care about saving the birds and the bees? [...] By spending your money, you are using your voice".[73]

6 Concluding Remarks

On 31 January 2002, the French Presidency of the Council of the European Union organized a high level conference on "The Economic Empowerment of Women: Key to substantive gender equality", which gathered the EU ministers for equality along with the European Commissioner for Equality. This was one of the first conferences organized by the French Presidency at the very beginning of its 2022 semester, with the aim to "formulate concrete solutions to support women's economic empowerment".[74]

Girls, Halifax survey finds' (*The Guardian*, 3 June 2016) <https://www.theguardian.com/money/2016/jun/03/boys-get-more-pocket-money-than-girls-halifax-survey-finds> accessed 29 November 2021; and Lucy Warwick-Ching, 'Gender Pay Gap Apparent in Pocket Money Data' (*Financial Times*, 23 July 2019) <https://www.ft.com/content/28017f78-a7ce-11e9-984c-fac8325aaa04> accessed 29 November 2021.

72 See in this respect, Mara Harvey, *A Smart Way to Start*, followed by other four books in the series (*A Smart Way to Save*, *A Smart Way to Spend*, *A Smart Choice to Make* and *A Smart Way to Start Doing Good*, *2019*), which are intended to build up financial literacy for kids. See for more information the official website <https://smartwaytostart.com/>.

73 Mara Harvey, *A Smart Choice to Make*, https://smartwaytostart.com.

74 French Presidency of the Council of the European Union, 'Conference on Economic Empowerment, Key to Gender Equality' (*News*, 31 January 2022) <https://presidence-francaise.consilium.europa.eu/en/news/ministerialpress-release-conference-on-economic-empowerment-key-to-gender-equality/> accessed 11 February 2022.

The interest in this conference by the EU and its member states follows a number of similar international initiatives – as we have recalled in the above paragraphs – that have been calling for increasing action for achieving financial equality. Indeed, enhancing financial literacy and facilitating economic gender equality is a huge opportunity for all countries and the "gender mainstreaming" approach to fiscal policies is a commitment that countries have been making in international *fora* for decades.

However, advancing women's economic empowerment in the financial sector is not only a matter of making the full range of financial instruments available to women; it is also a matter of financial education. As this chapter has illustrated, we need a new narrative for financial equality to effectively address the barriers that women are still facing.

Indeed, finance has usually been a male-dominated field: it is quite telling to recall a research carried out in Sweden in 2018, based on interviews of finance professionals, where "interviewees pointed to a masculine and unwelcoming culture as the main reason for why there weren't more women in certain fields of finance".[75]

Starting to develop a new narrative around financial matters at an early age – both in the family environment as well as at school, with dedicated finance literacy programmes to be included in the relevant curricula since primary schools – can help to successfully address the gender gap and enable girls and women to build up and reinforce their financial confidence. Indeed, "[i]t's time to make money equal".[76]

References

Ackermann N and Eberle F, 'Financial Literacy in Switzerland', in Aprea C et al. (eds), *International Handbook of Financial Literacy* (Springer 2016).

Behrman JR et al., 'The Effects of Financial Education and Financial Literacy: How Financial Literacy Affects Household Wealth Accumulation' (2012) 102 American Economic Review 3, 300.

Chinkin C, 'Gender and Economic, Social, and Cultural Rights', in Riedel E et al. (eds), *Economic, Social, and Cultural Rights in International Law: Contemporary Issues and Challenges* (Oxford University Press 2014).

75 Mary King et al, 'What Will It Take to Make Finance More Gender-Balanced?' (*Harvard Business Review*, 10 December 2018) <https://hbr.org/2018/12/what-will-it-take-to-make-finance-more-gender-balanced> accessed 11 February 2022.

76 Anne Boden, 'Why We Need to #Makemoneyequal' (*Starling Bank Blog*, 13 March 2018) <https://www.starlingbank.com/blog/make-money-equal/> accessed 29 November 2021.

D'Alessio G et al., 'Financial Literacy in Italy: The Results of the Bank of Italy's 2020 Survey' (*Banca d'Italia – Questioni di Economia e Finanza. Occasional Paper No. 588*, December 2020).

Fackelmann S and De Concini A, *Funding Women Entrepreneurs. How to Empower Growth* (European Investment Bank June 2020).

Harvey MC, *Women and Risk: Rewriting the Rules* (Nicolai Publishing & Intelligence 2019).

Jarecke J et al., 'Financial Literacy Education for Women' (2014) 2014 (141) New Directions for Adult and Continuing Education. Special Issue: Financial Literacy and Adult Education 37.

Kanze D et al., 'Male and female Entrepreneurs Get Asked Different Questions by VCs – and it Affects How Much Funding They Get' (2017) Harvard Business Review.

Kaufmann C, 'Marriage Law Revision. Occasion for Hope?' (1986) 9 (1) Women's Studies International Forum 35.

Lusardi A and Mitchell OS, 'The Economic Importance of Financial Literacy: Theory and Evidence' (2014) 52 (1) Journal of Economic Literature 5.

Stotsky JG, *Using Fiscal Policy and Public Financial Management to Promote Gender Equality. International Perspectives* (Routledge 2020).

Zakrzewski A et al., 'Managing the Next Decade of Women's Wealth' (*BCG Publications*, 9 April 2020).

PART 3

Women's Participation at the International Level and Institutional Encounters

CHAPTER 9

Gender Equality in the Judiciary – with an Emphasis on International Judiciary

Catherine Kessedjian

1 Introduction

According to the World Economic Forum, if all goes well, 2234 will be the year in which the economic gender gap will be filled. I have not calculated whether the same year will see the gender gap in the judiciary vanish, but I have a sense that this may not be the case. This is because the present picture seems quite gloomy, even though 143 out of 197 United Nations Member States have included gender equality in their constitution[1] and, at the UN level, diversity, gender equality, and inclusion are among the 17 Sustainable Development Goals adopted in 2015.

Before I go further into the analysis, I must clarify that I am not a gender scholar. Some of my colleagues have become specialists in gender issues in international law. I am not one of them. I am a generalist in international law, having studied both public and private international law, but my specialty is international private law, international dispute resolution, arbitration, and mediation. This is the background I come from.

Why did I become interested in gender issues? As Anna Calman (the young Ingrid Bergman) says in the movie *Indiscreet*: 'I am a woman, you know'. Well, I became interested in gender issues because I am a woman! More seriously, when I was invited to give the first Hague Academy Winter Session General Course and had decided to reflect on Neutrals in International Law,[2] it became self-evident that I had to discuss the manners in which judges and arbitrators

---

1 Institut du Capitalisme Responsable, '6 Mesures Concrètes pour Accélérer la Mixité dans les Organisations' (2020) L'Observatoire de la Mixité <www.capitalisme-responsable.com/wp-content/uploads/2020_OMix_livre_vert_10122020-2.pdf> accessed 18 June 2021. 'L'Observatoire de la Mixité' is a body composed of experts and representatives of different institutions with competences in the field of gender equality, which proposes solutions to quickly achieve gender equality in companies.

2 Catherine Kessedjian, 'Le Tiers Impartial et Indépendant en Droit International – Juge, Arbitre, Médiateur, Conciliateur' (2019) Recueil des Cours 409.

are chosen, who they are and whether they are representative of the population of the world. Hence diversity became one of the focuses of the Hague lectures.

The scope of this chapter is limited to gender diversity.[3] This does not mean other diversity issues are of no interest to me. By 'other diversity issues', I mean: culture, colour, religion, and ethnicity, among others. Because international law, as we know it now, was shaped by and large by occidental scholars and actors in the XIXth century, mostly with the rise of the Industrial Revolution, it is all too easy to forget that the whole world does not resemble this fairly small club. This is why general studies – such as the one conducted by Freya Baetens[4] or, for racial diversity in arbitration, by Benjamin Davis[5] – are essential to the full understanding of the subject matter.

This chapter is divided into four sections each of which addresses one of the following questions:

1. Why is gender equality so important in rendering justice?
2. What is the present situation for women in international courts and tribunals?
3. What are the reasons for the present situation?
4. What can we do to improve the situation?

2 Why Is Gender Equality So Important in Rendering Justice?

I can only quote from former President of the UK Supreme Court, Lady Hale of Richmond:

> I take the view that "difference" is important in judging and that gender diversity, along with many other dimensions of diversity, is a good, indeed a necessary, thing for several reasons. The principal reason is democratic legitimacy – the judiciary should reflect the whole community, not just a small section of it; the public should be able to feel that the courts are their courts, that their cases are being decided and the law is being

3 International Council for Commercial Arbitration, *ICCA Reports No. 8: Report of the Cross-Institutional Task Force on Gender Diversity in Arbitral Appointments and Proceedings* (ICCA & Kluwer Law International 2020).

4 Freya Baetens (ed), *Identity and Diversity on the International Bench – Who is the Judge?* (OUP 2020).

5 Among others, see Benjamin Davis, 'The Color Line in International Commercial Arbitration: An American Perspective' (International Arbitration Committee, Association of the Bar of the City of New York, 2004) <http://aria.law.columbia.edu/racial-diversity-in-international-arbitration/> accessed 29 November 2021.

> developed by people like them, not by alien beings from another planet; and this should enhance rather than undermine public confidence in the law and the legal system.[6]

I could not have put it better. However, this statement must be backed by some context. It is crucial that justice is rendered by people who represent a cross-cutting sample of society at large because of the unique role judges and justice have taken in our society. It has always been true that justice was an essential part of a society matrix. However, it has become the keystone (*la clef de voûte*) of the construction of the law. Legal rules have become essential to our modern societies: they have become so complex, as well as being complicated by additional standards and soft law rules, that no one can pretend any longer to 'know the law' as the old saying goes.

In addition, there is a strong argument for considering the judiciary as a counter-power to the other two pillars of democracy, namely the executive and the legislative powers. The judiciary, being the third pillar of democracy, must be independent, strong, and representative, particularly because most judges are not elected. Even if they are elected, like for the International Court of Justice, the election takes place within the community of States, which do not always represent an example of diversity themselves. Arguably (at least some of the) decisions rendered by the International Court of Justice (ICJ) have an impact on millions of citizens around the world. Consequently, if one wants to ensure respect for their decisions, judges rendering these decisions must represent a cross-section of the communities at large. This is a matter of trust in the judiciary. The same analysis applies to arbitration whether in investment matters[7] or in commercial cases.[8]

---

6 Lady Hale of Richmond, 'How Diverse are Judges?' in Jeremy Cooper (ed), *Being a Judge in the Modern World* (OUP 2017) 184. See also Vanessa Ruiz, 'Le Rôle des Femmes Juges et d'une Prise en Compte des Questions de Genre pour Assurer l'Indépendance et l'Intégrité du Système Judiciaire' (2019) ONUDC <www.unodc.org/dohadeclaration/fr/news/2019/01/the-role-of-women-judges-and-a-gender-perspective-in-ensuring-judicial-independence-and-integrity.html> accessed 29 November 2021.

7 The electronic list of arbitrators and conciliators maintained by ICSID shows 791 names out of which 469 have been appointed in at least one ICSID case. Among that group, only 54 are women: see <https://icsid.worldbank.org/sites/default/files/publications/ICSID10.pdf> accessed 20 August 2021. For a brief analysis, see Gus Van Harten, 'The (lack of) Women Arbitrators in Investment Treaty Arbitration' (Columbia FDI Perspectives No. 59, 6 February 2012) <https://ccsi.columbia.edu/content/columbia-fdi-perspectives> accessed 29 November 2021.

8 See Queen Mary University and White & Case, 'International Arbitration Survey' (2021) <https://www.whitecase.com/publications/insight/2021-international-arbitration-survey/appendices> accessed 29 November 2021. See also the controversy that arose after

However, I am not implying that one should only be judged by one's peers. Or that judges must resemble on all fronts the people addressed by their decisions. This would be contrary to my conception of diversity, impartiality, neutrality, and lack of bias. But there must be enough diversity on the bench to be representative of the society for which that particular court or tribunal was formed. In the end, this is a matter of legitimacy.

3 What Is the Present Situation for Women in International Courts and Tribunals?

Before we turn to the present situation, I will provide a brief broad-brush overview of history. Contrary to what is often believed, women were not prevented from rendering justice at all times. The Bible mentions Deborah who was active in resolving conflicts between the sons of Israël.[9] She is often portrayed as sitting under a palm tree (symbol of peace)[10] between Ramah and Bethel in Mount Ephraïm. She is a prophetess, an advisor, a judge, an arbitrator, and a mediator. But, more ambiguously, she is also a warrior when need be.

This promising beginning was ended by the *Corpus juris civilis*[11] whereby women were banned from the city governance because they were considered as weak persons. From that time on they could not be appointed as arbitrators. This situation persisted for many centuries. This is why '[*m*]*algré les textes égalitaires des Evangiles, la femme est tenue enfermée dans un étroit carcan juridique à l'époque médiévale, sa capacité juridique étant opacifiée par celle de son mari. Elle trouve cependant grâce aux yeux de certains auteurs de droit savant ou de droit coutumier qui admettent qu'elle peut trancher en équité et non pas en droit. Elle ne peut jouer ce rôle que dans trois cas: lorsqu'elle possède le droit de juger,*

the appointment by the European Union of the Comprehensive Economic and Trade Agreement (CETA) and other bilateral trade agreement arbitrators. They can be searched in the online database ITALAW at <https://www.italaw.com/> accessed 29 November 2021. See also Arbitration Institute of the Stockholm Chamber of Commerce (SCC), the 'Temperature Check on Diversity in Arbitration' (2021) <https://sccinstitute.com/about-the-scc/news/2021/new-scc-report-temperature-check-on-diversity-in-arbitration/> accessed 29 November 2021.

9 See the 'Book of Judges' in *The Hebraïc Bible* (also called the *Old Testament* by Christians), chapter IV-4: 'Deborah, a prophetess, the wife of Lappidoth, was leading [1] Israel at that time. She held court under the Palm of Deborah between Ramah and Bethel in the hill country of Ephraim, and the Israelites came to her to have their disputes decided'.

10 See also the tree as a symbol of justice in many epochs.

11 Justinian Code, VIe siècle – C.II.6.56.

ou est autorisée par la coutume, ou est une personne d'un rang social éminent'.[12] It was not until the XIIIth century, with the papal authorisation, that women acquired the right to be appointed arbitrators.[13]

Jumping ahead to modern times, it is no wonder that there are so few women in the judiciary. Indeed, in order to render justice, a woman needs to enjoy her civil rights. Women acquired these rights very late. To take only the example of France, after a short period thanks to the 1789 Revolution, women had to wait until 1945 to be allowed to vote. In Switzerland, 1971 is the date at which the right was granted at federal level, although some cantons provided for women's voting in 1959.[14]

Also, if one wants to become a judge, one needs first to be trained as a lawyer. And this is not so easy. To take one example from the United States, in 1869 the Supreme Court of Iowa decided that the State could not prevent Arabella Mansfield from taking the bar exam just because she was a woman.[15] However, four years later, the Supreme Court of the United States decided in the opposite direction by upholding a decision from the Supreme Court of Illinois forbidding a woman from taking the bar exam. A quote from the concurring opinion reveals the prejudices: '[16] The paramount destiny and mission of woman (sic) are to fulfill the noble and benign offices of wife and mother. This is the law of the Creator. And the rules of civil society must be adapted to the general constitution of things, and cannot be based upon exceptional cases'.[17] Barring women from practicing law was prohibited in the USA only in 1971.[18]

---

12 'Despite the egalitarian texts of the Gospels, woman is kept in a tight legal straitjacket in the medieval period, her legal capacity being opaque to that of her husband. However, she finds favour with some authors of soft law or customary law who admit that she can decide in equity and not in law. She can only play this role in three cases: when she has the right to judge, or is authorized by custom, or is a person of eminent social rank' (translation provided by the author); Yves Jeanclos, 'La Pratique de l'Arbitrage du XIIe au XVe Siècle – Eléments d'Analyse' (1999) 3 Revue de l'Arbitrage, 445.

13 ibid 446. See the examples mentioned by Jeanclos.

14 The latest date for cantons was 1990. A few States were pioneers: New Zealand 1893, Australia 1901, Finland 1906, Norway 1913, Denmark 1915, Russia 1917, USA 1920 (XIXth amendment of the Constitution but only for white women), Brazil 1932. For an exhaustive timeline, see *Encyclopaedia Britannica*, 'Women's suffrage' <https://www.britannica.com/topic/woman-suffrage> accessed 29 November 2021.

15 See Kristin Corey, 'Arabella (Belle) Babb Mansfield' (Iowa Department of Cultural Affairs) <https://iowaculture.gov/history/education/educator-resources/primary-source-sets/government-democracy-and-laws/Arabella> accessed 20 August 2021.

16 *Bradwell v Illinois* 83 US 130 (1873).

17 ibid 141–2.

18 See The American Bar Association, 'In their Own Words – Experienced Women Lawyers Explain why they are Leaving their Law Firms and the Profession' (April 2021)

To make my point, I only need to recall that it was as late as 1981 that the first woman was appointed as a judge at the Supreme Court of the United States (Sandra Day O'Connor)[19] and not until 1982 for the Supreme Court of Canada (Bertha Wilson). The first female *juge en chef* of the Supreme Court of Canada was appointed in 2000 (Beverley McLachlin).[20] The French *Cour de cassation* has had only two women as *Premier Président*: one in 1984 (Simone Rozès) and one in 2019 (Chantal Arens).[21] The overall statistics are not so bad in France. Indeed, in 2015, 66% of all judges were women. However, this number deserves a closer look. The *Ecole de la magistrature* (the principal avenue to become a judge in France) shows that 80% of the students are women. However, when one looks at the statistics of judges appointed to the bench, in the age group 30–34 years, only 29% of judges are women. The higher in the hierarchy one looks, the worse the situation becomes. Only 30% of judges at the *Cour de cassation* are women; four are at the head of a Court of Appeals and only 89 out of 390 Presidents of Courts and Tribunals are women.[22]

<www.americanbar.org/groups/diversity/women/initiatives_awards/long-term-careers-for-women/in-their-own-words/> accessed 29 November 2021.

19 Brian P. Smentkowski, 'Sandra Day O'Connor' (*Encyclopaedia Britannica*) <https://www.britannica.com/topic/judge-law/Professional-judges-in-the-common-law-tradition> accessed 25 August 2021. Ratified in 1920, the Nineteenth Amendment granted women the right to vote. During this time, women began assuming judgeships, through both appointment and election. One such woman was Mary O'Toole, who became the first woman municipal judge of the United States when she was appointed Judge of the Municipal Court of Washington, DC by President Harding in 1921. See Minnesota NOW, 'US Judicial Women Firsts' (10 April 2021) <https://www.britannica.com/topic/woman-suffrage> accessed 25 August 2021.

20 See Canadian Chapter of the International Association of Women Judges, 'Women Chief Justices of Canada' <https://iawjcc.com/women-in-the-spotlight/chief-judges/> accessed 29 November 2021.

21 This is the case even though women have been authorised to become judges since 1946. In France, the first female (Charlotte Béquignon-Lagarde) who wanted to take the '*agrégation*' (the highest competitive exam to become a full university law professor) had to ask for the authorization of her husband. She was born in 1900, the year when women were authorised to become a pleading attorney. In 1931 she became the first woman '*agrégée*' (private law). She later (in 1946) became the first and only female judge at the *Cour de cassation*. In public law, the first woman '*agrégée*' was Suzanne Basdevant-Bastid. See Gwenola Joly-Coz and Sophie Tardy-Joubert, 'L'Institution Judiciaire a Effacé les Traces des Premières Femmes Magistrats' (Actu-Juridique.fr, 21 August 2020) <https://www.actu-juridique.fr/professions/linstitution-judiciaire-a-efface-les-traces-des-premieres-femmes-magistrats/> accessed 29 November 2021.

22 The numbers in the UK are similar: In 2015, 8 out of 38 Court of Appeals judges and 21 out of 108 judges at the High Court were women. In the USA, women counted for 20% of

For the international judiciary, the situation is similar or perhaps somewhat bleaker. Concerning the ICJ,[23] despite a complete renewal of the judges between 1945 and 1969, no woman was elected until 1995 (Dame Rosalyn Higgins). In 2021, three women out of a total of 15 are on the bench: (by order of election) Joan E. Donoghue (2010), now the President, Xue Hanqin (2010), and Julia Sebutinde (2012). There are almost no women ad hoc judges at the ICJ.[24] The Tribunal for the Law of the Sea (Hamburg) is composed of 21 judges, five of whom are women. At the International Criminal Court, the situation has worsened: at the initiation of the court there was an equal number of women and men. However, in 2019 women accounted for only one-third of the bench. A decrease has also been seen at the European Court of Human Rights despite the policy announced by the Council that it would not be acceptable for Member States to propose a list that does not include at least one woman.[25] The World Trade Organization (WTO) panel members did not include a woman until 2003.[26]

Some signs of positive evolution are evident in arbitration; however, the road is still long for tribunals. For the first time in its history, the International Chamber of Commerce (ICC) Court of International Arbitration achieved gender equality in 2018.[27] In 2015, the Court appointed or confirmed 136 female arbitrators and in 2016 the number was 209. They represent only 14.8% of all arbitrators appointed under the ICC regime even though the percentage has

---

the Circuit Judges (Federal Court of Appeals): see Yoann Demoli and Laurent Willemwz, 'Les Magistrats: Un Corps Professionnel Féminisé et Mobile' (2018) 161 Infostat Justice, Bullettin d'Information Statistique 1.

23 There was no woman on the Permanent Court of International Justice, the predecessor to the present court.

24 Out of 19 positions in current cases only 2 are held by a woman. Many of the male ad hoc judges are repeat players. See Peacewomen, 'ICJ International Court of Justice' <https://www.peacewomen.org/content/international-court-justice> accessed 25 August 2021.

25 At the ECHR, out of the six senior positions, only two are held by women. The Court has never been presided over by a woman. In 2021, out of the 47 judges (one judge per Member State) only 15 are women.

26 A survey on the female composition of international courts and tribunals was carried out by GQUAL in 2015. See the results of the survey at GQUAL, 'The Current Composition of International Tribunals and Monitoring Bodies' (14 September 2015) <http://www.gqualcampaign.org/1626-2/> accessed 29 November 2021.

27 International Chamber of Commerce (ICC), 'ICC Celebrates 5 Years of Progress Since Arbitration Gender Pledge' (19 May 2021) <https://iccwbo.org/media-wall/news-speeches/icc-celebrates-5-years-of-progress-since-arbitration-gender-pledge/> accessed 29 November 2021.

doubled since 2011. Co-arbitrators appointing a chair only chose a woman in 12.4% of cases. But women make up one-third of emergency arbitrators.[28]

The proportions of male and female mediators/conciliators and arbitrators appointed by the Secretary-General at the International Centre for Settlement of Investment Disputes (ICSID) are also fifty-fifty. However, the picture is less bright when one considers the lists of conciliators and arbitrators appointed by Member States. Very few States achieve equality. Only one State[29] has appointed only women on its list, while many States (56 out of 155) have no women on their list.[30]

4 What are the Reasons for the Present Situation?

Historical, cultural, and traditional stereotypes are hard to combat. By their very nature, because they are fixed in people's beliefs without nuance, stereotypes influence people's judgement and function as an unconscious bias that influences our actions. If one adds to stereotypes the fact that people who are already in place have no incentive to change a system that benefits them,[31]

---

28 ICC, 'ICC Court Sees Marked Progress on Gender Diversity' (31 May 2017) <https://iccwbo.org/media-wall/news-speeches/icc-court-sees-marked-progress-gender-diversity/> accessed 29 November 2021.

29 The Bahamas, see ICSID, 'Members of the Panels of Conciliators and of Arbitrators' (26 August 2021).

30 See Arbitral Women, 'Latest Designations to ICSID Panels: A Mixed Bag for Gender Parity' (22 February, 2020) <https://www.arbitralwomen.org/latest-designations-to-icsid-panels-a-mixed-bag-for-gender-parity/> accessed 29 November 2021 and Meg Kinnear and Otylia Babiak, 'International Investment Arbitration Needs Equal Representation' (Centre for International Governance Innovation, 9 April 2018) <https://www.cigionline.org/articles/international-investment-arbitration-needs-equal-representation/> accessed 29 November 2021.

31 In order to write this section, I benefited from diverse sources of information: for my 2019 Hague Lectures, I reviewed a number of sociological studies. During my stay in the Hague in January 2019, I was invited to give a lecture at the ICC and the critical discussion that followed helped me understand a number of issues faced by women working in the international judiciary. I also benefited from discussions with women working in a challenging high-level environment, notably in large corporations. I consulted a study (published in February 2020) conducted by a French human resources tech company (EDHEC) that mapped out more than 65,000 tests taken by candidates between 2017 and 2019: EDHEC NewGen Talent Centre, 'Femmes & Carrière Quels sont Leurs Atouts et Leurs Motivations?' <https://careers.edhec.edu/news/etude-femmes-carriere-quels-sont-leurs-atouts-et-leurs-motivations-fevrier-2020-edhec-newgen> accessed 20 August 2021. These tests were taken by 54% women and 46% men. They tested 28 aspects of

improving the situation will take more time and effort than one may think at first.

Biology is also pertinent to the importance of culture, life experience, and the social environment in the way each one of us appraises a given situation. At birth only 10% of neurons are connected. This means that 90% of neurons are connected thanks to social interaction.[32] Consequently, the difference between girls and boys is constructed little by little, all through childhood and early adulthood, giving substance to the well-known statement by de Beauvoir '*on ne naît pas femme on le devient*'.

Psychology, sociology, and related cognitive sciences would be helpful in assessing why equality between men and women is so difficult to achieve, particularly when the positions at stake include power and high pay.

(a) Cognitive sciences teach us that women are less assertive than men.[33] Their education leads to that outcome. Boys are encouraged, at an early age, to speak, particularly in public. Studies show that those who are used to speaking in public assume leadership roles more easily.[34]

Women need nudging in order to put themselves forward as a candidate for any high-level position. And often, women do not have the kind of network that would give them that nudge. Men do not hesitate to put themselves forward, sometimes even overestimating their capacities (whereas women tend to underestimate them).

(b) Because of childbearing and tradition, women assume the primary responsibility for children and family. This explains why women's careers advance more slowly than those of men on equivalent career paths. Therefore, once the children are older and less demanding, and women themselves attain the age at which they might be considered for

the respondents' personality. I also consulted a study started in 2015 by McKinsey & Company and Leanin.Org, for corporate America: McKinsey & Company, 'Women in the Workplace 2019' (October 2019) <www.mckinsey.com/~/media/McKinsey/Featured%20Insights/Gender%20Equality/Women%20in%20the%20Workplace%202019/Women-in-the-workplace-2019.ashx> accessed 29 November 2021. I thank Hélène Boulet-Supau for having called my attention to these two studies and more.

32 Riita Hari et al., 'Centrality of Social Interaction in Human Brain Function' (2015) 88 Neuron 181.

33 See Emily T Amanatullah and Michael W Morris, 'Negotiating Gender Roles: Gender Differences in Assertive Negotiating are Mediated by Women's Fear of Backlash and Attenuated When Negotiating on Behalf of Others' (2010) 98 Journal of Personality and Social Psychology 256.

34 See also, Maria de Paola et al., 'Do Women Shy Away from Public Speaking? A Field Experiment' (2021) Institute of Labor Economics Discussion Papers 12959 <https://ideas.repec.org/p/iza/izadps/dp12959.html> accessed 18 June 2021.

appointment to leadership roles, they have not reached the level where they can compete for higher positions.

It is true that men are increasingly undertaking a larger share of the family duties to facilitate their wife's career, but such examples are far from being the majority. I would venture to say that it is the exception that confirms the rule. This has been reaffirmed during the 2020–2021 coronavirus pandemic, particularly in France, during which time women had to work from home, home school their children, and continue to shop and produce meals.[35] The extra duties falling to women prevent them from spending time networking, which is vitally important if one wants to assume higher positions.

(c) Women are more transparent, sincere, and authentic when it comes to the information they communicate about themselves and their experience. They are more concerned about objectivity and that trait increases (+5%) with experience.[36] When one knows becoming a member of an international court or tribunal usually happens after the second phase of one's professional life, it shows that a level playing field for competition is not guaranteed. In addition, 'women are more modest than men (17%)' and the more mature they become the more modest they get (an additional 12%).[37]

(d) More flexible and having a greater capacity to listen to arguments that run counter to their own ideas, women are the best mediators and problem solvers.[38] However, when it comes to defending their own position, they are more readily convinced to withdraw from competition.

(e) Stability is more important to women than men.[39] They have a greater sense of respect for the institution and a safe work environment. This would function as a deterrent to mobility when mobility (particularly international mobility) is often the price to be paid for higher positions and a change of work environment. In addition, when the ratio at senior management level is 1 to 3 in favour of men, the majority of women think they are well represented and an even greater majority of men think likewise.

---

35 This *tour de force* may also be explained by the fact that women are more efficient than men: when confronted with many tasks to be accomplished, they plan and organise better than their male counterparts.

36 See EDHEC NewGen Talent Centre (n 31).

37 ibid 19.

38 ibid 7.

39 This is also because women are more likely than men to accept a change of location if that would help their spouse progress in their profession.

(f) Women demonstrate greater emotional sensitivity than men.[40] In a group, they are likely to show more empathy to their colleagues. When it comes to defending their own interests, this characteristic may become a handicap. In the same vein they are more interested in others' wellbeing than their own and would rather help somebody who needs it than first consider whether it may have a counter-effect on their own position.

(g) Women are respectful of rules and have difficulties when they need to act in an environment where rules are obscure, paths are all but straight, politicking and manoeuvring are a necessary course of action.[41] In one of many films produced about the life of the late Ruth Bader-Ginsburg, she would say that her appointment from academia to judgeship was made possible thanks to her husband's networking for her, whereas he would say that it was possible because of her highest level of expertise and integrity. They were both correct.

(h) Life events do affect women more than men. And when these life events require that someone in the family must take leave of absence, it is more often the woman who does so. However, taking leave of absence is likely to have a bigger negative impact on a woman than on her male equivalent. Studies show that while paternity leaves have increased in the past decade or so, maternity leave has been stagnant.[42] Work–life balance is more important for women than for men. Therefore, women may hesitate to apply to positions that might entail sacrifices in their personal life that they may not be ready to make.

(i) Power is still the prerogative of white men aged over 50 years. They have no reason to give up a system that has worked to their advantage for decades. In other words, white men are privileged but they are privilege-blind. Most of them would be the proper vehicle for change.

5 What Can We Do to Improve the Situation?

As seen in section 3, in many cases, the absence of women is deeply rooted in psychological and social history. Hence, the most needed change concerns education.

40 Fischer AH et al., 'Gender Differences in Emotion Perception and Self-reported Emotional Intelligence: A Test of the Emotion Sensitivity Hypothesis' (2018) 13 (1) PLoS ONE.

41 See also Rolf Einar Fife, 'Generating Incentives to Appoint Women to the International Bench. Experiences with State Practice' in Baetens (ed) (n 4).

42 McKinsey Study (n 31).

And this must be an effort that continues throughout women's professional life. The McKinsey study I cite above shows that companies need to focus their efforts earlier in the pipeline to make real progress.[43] The role of corporations is essential. The Commitment to Diversity published by the Coca Cola Company on 28 January 2021[44] addressed to its outside counsels is a testimony to concrete steps that can be taken towards more diversity in the workplace.

Another example of concrete actions may be found in the Equal Representation in Arbitration Pledge adopted in 2015 that had gathered 3757 signatories as of November 2019. It is valuable to reproduce here the text of the Pledge:

> As a group of counsel, arbitrators, representatives of corporates, states, arbitral institutions, academics and others involved in the practice of international arbitration, we are committed to improving the profile and representation of women in arbitration.[45] In particular, we consider that women should be appointed as arbitrators on an equal opportunity basis. To achieve this, we will take the steps reasonably available to us – and we will encourage other participants in the arbitral process to do likewise – to ensure that, wherever possible:
> – committees, governing bodies and conference panels in the field of arbitration include a fair representation of women;
> – lists of potential arbitrators or tribunal chairs provided to or considered by parties, counsel, in-house counsel or otherwise include a fair representation of female candidates;
> – states, arbitral institutions and national committees include a fair representation of female candidates on rosters and lists of potential arbitrator appointees, where maintained by them;
> – where they have the power to do so, counsel, arbitrators, representatives of corporates, states and arbitral institutions appoint a fair representation of female arbitrators;

43 This is also one of the conclusions to be drawn from Rolf Einar Fife's contribution to Baetens (ed) (n 4).

44 'Commitment to Diversity, Belonging, and Outside Counsel Diversity' (28 January 2021) <www.coca-colacompany.com/media-center/bradley-gayton-on-commitment-to-diversity> accessed 20 August 2021.

45 The pledge is somewhat modest as it does not require gender equality in terms of of actual numbers but as a matter of "equal opportunity" showing the influence of John Rawls' writings.

- gender statistics for appointments (split by party and other appointment) are collated and made publicly available; and
- senior and experienced arbitration practitioners support, mentor/sponsor and encourage women to pursue arbitrator appointments and otherwise enhance their profiles and practice.[46]

But numbers are not enough. The pledge should stress equal opportunity and fairness in the work environment, work–life flexibility, and a safe respectful workplace. This last point is crucial to allow greater diversity among those occupying the highest positions of society. Organising the workplace so as to cater for women's needs, particularly at a younger age, is essential to secure a better gender balance at a later stage. This necessitates a very coherent policy as well as the engagement of the highest authorities in the work environment.[47] It includes a diversity plan actively supported by the highest authorities in the organisation, together with reporting procedures and grievance mechanisms.

Mentorship programmes are crucial to this effort. Big Sister (or Brother) mentorship and sponsorship is essential. As an arbitrator, I rarely witnessed a male senior partner distributing pleading roles to his female team members and sharing the podium with them. This has happened only a few times. I can testify, however, that following the careers of the women who benefited from such a sponsorship shows that this is the kind of mentorship that would help women climb the ladder.

Changing the way judges, arbitrators, and mediators are appointed could be another useful measure. However, this may prove trickier to organise. This immediately raises the question: Do we need quotas? It is known that if one gets over the famous 'smurfette or Snow White principle'[48] and appoints women in cohorts, so that they form a significant percentage of the workforce,

46 See the whole text of the Pledge at <www.arbitrationpledge.com/take-the-pledge> accessed 29 November 2021.

47 This is one of the six measures advocated by the French *Observatoire de la Mixité* (n 1) because among the 32 measures that have been tested in France to determine their effects on gender diversity in companies, these are the ones that work best to ensure a change in women's place in the company.

48 The '*smurfette* principle' occurs when one woman is appointed to the top, is alone in a group of men so that she is cornered in the position of "*faire valoir*" (something like being a foil for the men). See Liesbeth Lijnzaad, 'The *Smurfette* Principle. Reflections about Gender and the Nomination of Women to the International Bench' in Baetens (ed) (n 4).

they advance more successfully to the top of their profession. Consequently, as a temporary measure, quotas may be necessary in order to overcome the obstacles that women experience when they want to advance.[49] This goes hand in hand with the need for numbers (and the evolution thereof) to be continuously monitored and published so that everyone concerned can understand the effect of the measures taken. It is noteworthy that none of the international courts publish any figures on diversity in the workplace. It would be interesting to have these figures, not only for judges (which are easy to count), but also for all the employees of the court.

6 Conclusion

As I was finalising this contribution in May 2021, I was heartened by the many positive signals received from the business environment. Even though there is still plenty of room for improvement, more women are reaching the top management of companies. If that trend continues, these women will want to work with more female lawyers and encourage the firms with which they work to appoint women at the top management level. Having had that kind of an experience, these lawyers will be more likely to increase their public profile and therefore be considered for judicial functions, particularly in countries where judges are selected from practising attorneys. It is to be hoped, therefore, that more female judges will be able to join the ranks of the international judiciary. *Rendez-vous* is taken for 2234!

Postscriptum

As we were going to press, we were informed that Prof. Hilary Charlesworth was elected at the ICJ making her the fifth woman only in the entire history of the Court.

49 The report published by the *Institut Montaine* (a French private think tank maintained mostly by large corporations that opines on public affairs) in 2019, promotes a form of quotas with a reasonable component to it, see: Institut Montaigne, 'Agir pour la Parité, Performance à la Clé' (July 2019) <www.institutmontaigne.org/publications/agir-pour-la-parite-performance-la-cle> accessed 20 August 2021. See also the measures advocated by the *Observatoire de la Mixité* (n 1).

References

Aolain NF, 'More Women – But Which Women? A Reply to Stéphanie Hennette Vauchez' (2015) 26 (1) European Journal of International Law 229.

Baetens F (ed), *Identity and Diversity on the International Bench – Who is the Judge?* (OUP 2020).

Baetens F (ed), *Legitimacy of Unseen Actors in International Adjudication* (CUP 2019).

Bjorklund AK et al., 'The Diversity Deficit in International Investment Arbitration' (2020) 21 (2–3) Journal of World Investment & Trade 410.

Chappell L, *The Politics of Gender Justice at the International Criminal Court: Legacies and Legitimacy* (OUP 2016).

Demoli Y et al., 'Les Magistrats: Un Corps Professionnel Féminisé et Mobile' (2018) 161 Infostat Justice, Bullettin d'Information Statistique 1.

Einar Fife R, 'Generating Incentives to Appoint Women to the International Bench. Experiences with State Practice' in Baetens F (ed), *Identity and Diversity on the International Bench – Who is the Judge?* (OUP 2020).

Elsig M and Pollack MA, 'Agents, Trustees, and International Courts: The Politics of Judicial Appointment at the World Trade Organization' (2012) 20 (2) European Journal of International Relations 391.

Grossman N, 'Achieving Sex-Representative International Court Benches' (2016) 110 American Journal of International Law 82.

Grossman N, 'Sex on the Bench: Do Women Judges Matter to the Legitimacy of International Courts?' (2012) 12 (2) Chicago Journal of International Law 647.

Grossman N, 'Legitimacy and International Adjudicative Bodies' (2010) 41 George Washington International Law Review 107.

Hennette-Vauchez S, 'Gender Balance in International Adjudicatory Bodies' *Max Planck Encyclopedias of International Law* (2019).

Hennette-Vauchez S, 'More Women – But Which Women? The Rule and the Politics of Gender Balance at the European Court of Human Rights' (2015) 26 (1) European Journal of International Law 195.

Jeanclos Y, 'La Pratique de l'Arbitrage du XIIe au XVe Siècle – Eléments d'Analyse' (1999) 3 Revue de l'Arbitrage 445.

Kenney JS, *Gender and Justice: Why Women in the Judiciary Really Matter?* (Routledge 2012).

Kessedjian C, 'Le Tiers Impartial et Indépendant en Droit International – Juge, Arbitre, Médiateur, Conciliateur' (2019) 409 Recueil des Cours 9–818.

Lady Hale of Richmond, 'How Diverse are Judges?' in Cooper J (ed), *Being a Judge in the Modern World* (OUP 2017).

Lijnzaad L, 'The *Smurfette* Principle. Reflections about Gender and the Nomination of Women to the International Bench' in Baetens F (ed), *Identity and Diversity on the International Bench – Who is the Judge?* (OUP 2020).

Rimmer HS and Ogg K (eds), *Research Handbook on Feminist Engagement with International Law* (CUP 2020).

Rubio-Marín R and Kymlicka W (eds), *Gender Parity & Multicultural Feminism. Towards a New Synthesis* (OUP 2018).

Schultz U and Shaw G, *Women in the Judiciary* (Routledge 2012).

Shikhelman V, 'Diversity and Decision-Making in International Judicial Institutions: The United Nations Human Rights Committee as a Case Study' (2017) 36 Berkeley Journal of International Law 36,3.

Sterio M, 'Women as Judges at International Criminal Tribunals' (2020) 29 (2) Transnational Law & Contemporary Problems 219.

Tulkens F, 'Parity on the Bench: Why? Why not?' (2014) 6 European Human Rights Law Review 587–595.

CHAPTER 10

Gender Equality in Crisis

Emerging Challenges for Women's Participation

Chiara Germano and Elisa Fornalé

1 Introduction[1]

The whole process of institutionalising the emergency regime has attracted severe criticism for its lack of a gender lens and the underrepresentation of women in decision-making processes.[2] A case in point was the Emergency Committee on COVID-19 set up by the World Health Organization (WHO), in which women accounted for less than 20% of the membership.[3] This imbalance was also evident in the all-men emergency task forces established at domestic level, which defined the institutional face of a 'mandemic response'.[4]

1 This Chapter draws upon the article Elisa Fornalé and Chiara Germano, 'La parità di genere nell'emergenza: un'analisi del carattere democratico-rappresentativo delle "Task Forces" alla luce del diritto internazionale' (2021) 1 Gruppo di Pisa 342. Elisa Fornalé was responsible for writing parts 1, 2, and 4 and Chiara Germano wrote part 3.

2 Coscieme L, et al. 'Women in Power: Female Leadership and Public Health Outcomes During the COVID-19 Pandemic', MedRxiv (2020). United Nations (UN), *Policy Brief: The Impact of COVID-19 on Women*, 9 April 2020; World Bank (WB), *Gender Dimensions of the COVID-19 Pandemic*, Policy Note, 16 April 2020; Alon et al., 'The Impact of the Coronavirus Pandemic on Gender Equality' (*Voxeu*, 19 April 2020) <https://voxeu.org/article/impact-coronavirus-pandemic-gender-equality> accessed 5 November 2021; Phumzile Mlambo-Ngcuka highlighted: "It is inconceivable that we can address the most discriminatory crisis we have ever experienced without full engagement of women" [...] "At the moment, men have given themselves the impossible task of making the right decisions about women without the benefit of women's insights. This needs to be set right without delay so we can work together on a future that is equitable, gender-responsive and greener." UN Women Executive Director. UN Women 'Women's Absence from COVID-19 Task Forces will Perpetuate Gender Divide', statement made on 22 March 2021.

3 Kim Robin Van Daalen et al. 'Symptoms of a Broken System: the Gender Gaps in COVID-19 Decision-Making' (2020) 5 (10) BMJ Global Health. Van Daalen et al. collected data related to expert and decision-making bodies created in 193 UN Member States, 12.

4 The USA, for example, established the "White House Coronavirus Task Force" with the purpose of monitoring, preventing and mitigating the spread of the coronavirus. The task force was replaced in January 2021 with the "COVID-19 Advisory Board" of which seven out of sixteen members are women. In addition, a so-called "COVID-19 Health Equity Taskforce" has been created to include members from disadvantaged groups (e.g. immigrants, LGBTQ+,

The available data highlighted that only 3.5% of the task forces created in 87 countries ensured gender parity.[5]

This imbalance in decision-making power affects the degree to which the specific circumstances of women are taken into consideration, by not allowing them 'to make the decisions that affect their lives'.[6] In the words of the United Nations (UN) Secretary-General 'when women are not consulted or included in decision-making on issues that have a direct impact on their lives, such as education, health, economic development and conflict resolution, policy outcomes are likely to be harmful and ineffective and to lead to the violation of women's rights'.[7]

Now that the recovery and response phase is being planned, the chapter aims to reflect on the critical issues raised by the pandemic emergency in relation to women's participation. Specifically, the analysis focuses on how the creation of temporary decision-making bodies, such as task forces, at international and domestic level has revealed that the adoption of the 'usual modus operandi' could reinforce gender inequality by severely limiting women's participation.[8]

2 Gender Equality and Participation

Participation, as 'an essential principle of governance', is vital for the functioning of democratic processes and for fostering coherent responses.[9] As recently stated by the UN Secretary-General 'the key to reinvigorated and reimagined

racial minorities); Clare Wenham et al. 'COVID-19: The Gendered Impacts of the Outbreak' (2020) 395 (10227) The Lancet 846.

5 Commission on the Status of Women, Women's Full and Effective Participation and Decision-making in Public Life, as well as the Elimination of Violence, for Achieving Gender Equality and the Empowerment of Women and Girls: Report of the Secretary-General (E/CN.6/2021/3, para 22).

6 Paola Profeta 'Gender Equality and Public Policy during COVID-19', CESifo Economic Studies (2020) 1–11; Karen Knop, 'Re/Statements: Feminism and State Sovereignty in International Law' (1993) 3 Transnational Law and Contemporary Problems 293; Alessandra Minello et al., 'The Pandemic and the Academic Mothers: Present Hardships and Future Perspectives' (2020) 23 European Societies 82.

7 Commission on the Status of Women (n 5) para 23.

8 Sandra Fredman et al., 'Transformative Equality: Making the Sustainable Development Goals Work for Women' (2016) 30 (2) Ethics & International Affairs 177.

9 Office of the United Nations High Commissioner for Human Rights (OHCHR), *Statement by Michelle Bachelet, UN High Commissioner for Human Rights. 75th Session of the UN General Assembly*, 25 September 2020, <www.ohchr.org/EN/NewsEvents/Pages/DisplayNews.aspx?NewsID=26298&LangID=E> accessed 5 November 2021.

governance lies with truly meaningful participation of people and civil society in the decisions that affect their lives'.[10]

In international law, participatory rights relating to women's equality are set out in the International Convention on the Elimination of All Forms of Discrimination Against Women (CEDAW).[11] Two provisions are particularly relevant. The first is article 7,[12] which defines the internal dimension of participatory rights and includes States' obligations to ensure women's rights to access to decision-making together with the right to participate in the formulation of government policy and in its implementation (article 7a). Article 7 includes the right to hold public office and to perform all public functions at all levels of government (article 7b), and the principle of non-discrimination with regard to the right to participate in non-governmental organisations and public life (article 7c).[13] The scope of the provision is very broad and it requires that women are not only part of decision-making bodies, but also 'that women be given the opportunity to have a real and viable input in all decision-making processes' by preventing future discrimination ('meaningful presence').[14]

The second of the provisions is in article 8, which concerns the participation and representation of women in international positions (the external dimension of participatory rights) and the 'CEDAW became the first international instrument to address explicitly the issue of women's participation at

10 United Nations Secretary-General (SG), *Secretary-General's Remarks at High-level Side Event: "Participation, Human Rights and the Governance Challenge Ahead" [as delivered]*, 25 September 2020, <un.org/sg/en/content/sg/statement/2020-09-25/secretary-generals-remarks-high-level-side-event-participation-human-rights-and-the-governance-challenge-ahead-delivered> accessed 5 November 2021.

11 The CEDAW entered into force on 3 September 1981 (1249 UNTS 13), and it has 189 States parties. Hilary Charlesworth and Christine Chinkin, 'Between the Margins and the Mainstream: The Case of Women's Rights', in Fassbender Bardo and Traisbach Knut (eds), *The Limits of Human Rights* (Oxford University Press, 2019) 205–222.

12 Article 7 of the Convention on the Elimination of All Forms of Discrimination against Women (A/RES/34/180) states: "States Parties shall take all appropriate measures to eliminate discrimination against women in the political and public life of the country and, in particular, shall ensure to women, on equal terms with men, the right: (a) To vote in all elections and public referenda and to be eligible for election to all publicly elected bodies; (b) To participate in the formulation of government policy and the implementation thereof and to hold public office and perform all public functions at all levels of government; (c) To participate in non-governmental organizations and associations concerned with the public and political life of the country".

13 Wittkopp Sarah, 'Article 7', in Marsha Freeman et al. (eds), *The UN Convention on the Elimination of all Forms of Discrimination Against Women* (Oxford University Press 2012) 198.

14 Marsha Freeman et al. (eds), *The UN Convention on the Elimination of all Forms of Discrimination Against Women* (Oxford University Press 2012) 198.

international level'.[15] It requires State Parties to 'take all appropriate measures to ensure to women, on equal terms with men and without any discrimination, the opportunity to represent their governments at the international level and to participate in the work of international organizations' (article 8).[16]

The duty to ensure gender equality covers the right of women to be appointed to positions that represent Member States in international organisations, such as diplomats, ambassadors, members of international tribunals and international organisations such as the UN, and that play 'key roles in developing international law and human rights'.[17] Member States are required to ensure equal participation through a two-fold approach: first, by guaranteeing that processes of appointment to international positions comply with gender equality criteria, and, second, by adopting at domestic level transparent selection processes to ensure equal opportunities for women, particularly if states nominate candidates for those positions.[18] By ensuring the opportunity to participate at international level, the articles reinforce women's right to non-discrimination.[19]

As clearly outlined in the above provisions, 'participation is not just to vote', participation requires having influence and a continous interaction between women and political power at the domestic and international levels to contribute to the way political power decides.[20] That is what makes articles 7 and 8 'powerful tools' for women specifically, in line with the two general recommendations (No. 23 and 25)[21] adopted by the CEDAW Committee to guide Member States on implementing these provisions.

---

15 ibid.

16 Article 8 of the Convention on the Elimination of All Forms of Discrimination against Women.

17 Claudia Martin, 'Article 8 of the Convention to Eliminate All Forms of Discrimination against Women (CEDAW): A Stepping Stone in Ensuring Gender Parity in International Organs and Tribunals' (*INTLAWGRRLS*, 13 January 2016) <https://ilg2.org/2016/01/13/article-8-of-the-convention-to-eliminate-all-forms-of-discrimination-against-women-cedaw-a-stepping-stone-in-ensuring-gender-parity-in-international-organs-and-tribunals> accessed 5 November 2021.

18 UN Human Rights Council, Current Levels of Representation of Women in Human Rights Organs and Mechanisms: Ensuring Gender Balance, Report of the Human Rights Advisory Committee, 21 May 2021, A/HRC/47/51.

19 "The appointment of women to international bodies is a prerequisite for women to influence, formulate, and implement international policy", ibid. para 24.

20 Commission on the Status of Women (n 5).

21 CEDAW, *General Recommendation No. 23: Political and public life* (1997); CEDAW, *General Recommendation No. 25, on Article 4, Paragraph 1, of the Convention on the Elimination of All Forms of Discrimination against Women, on Temporary Special Measures* (2004).

In General Recommendation No. 23, the CEDAW Committee explained that the political and public life of a country is a broad concept and can refer to the exercise of political power, in particular legislative, judicial, executive and administrative powers, all aspects of public administration and the formulation and implementation of policy at all levels.[22] In General Recommendation No. 25, the CEDAW Committee endorsed a mandatory nature of 'temporary special measures' for the fulfilment of *de jure* and *de facto* women's rights to participation in line with articles 7 and 8.[23] The Committee recommends a complementary reading of both provisions with article 4 that legitimates affirmative action.[24]

The question of how the COVID-19 emergency could influence the full implementation of women's rights became pressing. In particular, could an emergency situation limit women's right to access and to participate in decision-making bodies? To answer this question, the next section will explore how women's political participation and representation has been addressed during the pandemic.

3 The Impact of the Regulatory and Institutional Framework of Lockdown: The Composition of 'Task Forces'

As the lockdown became more globalised at the beginning of the pandemic, several governments assumed emergency powers. Women's participation have been curtailed for two main reasons: on the one hand an ongoing limitation of

---

22 Wittkopp Sarah, 'Article 8', in Marsha Freeman et al. (eds), *The UN Convention on the Elimination of all Forms of Discrimination Against Women* (Oxford University Press 2012) 198.

23 Ruth Rubio-Marín, 'Women's Participation in the Public Domain Under Human Rights Law: Towards a Participatory Equality Paradigm Shift', in Rubio-Marín R and Kymlicka W (eds), *Gender Parity and Multicultural Feminism, Towards a New Synthesis* (Oxford 2018) 66–96.

24 Article 4 of the Convention on the Elimination of All Forms of Discrimination against Women (A/RES/34/180) states: "1. Adoption by States Parties of temporary special measures aimed at accelerating de facto equality between men and women shall not be considered discrimination as defined in the present Convention, but shall in no way entail as a consequence the maintenance of unequal or separate standards; these measures shall be discontinued when the objectives of equality of opportunity and treatment have been achieved. 2. Adoption by States Parties of special measures, including those measures contained in the present Convention, aimed at protecting maternity shall not be considered discriminatory". Frances Raday, 'Article 4', in Marsha Freeman et al. (eds), *The UN Convention on the Elimination of all Forms of Discrimination Against Women* (Oxford University Press 2012) 198.

human rights, such as freedom of movement and association, which placed an ever-increasing workload and the burden of family care on women, and, on the other, a gradual and progressive reduction of women's active participation in managing the crisis and the subsequent reconstruction phase.

Against this background, our analysis attempts to clarify to what extent the creation of the new 'emergency' institutional set-up interfered with the exercise of the above-mentioned safeguards set out in CEDAW. Specifically, we focus on the establishment of the institutional mechanisms, the so-called 'task forces', in relation to their gender dimension. The involvement of these task forces is not an absolute institutional novelty, since in the past, *ad hoc*[25] bodies have been established during emergencies such as earthquakes or natural disasters, or to facilitate the achievement of specific goals.

Unsurprisingly, starting from February 2020, when the first signs of the Coronavirus emergency appeared, and even more so during the full-blown epidemic, multiple task forces were hastily set up with experts called to assist government bodies, both centrally and locally. These task forces were somewhat undefined and flexible, as confirmed by the names they were given: e.g. technical committees, study groups, working groups and control room, among others.[26]

3.1 *At International Level*

Data relating to the creation and composition of COVID-19 task forces by international institutions and organisations are rather limited and not easily accessible. Noteworthy among them is the task force created by WHO. At the beginning of 2020, WHO set up the 'Emergency Committee' to deal with the pandemic emergency implementing the International Health Regulations (a binding international law instrument adopted by WHO Member States in 2005). Initially 20% of the members of the Committee were women. This was contrary to the resolution adopted by the Executive Committee on 8 February

25 For instance, the Global Health Crises Task Force established by former UN Secretary-General Ban Ki-moon in 2016 to support and monitor the implementation of the recommendations of the High-level Panel on the Global Response to Health Crises; the Italian Education Ministry's task forces established in 2016 and in 2017 following the 2016 earthquakes in Abruzzo, the Latium, Umbria and the Marches (Decree n. 667/2016) or in 2017 following an earthquake on the island of Ischia.

26 We adopt the definition formulated by the COVID-19 Global Gender Response Tracker "A COVID-19 task force is any executive branch (temporary or permanent) created by a national government in response to COVID-19" and we extend this definition to international and/or subnational task forces (COVID-19 Global Gender Response Tracker, 'Women Remain Absent: COVID-19 Task Force Participation', 2021).

2020, which was only partly implemented, clearly urging Member States to '1.5 take action to engage and involve women in all stages of preparedness processes, including in decision-making, and mainstream gender perspective in preparedness planning and emergency response'.[27] Similarly, among the 25 members of the WHO–China Joint Mission on Coronavirus Disease 2019, which met in February 2020, less than 20% were women.[28] Moreover, the first and second WHO International Health Regulations (IHR) Emergency Committee had (5 women and 16 men out of a total of 21 members, i.e. 23.8%). Women's participation has improved, reaching the threshold of 37.5%, in the third IHR Committee, which had 32 members 12 of whom were women.[29]

Of the members of the Africa Task Force for Novel Coronavirus established by the Africa Centres for Disease Control and Prevention (Africa CDC) to oversee, at the continental level, preparedness and response to the epidemic, just over 10% were women (2 women out of a total of 16 members).[30]

The European Commission also created a specific task force on 16 March 2020 to assist in the implementation of existing European Union legislation, programmes and policies. Named the Commission's Advisory Panel on COVID-19, the task force comprised ten experts 'appointed by the President of the Commission on the basis of their acknowledged expertise' in specific fields set out by the Commission: 20% of the appointed members were women.[31]

In contrast, the Corona Response Teams launched at the beginning of March 2020 by the President of the European Commission, Ursula Von Der Leyen, to encourage a coherent approach to the situation from all 27 Member States and the European Union, had a majority of women (four of the six members),[32] but this is the only known instance of female overrepresentation.

---

27 The composition of the COVID-19 IHR Emergency Committee consists of 19 members, 7 of whom are women and, of the 12 Advisors, only 2 are women, see <www.who.int/groups/covid-19-ihr-emergency-committee> accessed 28 August 2021.

28 World Health Organization (WHO), *Report of the WHO-China Joint Mission on Coronavirus Disease 2019 (COVID-19)* (16–24 February 2020) <www.who.int/docs/default-source/coronaviruse/who-china-joint-mission-on-covid-19-final-report.pdf?sfvrsn=fce87f4e_2> accessed 29 November 2021.

29 ibid.

30 Van Daalen (n 3) 13.

31 European Centre for Disease Prevention and Control (ECDC), Commission's Advisory Panel on COVID-19 <https://ec.europa.eu/transparency/expert-groups-register/screen/expert-groups/consult?lang=en&groupID=3719> accessed 30 August 2021.

32 European Commission, 'Remarks by President Von Der Leyen at the Joint Press Conference with Commissioners Lenarcic, Kyriakides, Johansson, Valean and Gentiloni at the ERCC ECHO on the EU's Response to COVID-19' (2 March 2020) < https://ec.europa.eu/commission/presscorner/detail/en/statement_20_368> accessed 29 November 2021.

Remarkable is also the initiative of CERN, which created a task force with the aim of ensuring an effective and well-coordinated response to the emergency. The task force was called CERN against COVID-19 and composed of 21 members only three of whom were women.[33]

Despite the limited information relating to the international task forces and the gender of their members, there was clearly a significant absence of women in the bodies created to manage the pandemic at supranational level.[34] As early as April 2020, the UN had underlined, in its Policy Brief related to the first impact of COVID-19, the risk that this absence could affect the effectiveness of the COVID-19 response plans. It identified, as one of the three cross-cutting priorities, the urgent need to involve women in the decision-making process related to the pandemic and to 'ensure women's equal representation in all COVID-19 response planning and decision-making',[35] an exhortation which so far, however, does not seem to have been heeded.

3.2 *At Domestic Level*

The lack of women in all the COVID-19 task forces is also a concern at the domestic level. The recent mapping exercise undertaken by the United Nations Development Programme (UNDP), in partnership with the Gender Inequality Research Lab (GIRL) at the University of Pittsburgh, shows that only 24% of members of COVID-19 task forces were women and that only in 19% of the women held a leadership role.[36]

The percentage of women in COVID-19 task forces varies significantly by region, with a higher level of participation in 'Europe, North America, Australia and New Zealand (32%)' than in Latin America and the Caribbean (29%) and sub-Saharan Africa (20%).[37]

Considerable differences are also seen within regions, for example in Europe, 73% of members of the Albanian task forces are women and 63% of Estonian task force members are women. By comparison, in the Hungarian task forces the level of women's participation is only 7% and in the Belarusian

33 See <https://againstcovid19.cern/mandate/task-force-members> accessed 29 November 2021.

34 Van Daalen et al. (n 3).

35 United Nations (UN), *Policy Brief: The Impact of COVID-19 on Women*, 9 April 2020.

36 The datasets include data on 334 task forces created in 187 countries. United Nations Development Programme (UNDP), *COVID-19 Global Gender Response Tracker. Women remain Absent: COVID-19 Task Force Participation* (22 March 2021) <www.undp.org/sites/g/files/zskgke326/files/2021-06/UNDP-UNWomen-UPitt-COVID19-Task-Force-Participation-EN_0.pdf> accessed 29 November 2021.

37 ibid.

task forces it is 9%. Also, the average for female participation in the Italian COVID-19 task forces appears to be among the lowest in Europe (19%), a not encouraging finding, considering that Italy is apparently among the states with one of the largest numbers of COVID-19 task forces.[38]

We now turn our focus to the specific case of Italy to look more closely at the formation of some of the main COVID-19 task forces set up in its ministries during the emergency.[39]

3.2.1 Italy

Italy represents a significant example of the proliferation of task forces during the pandemic. The Head of Civil Protection started this trend on 3 February 2020 by creating one of the first COVID-19 task forces in Italy, which was composed entirely of men.[40] Faced with the urgent requests to explain the total absence of women, the Head of Civil Protection justified the situation as merely a consequence of the lack of women in the top positions in public administration.[41] It was not until May 2020 that six female experts joined the Committee.[42]

The Presidency of the Council of Ministers set up its own task force in April 2020[43] chaired by Dr Colao. Only four of the nineteen members, drawn from

38 ibid.

39 The list of COVID-19 task forces is by no means exhaustive.

40 The 'Operational Committee on the Coronavirus for Civil Protection' was in charge of ensuring the full coordination of actions to be taken during the COVID-19 pandemic. Article 2 of the Decree n°371/2020 states that 'the Committee consists of the following members: Coordinator of the Office for the promotion and integration of the National Civil Protection Service of the Civil Protection Department; Secretary General of the Ministry of Health; Director General of Health Prevention of the Ministry of Health; Director of the Office for the Coordination of Maritime, Air and Border Health Offices of the Ministry of Health; Scientific Director of the National Institute for Infectious Diseases 'Lazzaro Spallanzani'; President of the National Institute of Health'; article 3 also provides for the possibility of calling upon 'qualified experts' to attend meetings, selected in 'special cases at the discretion of the Head of the Civil Protection Department or at the proposal of the Coordinator of the Committee or its members'.

41 Head of Civil Protection, Press Conference of 28 April 2020.

42 Presidency of the Council of Ministers, Press release of 12 May 2020.

43 The experts of the 'Task Force for Reconstruction' were appointed by the Decree of the President of the Council of Ministers of 10 April 2020. The overall aim of the task force was to identify a 'catalogue' of solutions (the so-called Colao Plan) for the post-COVID-19 emergency and gradual recovery of the country. The Task Force created a sub-group to deal with 'Individuals and Families' which had the merit of advancing the debate on inequalities and identifying specific measures to promote gender equality and social sustainability (e.g. the adoption of the Gender Impact Evaluation, to strengthen inclusive welfare, and to improve education and employment opportunities for women).

professional and academic fields, were women. Five additional members, all women, were later appointed to the Committee because of the uproar following the blatant underrepresentation of women.[44]

The Ministry of Innovation, with the agreement of the Ministry of Health, established one of the largest Italian task forces. It comprised a multidisciplinary group of 76 experts from institutional and professional fields, with the task of analysing and studying socio-economic and health data relating to the impact of the epidemic: only 16 of the members were women.[45] The selection procedure was strongly criticised for a lack of information about the criteria adopted to identify the candidates.[46]

The Ministry of Economy and Finance together with other institutions operating in the financial sector 'informally' set up a task force to ensure the swift and efficient use of the cash support measures adopted by the government. The criteria for appointment to the task force – called upon to operate with 'informal methods and means, with a variable organisation and make up'[47] – were not disclosed.

The Ministry of Education set up two task forces. The first, which was established to deal with the educational emergency, seems to have had more than one hundred members, although there are no official data on their exact number and gender. The second, which was tasked with drafting ideas and

44 Decree of the President of the Council of Ministers of 12 May 2020.

45 The 'Anti-COVID-19 Technology Task Force' identifies, proposes and evaluates solutions 'for the management of the health, economic and social emergency' linked to COVID-19. This task force has promoted the development of a COVID-19 tracking application.

46 The question was raised in front of the Senate on 6 April 2020: the Minister was asked to clarify what procedures had been followed to select the experts and to guarantee the appropriate degree of impartiality, transparency and competence. In reply, the Minister merely repeated that 'Members, indeed, were identified precisely in consideration of the possession of the specific professional skills and qualifications required to carry out the activities assigned within the work group'. This appeared insufficient to clarify the issue: Senate of the Republic, 'Interrogazione sulla costituzione della task force dati per l'emergenza COVID-19. Risposta' ('Question on the establishment of the data task force for the COVID-19 emergency. Reply', authors' translation) (16 April 2021) <www.infoparlamento.it/tematiche/interrogazioni-interpellanze-risoluzioni-mozioni/senato-della-repubblica-403094-interrogazione-sulla-costituzione-della-task-force-dati-per-lemergenza-covid19-risposta> accessed 29 November 2021.

47 Parliamentary Commission of Inquiry into the Banking and Financial System, 'Iniziative della Task Force per assicurare l'efficiente e rapido utilizzo delle misure di supporto alla liquidità adottate dal Governo' ('Initiatives of the Task Force to ensure the efficient and rapid use of the liquidity support measures adopted by the Government', authors' translation) (29 April 2021).

proposals for the start of the new school year, had 18 members of whom eight were women.

The Undersecretary of State at the Presidency of the Council of Ministers set up a (more balanced) Monitoring Unit aimed to counteract the spread of 'fake news' on COVID-19, comprising 11 members, five of whom were women.[48]

In contrast, the Minister for Equal Opportunities and the Family appointed a task force called 'Women for the New Renaissance' composed of 12 experts, all women, with the mandate to develop proposals 'to increase the percentage of women in all areas of work, to overcome the barriers to progress in career paths'.[49] The outcome of its work, submitted on 25 May 2020,[50] was not unanimously accepted due to the significant absence of a long-term perspective on improving gender equality beyond the emergency situation.[51]

Interestingly, in May 2020, the issue of women's underrepresentation in the various task forces gave rise to a heated debate in Parliament, ending with the tabling of a motion in which the Italian Government was asked, among other things, to make transparent and available the criteria adopted to nominate the members of these bodies and to guarantee the gender balance without necessarily increasing the overall number of members appointed.[52] This request was not accepted.

3.3 *Main Challenges*

This brief overview identifies some specific challenges facing women's participatory rights in the specific context of the emergency task forces.

First, the creation of temporary decision-making mechanisms both at international and domestic level has had serious implications for the fulfilment of the right to non-discrimination and equal participation in all public spheres. The lack of formal channels for participation, in particular due to the lack of transparent public appointment procedures and objective criteria for recruitment to these bodies, has affected respect for the obligations arising from articles 7 and 8 of the CEDAW.[53] Most of the task forces were created through political expediency justified by the urgency of the situation, instead of adopting

48 Decree of the Undersecretary of the Council of Ministers of 4 April 2020.

49 Decree of the Minister for Equal Opportunities and the Family of 10 April 2020.

50 Department for Equal Opportunities, 'Women for a New Renaissance' (25 May 2020).

51 Jennifer Guerra, 'Per la politica la parità di genere in Italia esiste solo per le madri lavoratrici' (*The Vision*, 3 June 2020) <https://thevision.com/attualita/politica-parita-genere> accessed 29 November 2021.

52 Senate of the Republic, Act 1-00231 of 12 May 2020.

53 UN Human Rights Council (n 18).

consistent and formal nomination procedures for the selection of candidates. In several cases, the selection procedure was not even public; this also makes it possible to avoid disclosing the identities of candidates before the nomination. Interestingly, the so-called 'co-option method' was a prominent strategic choice and, as Dr Colao had warned, this method mostly favoured men. The creation of an opaque environment within which nomination procedures disregarded the gender balance could not be explained away by invoking the 'emergency situation' created by the pandemic. In fact, the CEDAW 'doesn't allow for derogation in time of public emergency, nor is the commitment to women's equality made subject to such "claw-backs" as protection of national security, public order, public health, morals or the rights of freedom of others'.[54]

The second concern relates to the effectiveness of measures adopted by these bodies. These bodies were created to respond to the crisis and should have reflected society as a whole, guaranteeing an equal and balanced presence of males and females as an expression of democratic representation.[55] This underrepresentation could not be explained by the argument that there was a 'limited pool of candidates available', because women were evidently precluded from having an equal opportunity to gain access to the selection procedures.[56] The lack of women playing an active role in the development of policies could affect the implementation of measures adopted at domestic and international level by undermining the democratic legitimacy of the COVID-19 closed-door governance.[57]

To face these challenges, and to make gender parity a priority both at the international and domestic levels, new mechanisms and changes to the normative frameworks will be necessary. As a possible way to implement successive changes, some scholars suggest the adoption of temporary measures, such as quotas, to strengthen a gender-balanced approach to the nomination

---

54 Freeman (n 14) 28.

55 Commission on the Status of Women (n 5), para 22.

56 'Claiming to not find any qualified women in global health is ultimately an unjustifiably poor excuse for excluding diverse perspective', Van Daalen et al., 14.

57 As highlighted by the UN Women Expert Group Meeting, the 'lack of social diversity and inclusion may undermine the perceived legitimacy of decision-making processes by elected and appointed bodies' from a general point of view. UN Women Expert Group Meeting, *The State of Women's Participation and Empowerment: New Challenges to Gender Equality; Background Paper prepared by Pippa Norris* (EGM/CSW/2021/BP1); UN Human Rights Council, *Current Levels of Representation of Women in Human Rights Organs and Mechanisms: Ensuring Gender Balance. Report of the Human Rights Council Advisory Committee* (A/HRC/47/51).

of candidates. Better access to information about available vacancies is also needed. The identification of 'appropriate measures' to reduce the persisting barriers that prevent women from being nominated could also include possible 'sanctions', such as the rejection of the whole list of candidates if it is not gender balanced.[58]

4 Conclusion

The COVID crisis has unquestionably demonstrated how the full enjoyment of women's rights continues to encounter obstacles and has highlighted that gender inequalities are still a global phenomenon. As recalled by Henn 'globally, women and girls face discrimination in every social and legal system. It is only the extent and multidimensionality of the discrimination, and its intersection with other grounds of discrimination such race and class that differ'.[59]

It is absolutely essential to continue to strengthen collective efforts to make visible the gender limits that persist in the institutional set-up.[60] In this sense, the composition of task forces offers an emblematic example of how certain established practices, such as co-option, may undermine effective participation of women and equal leadership opportunities at all levels of decision-making in political and public life.

To end on a positive note, the key critical issues in this contribution may provide fertile ground upon which to build 'gender-responsive institutions' at all levels. Institutions are called upon first to become aware of the need for women's participation in positions and places of power and, second, to actively encourage equal opportunities, starting with the adoption of transparent methods of appointment. As noted by the UN Secretary-General 'good governance and democracy require inclusive leadership and representation'.[61]

---

58 UN Women Expert Group Meeting, *Commission on the Status of Women; Temporary Special Measures, Including Gender Quotas – Types, Usage and Effects; Expert Paper prepared by Drude Dahlerup* (EGM/CSW/2021/EP3).

59 Elisabeth V. Henn, 'Gender Injustice, Discrimination and the CEDAW: A Women's Life Course Perspective' in Maarit Jänterä-Jareborg and Hélène Tigroudja (eds), *Women's Human Rights and the Elimination of Discrimination / Les Droits des Femmes et l'Elimination de la Discrimination* (Brill 2016) 12.

60 It is important to underline how global mobilisation, for instance, had a significant impact on changing the membership of several bodies.

61 Commission on the Status of Women (n 5) para 5.

References

Buhlmann M and Schadel L, 'Representation Matters. The Impact of Descriptive Women's Representation on the Political Involvement of Women' (2012) 48(1) Representation 101.

Charlesworth H and Chinkin C, *The Boundaries of International Law, A Feminist Analysis* (Juris Publishing, 2000).

Criado Perez C, *Invisible Women: Exposing Data Bias in a World Designed for Men* (Abram Press 2019).

Dahlerup D and Leyenaar M, *Breaking Male Dominance in Old Democracies* (Oxford 2013).

Dahlerup D, *Has Democracy Failed Women?* (Polity 2017).

Fredman S et al., 'Transformative Equality: Making the Sustainable Development Goals Work for Women' (2016) 30 (2) Ethics & International Affairs 177.

Fredman S, 'Substantive Equality Revisited' (2016) 14 International Journal of Constitutional Law 712.

Freeman M et al. (eds), *The UN Convention on the Elimination of all Forms of Discrimination Against Women* (Oxford University Press 2012).

Henn EV, 'Gender Injustice, Discrimination and the CEDAW: A Women's Life Course Perspective' in Jänterä-Jareborg M and Tigroudja H (eds), *Women's Human Rights and the Elimination of Discrimination / Les Droits des Femmes et l'Elimination de la Discrimination* (Brill 2016).

Knop K, 'Re/Statements: Feminism and State Sovereignty in International Law' (1993) 3 Transnational Law and Contemporary Problems 293.

Lépinard E and Rubio-Marín R (eds), *Transforming Gender Citizenship. The Irresistible Rise of Gender Quotas in Europe* (Cambridge 2018).

Minello A et al., 'The Pandemic and the Academic Mothers: Present Hardships and Future Perspectives' (2020) 23 European Societies 82.

Peter A, *Women, Quotas and Constitutions, A Comparative Study of Affirmative Actions for Women Under American, German, European Community and International Law* (Kluwer Law International 1999).

Rubio-Marín R and Kymlicka W (eds), *Gender Parity and Multicultural Feminism, Towards a New Synthesis* (Oxford 2018).

Schoop-Schilling HB and Flinterman C (eds), *The Circle of Empowerment* (The Feminist Press 2007).

Van Daalen KR et al., 'Symptoms of a Broken System: the Gender Gaps in COVID-19 Decision-Making' (2020) 5 (10) BMJ Global Health 1–19.

Wenham C et al., 'COVID-19: The Gendered Impacts of the Outbreak' (2020) 395 (10227) The Lancet 846.

Index

www.ingramcontent.com/pod-product-compliance
Lightning Source LLC
Chambersburg PA
CBHW071226230926
51849CB00001B/41
* 9 7 8 9 0 0 4 4 6 7 6 7 5 *